To Ted-

Wishing you a very
happy birthday!

much love-

Jane, Doug, Annie and Tom

18 February 1984.

Skiffs And Schooners

Skiffs And Schooners

by
R. D. Culler

International Marine Publishing Company
Camden, Maine

Contents

Preface

There have been so many books on boats and boatbuilding — and good ones too — by experts and some near experts that it may seem almost ostentatious for a person to write another. However, being of an age whence I can look back on a good many years at just plain messing around with boats and on the experience acquired thereby — you can never get enough experience at anything — I feel the urge to put down some things connected with boats and their building. None of it is new; most of it is half forgotten; all of it can be useful. Best of all, most of it is very simple.

Realizing that boats, like whiskey, are all good, I make no attempt nor have any intention of making adamant statements of how things should be done, or of preaching dogma until it sounds almost like truth. I put down things our forefathers knew and acquired the hard way, things we have been exposed to, often the very same hard way. One learns by his mistakes. If I have produced anything, however small, of further use to the World of Boats, it will make my efforts worthwhile. All whiskey has its place.

R. D. Culler
Hyannis, Massachusetts

Skiffs And Schooners

I

Experience Starts When You Begin

My early exposure to boats involved expeditions that we glorified with the name "cruises." I would pick a buddy with like inclinations and we would prepare for the trip with care. Once our big skiff was ready, we'd Head Out.

We took long rows with some assistance from sail to likely beaches or surf-barred slough entrances, all deserted. We became rather good at surf work. Usually these voyages were just after the winter gales, so there was much plunder to pick up on the beaches. When the bacon and pancakes ran out and the craft had such a load that it was hard to launch her off, we made for the home port. On these trips it was not the feet suffering near the end, but the hands and back! I think our greed was part of it; we just couldn't pass up another steamer deck chair, or a couple more lobster buoys, and that part of an old net was very necessary to have. An overloaded skiff of good size, built of Oregon pine, made the last mile sort of desperate. Fees, permits for fires or for anything else were unheard of, and on land or sea we never saw another soul, except for an occasional steam schooner far offshore. I wonder if such goings on are possible anywhere now?

While we no doubt caused worry at home, I cannot recall ever being in real danger or experiencing any sort of near disaster. We knew nothing of drugs except that they were something connected with Orientals. Booze was for grown-ups. In many ways we were quite grown up, though by some of today's standards we were just babes. We did know a lot about tobacco; all our tutors smoked pipes or chewed. These men took time for boys who were boat crazy; looking back on it, I think they remembered how it was when they were boys.

There was Pop Cannon, master shipwright retired, who took a small job now and then. Eighty, frail-looking, and blue-eyed, he could turn out much more work in a day than many younger men. He knew considerable about ballasting and trim, rake of masts, and the tuning of a vessel. There was Nick, the loner cod fisherman with his handsome power dory. He was a squat, swart, powerhouse of a man. From him, we learned "the marks" for Eleven Mile Reef, and the art of mackerel trolling. There was Jeemy, the Italian seacook, who, true to type, was full of bombast, and noise, and sea lore. There was Mario, of the pretty little seiner; he knew much about reading the weather. And above all, there was Captain George, large, paunchy, and gruff. He was a thorough seaman and superb boat handler, under oars or sail. His disgust with "farmers" and "backwoodsmen" around boats was something to behold. I think he kept an eye on us at all times, though he was not obvious about it. If we pulled off a difficult bit of boat handling in nasty conditions, Cap would grunt and say as how "it was a mite airish." If we bungled, even slightly, we were Hair-Brained Yazzoos, whatever they are.

Becoming accepted as boatmen with some surf experience, one summer my school mate and I turned pro. We crewed on a fine motor craft that was chartered to "take scientific fellers about." We felt quite some stuff, for this was offshore work at times, and there was much surf work and ferrying of gear and scientific finds. We launched off with many a load of bones, some of them human. We were always wet, tired much of the time, and occasionally somewhat seasick. Oh, it was a fine life! The vessel was nearly new, had a handsome Frisco Standard engine, and a master who was all seaman and a stickler for neatness. In idle moments, we soogeed white paint; the hooker seemed to have miles of it.

Seamanship was thrown at us in chunks, for where we worked was the real thing, no mill pond. There were some desperate times, for we went into desperate places with the weather turning bad to pick up men who had been there weeks with their grub running low. They and their collection had to be boated off. We learned of embayment and of having to clear out in the wee hours of the wildest night, working on the jumping foredeck and securing great anchors as we went, for there was no time to lose; the whole place was a mass of white. We were pooped once, and we broached another time and nearly lost a man. Near the end of our season, we were pounding along in a fierce nor'wester, ship and all a smother of white. We had strict orders; no one on deck. So we young crew are in our "quarters," the forecastle, same as two walnuts in a rolling tin can. Sleep is impossible, so we puff a pipe, talk a bit, and make an occasional trip through the engine room, where the never-failing Frisco is thumping away (I think she turned 275), to tend the stove and have a mug. It was pretty heady in that engine room, but we felt tough and salty. I suppose to some extent we were.

Later I became the lone paid hand on a nice sailing craft whose design was based on that of a small fishing boat. That was quite a berth. I

was also the engineer, for she had a one-jug Bridgeport of monumental stubbornness. Without knowing really why, I could make her go.

This boat needed her wire rigging replaced, which, as yet, I was not up to, though I was much interested in marlinespike seamanship. The services of Captain Barrie were obtained. This handsome Scot was then 85, a huge man with a white trimmed beard that made him look very like King George V of England. He started his sea career at the age of nine in collier brigs. He had learned his seamanship under men who had sailed with Nelson. This at first seems improbable, but it was the mid-1920's, and 1805 was not so far away! Rigging wire did wonderful things under his powerful hands, and, of course, I learned much of brigs. The full-rigged collier brig was a handy craft to use in narrow, congested waters. She was short and dumpy, and her square rig made it possible to back, haul, and box about in the tightest places. Under the command of such men as this, I'm sure it was so. Captain Barrie was a good carpenter and sailmaker too, and knew all about overlapping jibs, which were not around on yachts in those days. He called them "tow fores'ls." His own vessel at this time, a partially decked sloop, seemed to give him great pleasure. Though plumb in the ends and with a single stick, she somehow had the smack of a brig! He made his own oilskins; they had no buttons, but instead, wood toggles and loops, and they were waterproofed with a fearsome mixture of pine tar, beeswax, kerosene, tallow, linseed oil, and I don't know what-all else. Boarding the street car (yes, they were around then) after a wet day of it, these oilskins made the car smell like a brig's forecastle.

Yes, it was wonderful to have such teachers, and they seemed to enjoy telling how to do it right. I think this kind of teaching has not changed much. Nelson's time is further away. Those men I mention are gone; a later set of old timers is around — some call 'em old fools — men who have learned from men who learned from Nelson's men. I find for the most part that they are a friendly lot, willing to talk and

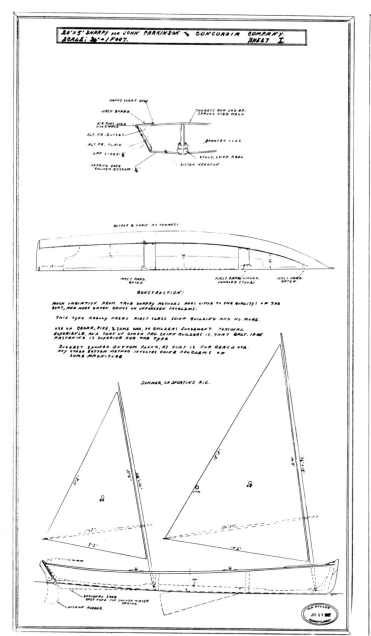

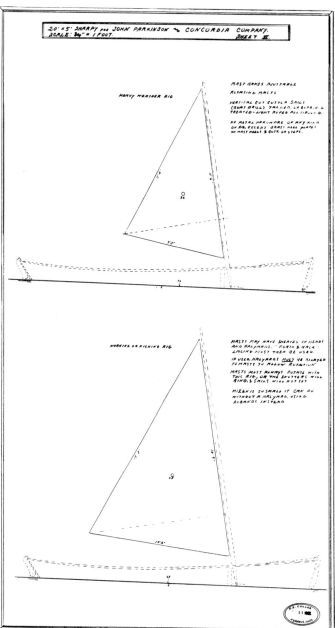

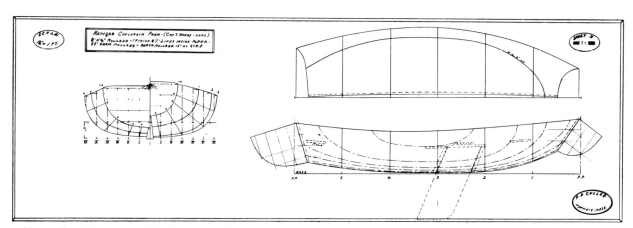

All of the plans in this book, with the exception of those of the
Spray, are the author's drawings of boats he has designed.

5

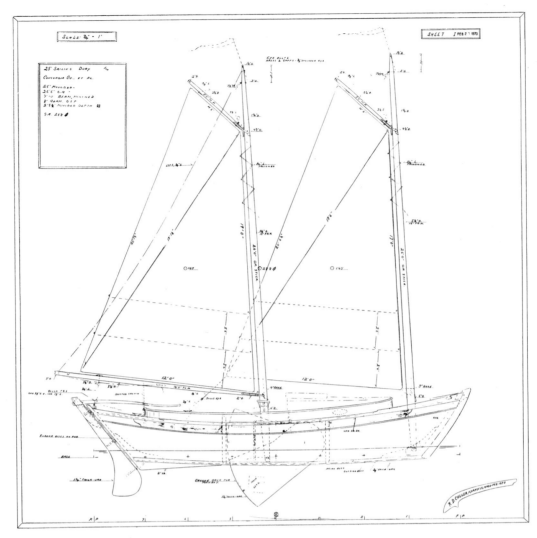

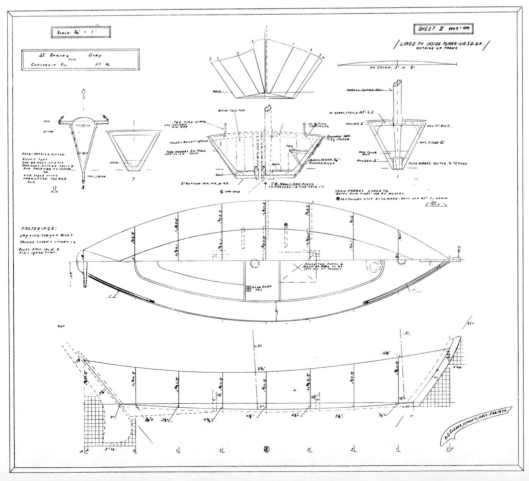

teach. They all agree that the Sea has not changed, only the way of going on it, and that in very small vessels and boats, the way has changed the least.

My Old Man I think had hope for me in the ministry. Higher learning was available, but it did not appeal to me. So he said if I was so wrapped up in boats as to make boating a career, I had better learn it inside out and stick with it. As a medical man, he felt that to be good around boats, you should have a thorough grounding in their anatomy. He could draw anatomy, human or animal, and see it, feel it, sense it. In his day, he was much sought after as a diagnostician. He felt boats were to be approached in about the same way as medicine, and he was right. I spent many happy, often tiring, wet and dirty years exposed to boats in yards, machine shops, sail lofts, and foundries, along with plenty of sailing. It was certainly no way to get rich, except in varied experiences, which are often the greatest riches of all.

When I passed 50, I thought it time to see if I had any designing ability. The mechanics of it are not much different than what I'd done in mould lofts time and again, laying down, taking up, and converting into craft of some sort. In fact I had found long ago that some designers had little knowledge about deadwoods, and rabbets, and fairing in to heavy timber; they left that to the builder, who as a rule took it as a matter of course and used his judgement. I found I had a feel for form within the limit of those types of craft in which I was really interested. After all, I had scrubbed and painted many a bottom when I was "copper paint man." To learn any trade, you used to start at the bottom! Many of these boats were fine designs, often by unknowns. Having gone over them first with a broom, then scraper, and often more

brooming, and finally paint, was a good way to get a feel of their shape. Some were worth more study, and sometimes I came back after supper and looked at the vessel's lines some more. She might be a classic, living on borrowed time, barely supported by a dying trade. She might never come to haul up again.

With a building background, I saw no point at all in drawing lines to outside of plank, as is now the only way. Why draw some line that has to be altered, sometimes with error? The old way was to draw to inside of plank and back rabbet, which is what the builder was interested in and still is. Some folks say drawing to inside of plank fouls up displacement calculations. There is a readily available formula for this if you like such things, or there is the old builder's rule, once much used and quite simple. If you figure displacement by both methods, you find that they agree closely.

You may wonder why I give all this background about my doings with boats, much of it probably not very interesting, and most of it, by certain standards, outdated. That's the point; this is like it was and like it can be for the man who is going to do it himself, and by this I mean Do It.

That's what it's all about: Any man who wants to can produce a good boat. It takes some study, some practice, and, of course, experience. The experience starts coming the minute you begin, and not one jot before. I sometimes hear the wail, "I have no experience." Start. Start anything, and experience comes. Some say building a boat is one of man's nobler efforts. Maybe so; it's a lot of fun, anyway. As one of my builder friends says, "It's only a boat; go ahead and build it." If the first effort is a bit lumpy, so what? There will be another much less lumpy later on.

II

Building the Spray

Looking back forty-three years to the building of a wooden vessel, in what was then considered a somewhat backward part of the country, and then comparing it to one built in the early 1960's in a highly industrialized area, is most interesting. I was a learner on the first vessel and head shipwright on the later one. I'm struck by the very little difference between the two jobs. Both vessels were built outdoors, which, I think, has some advantages. There were some things available to work with in the later craft that were unheard of when the early one took shape, such as a heated shop for a mill and work room. In practice these "advantages," if they can be called so, were of little use. Some were discarded, some were used mostly just because they were there and are now the custom. The heated shop was a total flop until the heat ducts were blocked off. Men can't do real work in what is now considered the proper temperature in a modern shop.

The early vessel was a reproduction of Captain Joshua Slocum's *Spray,* and, as she's been discussed, hashed over, and fought over for years, I won't go into the reasons for choosing the model. There was money available for the project, about what a half-way-decent daysailer now costs. Some study was given to locations for building, timber, and men skilled in constructing such a craft and in shipbuilding in general. Around 1929, there were many skilled yards on

the East Coast; however, a part of the country where the economics were suited to the type of craft was very important. The model was not a type suited to or needing the skills of such as Lawley or Nevins.

The Eastern Shore of Chesapeake Bay was chosen, and Oxford, Maryland, a very small village devoted to the oyster trade, was picked. After all, the old *Spray* was considered by some folks to be "only an old oyster boat," so what better set-up? The community at the time was said, by those who knew, to be very much like small New England coastal villages in about 1870. There were great changes just around the corner, however, and in a very few short years all was different. Progress caught up, and, to my way of thinking, the place was spoiled forever.

The master builder, Alonzo R. Conley, was a man of much skill and long experience. He had several large vessels to his credit, both in design and building. He was willing to take me on as a learning apprentice; what I produced I saved on the vessel. Let it be said he was a fine teacher. Though of small formal education, this man had a vast working knowledge of his trade and was quite familiar with many of the older written works on the subject; he promptly lent me some classic books on shipbuilding.

The business arrangement was simple, and

one which I still find good for a builder who really knows his stuff and a client who is honest about his own finances. The arrangement was this: The builder thought the vessel "would not cost over so much." He was right; she was a little less. The work on her was not to interfere with the seasonal work required on the oyster fleet and freighters, most of these still being sailing vessels, though some were cargo power craft. There would be slack periods on my vessel on this account, when I would go it alone when and where I was able. Payment was to be so much a month; sometimes I was ahead, sometimes behind, but for the most part it ran pretty even, and no one was hurt.

There was plenty of good timber. This was white oak country, and hard pine was available in baulks from "the city." White cedar came in by boat, and in those days yards stocked ahead. Hardware was no problem, or sails either, as there were both shipsmith and sailmaker right next door.

Alonzo R. Conley, the master builder at the yard at Oxford, Maryland, where the author's replica of the Spray *was built. (Courtesy Mrs. James Conley and the Mariner's Museum, Newport News, Virginia.)*

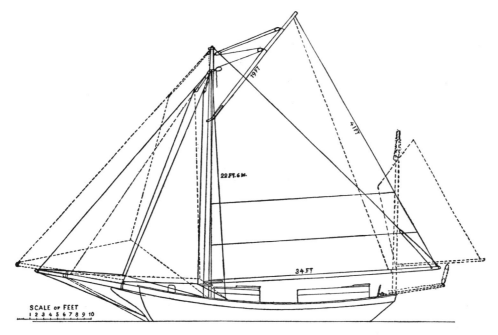

SCALE of FEET
1 2 3 4 5 6 7 8 9 10

The Spray's *sail plan, taken from Joshua Slocum's book,* Sailing Alone Around the World. *The solid lines show how she was rigged when she started the voyage, and the dotted lines show the modifications Slocum made during the cruise to make the rig easier to handle.*

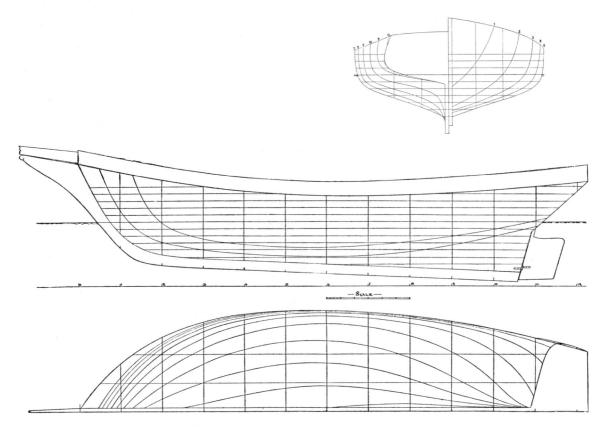

The Spray's *lines as presented by Slocum in his book. They were drawn by Charles D. Mower from a model made by a Captain Robins from measurements he made from the* Spray *when she was hauled at his yard at Bridgeport, Connecticut, for the purpose.*

The yard layout was about what was customary then. There was sloping land to a creek and anchorage, with several big shade trees and plenty of room, two railways, and space to set up three or more new vessels. The main building was a stark old post-and-rail affair, framed with local gum wood so hard with age it would refuse a nail, sheathed with vertical boards, battened, and covered with a ternplate roof. The building was the traditional ochre color. One small corner was the office and store room and had wonderful smells. The other end was the mill, which had a shipsaw and planer only, these being the total machinery and both very old. The rest of the lower floor was devoted to work benches, tool boxes, and space to work timber or build a motor yawlboat. Large sliding doors were in many places in the building, so there was always a clear shot for getting big timber to the machines.

There was a loft upstairs for laying down and a small room off it for oakum and for storing the large jeer blocks (each filling a wheelbarrow) and fall used to rig the big sheer legs on the end of the dock. (A wooden, walk-around capstan was near the sheers.) At the other end of the loft was a home-built wood lathe of large capacity, driven by a tiny hopper engine that was quite short-tempered on a cold morning.

Outside, the yard had a cluttered and messy look by some standards, for there was much work going on. There would be time enough to clean up when things were slack. Winters were cold, and there was much need of firewood. Much good ship timber was about, piled everywhere, and carefully "stuck." There were timber wheels, peaveys, many clamps, some of them huge, and, of course, "planking jacks." The railways were driven by locally-made, single-cylinder, hit-and-miss, gas engines, cooled by toted creek water kept in pickle barrels. These engines were rated at 5 h.p. each. There was the outhouse, which hung over the end of a bulkhead at a rakish angle. It was fearsomely cold or hot inside it, depending on the season, but it never needed maintenance. There was no electricity at all in the yard, though the owner's house next door and most of the village had it, made locally, as was the custom then. Hand-held power tools were unknown. Water for drinking came from the ice house next door, where it ran in a fine cool stream. Each workman went for his own water with a "can," which was really a half-gallon mason jar of the bootleg era.

How, many folks ask now, can you build a vessel with such a crude setup? You can, and they did, and, sad to say, the man-hours per ton of vessel then were less, sometimes very much less, than they are now. Lest you might think the work was crude, let me say it was just the opposite. The yard was known for the fair hulls, fine planking, and excellence of fastening on

the craft it turned out. There seemed to be no great effort to accomplish this; all hands just knew how.

Everyone walked to work, for the village was small, few people owned autos, and all was geared to the yards and oyster trade. You worked at what the place offered, or left for greener fields. Few left. There were few amusements; we didn't need any, for the country store was the men's social place. For yarns of hard sailings, great feats of hunting, gossip, lies, and all sorts of exciting things, you went to the store evenings. The layout was just like the pictures of a real country store. The smoke got pretty thick (many of the men smoked black Five Brothers) and things got pretty deep, but we all wore boots!

Looking back on it, knowing there were what would now be considered great discomforts, it was still a good way to live, maybe because we did not know any better. To hear "Captain Harry" get going and take the floor for a full evening (being baited now and then to keep it hot) was a far better show than any purveyors of the boob tube can put on now!

Grub was hearty; oysters in many forms were commonplace at table, cooked by experts. Nowadays, oysters cost a fortune, and the cooks louse 'em up. A breakfast of biscuits, or "corn cake and aigs" with fried fatback was fit to do hard work on. The dinner bucket carried solid food

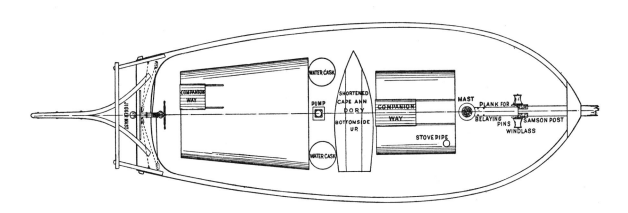

The Spray's *deck plan as shown in* Sailing Alone Around the World.

too. There were no thermos bottles; coffee was brought in an ordinary bottle and cuddled close to the office stove in winter so it was just right at noon. Sometimes it almost froze on the way to work. In summer, and it can be frightfully hot on the Bay, the kindly engineer in charge of the nearby ice house made ice tea or coffee commonplace. You could even have it frozen if you wanted. Working hours were longer than they are now, based on available daylight. There were no rules for workmen, no regulations, except what the Master made. This was the pre-Roosevelt era, and the yard was fairly isolated from city ways. There was no insurance of any kind, no guards on the belts, no fire equipment. It was probably not much different from, say, a farm a hundred years ago. Everyone knew his work, and accidents or mishaps of any kind were most rare.

A yard must have a crew of workmen; this crew was small and was supplemented at times of much work by some old timers from what had once been a very active shipbuilding area further down the Bay. These fellows came for a specific job, saw it through, and departed, to return later on for some other project. They were highly skilled, experienced in large work, and could pretty much run any job without supervision. The boss of this little yard was shown considerable deference by these seasoned old timers, though he was younger than they, for he had once been a designer and builder in the Big Time, and these men had been under him. He had something they lacked.

The regular crew were, as they always are, varied in looks, build, and personality. The common trait was that they knew their work and very much knew that the Master Shipwright knew his. There was Hamilton, a leathery, sparse man of excellent ability in all phases of his trade, besides being an accomplished rigger. Edward, who was black, though his head was quite white, was no doubt much older than he looked. Caulker and fastener extraordinary, he lent magic to a pin maul with his hands. Isaac, short, round, and strong, though his legs were giving out, had a Santa Claus face without the

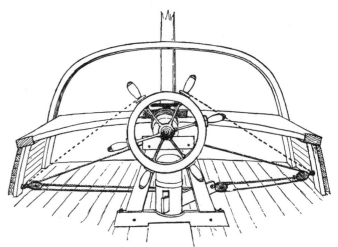

A drawing from Sailing Alone Around the World *showing the* Spray's *steering arrangement and the strongback that braced the mizzen mast.*

whiskers. He could dub and hew accurately with the dispatch of a machine, and from the most impossible positions. In his retirement years, he kindly sold me one of his fine adzes for one dollar. I've used it for years, and still do occasionally. The bell-like ring that is its trademark is still with it! Tom was addicted to bad whiskey; it was an unwritten rule that he was not to show up when in bad shape. To make up for his tardiness, he would turn out at one o'clock in the morning, if necessary, to man the railway to haul some leaking craft that was about to go down. Going overboard in the total darkness of a winter night to find out what was ailing a sticking poppet bothered him not at all. Wedges, clamps, jacks, and all sorts of heavy work was his specialty. Tom was not very robust looking, probably couldn't see out of one eye, and was racked by demon rum, but none of these ailments seemed to cramp his style any.

Edgar, somewhat younger than the others, was the foreman. He kept time for all and rang the old, dismal, cracked bell for starting work and knocking off. He generally kept the run of the others' work and did most of the spiling and laying off, once a job was started. Edgar maintained the mill and engines, for which he had a great knack. He set and filed the miles of bandsaw blades. He did most of the interior joiner-work, including fine, paneled doors. There was no small machinery for joinerwork; it was all done by hand, rapidly, and in good style. Edgar owned a Stanley 55 plane, "a joiner shop in itself," if you get behind it and push! Besides all this, he was a sawyer, and a wizard at it.

So money was passed, and I was put to work in the loft with a broom. Then I was introduced to the fine points of lofting, many of which seem not to be found in books. I flattened the points of hundreds of thin wire nails. Though the floor was old and dark, it was treated with respect. The flattened points left little or no holes and had other advantages. Much work was done with chalk, and I learned you can work quite accurately to chalk lines, once shown how. I also learned what "fair" is, a thing many of the highly skilled can still argue about. A master can show you just what a very slight adjustment can do for a line that seems good already. I learned about lifting the bevels, for my vessel was to be a sawn-frame craft. I had never seen a bevel-lifting instrument; no shipbuilding books I've seen show such a thing. The Master had built it. I've since built one and have had it for a good many years. I learned mould making; the whole backbone and all the frames had moulds, for this was all gone about as if she were a big four-master. This is, in the end, the fastest, most accurate way to build a sawn-frame vessel.

Nailed on one wall, looking down on all this, was the profile and sail plan of a fine four-masted schooner, the past work of my designer-builder-teacher. She had made some maritime history as "The Ship The Sea Couldn't Kill." Her sails and all spars and rigging were made from this plan; it was drawn in pencil on common matchboarding. Men of these skills got right at the heart of the matter without the frills of offices, tidy draftsmen, and much paperwork, and they never failed to be artistic in their work.

There was plenty of stock on hand for framing. During the lofting, a most battered truck came with the keel, stem, and deadwood stock

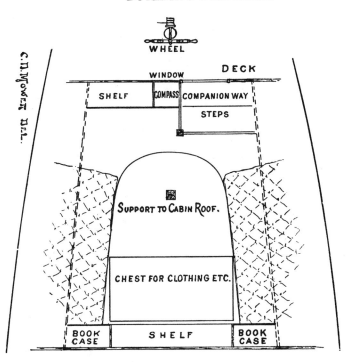

The plan of the Spray's *cabin shown in* Sailing Alone Around the World.

from a backwoods mill by some swamp. All mill trucks were battered, but this one was special. The mill owner unfolds from the cab, an elderly Mennonite in the garb of his sect. Immediate haggling follows between shipwright and mill owner, as, though both are good churchmen, neither trusts the other's lumber tally. Some Eastern Sho' white oak won't float when green, and, while the haggle proceeds, a huge giant, unshorn since birth, unloads this great pile in short order, singlehanded, with a peavey and a simple (so it seems) twist of the wrist. He's an astonishing fellow. He thinks maybe he's thirty-six years old. His boss says he has eighteen children. It's rumored that he lives in a true serfdom under this small lumber baron.

This timber is soon converted. There is much screeching from the ancient bandsaw and bellowing from the engine. Both are quite up to it and labor not at all. There is considerable adz work, rabbet cutting, drifting, and then setting up. The mysteries of setting to drag and plumbing up were fully explained, doing it in

THOMAS FOGARTY.

A drawing by Thomas Fogarty from Sailing Alone Around the World. *The caption was, "It'll crawl!" Slocum had plenty of spectators as he rebuilt the* Spray, *and the gent with the heavy basket evidently disapproved of Slocum's caulking technique.*

a wind, too! The ground where the backbone was set up was traditional to these yards, a hard-packed, unknown depth of adz and axe chips from 125 years of building by various men on the same site. The old railways had seen all kinds of power. First a horse walk-around, then steam, now gasoline engines.

It was soon time to frame up, and getting cold. The oyster season was well started and all the craft were on the beds. Framing is an all-hands job. The Master moulded. Much flitch was spread around for his easy access. The timber wheels were much in use. As he moulded, the work was taken to the saw. Four-inch white oak flitch is heavy.

To this day I very much enjoy the sawing of frame for a vessel. Usually there is a cold wind sweeping across the huge saw table. There is the heady smell of new-sawn oak, the rumble of rollers as the flitch is jockeyed into position to start the cut. There is the idling saw, veteran of a billion cuts, and the loafing engine, sounding sort of slack in the rod. The saw is rolled

down to the proper starting bevel, the motions from the sawyer's hand guiding the crew in lining her up, and the roller crank is then rigged. And the cut starts, hesitantly at first, then, as she's lined up, the big saw cuts in earnest, and the machinery and crew settle into stride. With gentle motions occasionally from the sawyer's hand, the saw gradually lays back more and more as the bevel increases. There is much sawdust in the eyes, as it's windy, and an occasional spark from the saw guides. It's through, the tempo of the machine slacks off again, the bevel man stands her up and she rumbles back to get the other side.

If it's a cant frame with rapidly changing shape and bevel, things can become quite tense. The bevel man can only just keep up with the changes and cranks the wheel for all he's worth. Usually the sharpest curve is at one end, when the crew is carrying most of the weight of the timber. The sawyer's signals become somewhat rapid, the old saw is almost lying on its back, a stream of sparks strikes from the blade, she whines and yammers, there is a hysterical shriek from the drive belt with much slapping, and the old engine thumps manfully. Then she's through, right on the line. There's little dubbing to do with this kind of work.

Yes, it gets in the blood, and though modern ship saws have improved slightly, with their heavy, solid lower wheels to act as a flywheel and their swage-tooth blades, driven by five vee belts connected to quiet electric motors that need no water or gas toted by hand for them, there is little other change. New-sawn oak smells the same, and the saw blade has the same screech. I am glad to have heard the fine slap of the big, totally-exposed, flat belts and the bark of a steam mill exhaust when the engine's governor said "go to work," and to have seen the drunken rocking of the big upright gas engines when they were Laying Into It. Wooden shipbuilding sounds and smells good!

Framing up took just a week; this sounds fantastic to many folks who have not experienced such things. Men who knew their trade, rugged though very simple equipment just suited to such work, and a vessel of only 15 tons made this possible. The fact that she was framed much heavier than usual for a craft of her length made no difference; the same motions had to be gone through. The main reason for the heavy framing was that the vessel is of a naturally weak shape and maybe overly stiff, so it seemed well to build some of the ballast into her. Much subsequent use proved this approach.

There was a coaster waiting her fate anchored off the yard. Old and worn with work, she was a sad sight, with drooping stern and other signs of a hard life. It was suddenly decided to rebuild her, as at this time there was a local economic reason to rebuild old vessels, some being converted to power. It later turned out that this was the last big effort at this sort of thing on the Bay.

Another Fogarty drawing from Slocum's book showing the Spray *being passed by the U. S. battleship,* Oregon, *on her way from Puget Sound round Cape Horn to help the Navy fight the Spaniards in the Caribbean in 1898.*

The author's replica of the Spray *stretching her sails off Oxford, Maryland, on September 4, 1933. (Photo by Robert H. Burgess.)*

As the schooner job was urgent, it was decided to let the *Spray* frame set for the winter, and "find and set" itself, to be horned and trued again when work started on her later. I still think this is a good practice; it was once common in first-class housebuilding too. "Lets the snow work the sap out."

I was put to work on deck beams, beams for the cabin trunk, parts for hatches, and spars, all under the Master's direction. Prefab was well understood here. I went alone, mostly in the old drafty loft, the ternplate roof rattling dismally to winter Nor'westers that turned the river "feather white."

Meanwhile, the schooner was hauled on the big railway and prepared for her major operation. This in itself was quite a project, salted with much know-how. Her ends were knocked out, and most of her topwork taken off to the waterline. Old bottoms usually are in good shape, except for the ends. Her deck was cut loose from her sides with her masts still in her. She was all jacked, shored, and stayed to deadmen buried in the yard, of which there were many, some dating back to the beginning. I had an excellent view of all of this from the loft, for the vessel was right below me, with her headstays secured to the head of the railway. I began to realize I was witnessing The Big Time, a master shipwright at his best. The battered mill truck and giant were frequent visitors with huge piles of oak. The stem liner, otherwise known as an apron piece, arrived. It was a noble chunk, 18″ x 24″ x 20 feet. Isaac, the axe wizard, was put on it, and some of the days were so cold it's a wonder his axe stood it.

The author's Spray *under power.*

The old timers from Down the Bay showed up, all of 'em, and boarded locally in the village during the working week. Captain Bill, framer-planker-ceiler extraordinary, was sort of chief, under the Master. His hands were so big that cotton work gloves covered only a little more than half of them. John, aged 74, who "could lay off work for 25 head of men and do a full day's work besides," could and did! His brother, 72 and hunch-backed, had a 42-inch handle in his maul and could do anything with it. No one else could do a thing with the tool. It was just too long. Pap, who was supposed to be 84, was so shrunken and withered it was said he had a brick in each pocket to keep from blowing away, yet he was right in it with the rest. There were a couple of younger men making up, with the yard steadies, quite a crew.

The mill roared, and the old building creaked with its efforts, as all the strain was transmitted to the frame through the big overhead line shaft. I heard the ring of pin mauls, the chunking of adz and axe, and the constant rumble of rollers moving heavy stuff. Then a sick cruiser showed up, and this job was taken on. One of the younger men from Down the Bay was put to "opening her up." The Master stopped by daily to check my lone progress, and he seemed satisfied. One day he said, "Harly needs help on the cruiser." Would I give him a hand? I was part of the crew the rest of the winter, and the cruiser turned out well after we gave her a new stem and re-planked her topwork. Harly knew considerable about yacht planking.

By early spring the schooner was about finished. Soon she was launched. She had the yard's handsome, springy sheer and was every inch a smart coaster. Her new master had been by her all winter. A thorough seaman and somewhat of a dude (always wore a store suit), he was a stickler for doing it right, and she was properly rigged and fitted out in record time. One day she sailed, in half a gale. She made a short board across the creek, went about with much volleying from the new canvas, and then she was standing down river, leaving "a wake as wide as the State Road."

The *Spray's* hull in frame was worked on as the oyster fleet's spring repairs allowed, and, as it got warm, planking and ceiling started in earnest. A steam box was, of course, used, as hard pine is stiff, and the curves were full. Right here I learned about ceiling run and planking run too, things which seem to be overlooked in books and seem to have been forgotten. Later on, in the World War II years, this fact began immediately to show up. In that era, I suddenly found myself as Boss Planker "with twenty-nine head of men under me," a most successful one, they said, and I lay it all to the teaching of those who really knew.

Soon beams were going into the *Spray,* and waterways, decks, and the trunk were started. When she was about together on top, it was time to think of getting her tight so work could go on below in bad weather, for fall storms were not far away. It was time to caulk her hull, too. Edward, the caulker, got a couple of his crew from the old days from Down the Bay, and they went at it. This was quite a show in itself. Caulking was a trade of its own and took much learning. Morning starts were slow and hesitant, especially if it was a bit chilly. Then the tempo would increase slightly, the magic black hands feeding the cotton and oakum like machines. There would come a moan from somewhere under her, an answering hum, and shortly a hymn would start, lightly at first, in time with the mallets. Each mallet had a voice of its own. The tempo would increase, with much punctuation from the mallets. The crab pickers next door would pick up the hymn, and soon there would be a real old rouser going. At some mys-

tic signal from the boss mallet, all would stop; at a cry from it another would start, a real old foot-stomper this time! By then, the sun would be beating down, happy looks were on the shiny black faces, and the real fun would start. Suddenly all mallets would stop but one, he would solo with much art and many flourishes, and then the chorus would come in again, until some other would do his solo. This went on all day until she was caulked; no wonder it did not take long.

I asked Edward how it was in the days of the big vessels. His face lighted up. "When 'e done the *White,* had a thick oak bottom, first-class seams, and twenty head of men under her. Man, that were Music!" He was referring to the fourmaster, the *Purnell T. White.* My vessel was, of course, tight, and stayed so. Fifteen years later she was "set back" for the first time. Ancient Ed was still around, though others did the job. I had consulted him about it, and he thought "it was about time."

Deck details were worked on as the weather allowed, and, as it was getting cool, the stove was set up below. On bad days, we built the cabin around it. Simple though attractive, it was a vessel's cabin. Then there was much bunging and painting outside, with much effort on the seams, which were all rodded back. She sat at the edge of a bulkhead near the sheers. A big November tide was needed, as otherwise there was quite a drop and not much water ordinarily.

The line of the launching just cleared the old backhouse. It was a true shipways launching, on grease, as that was the custom, even for very small vessels. Ways were built, and she had the customary trial packing. Then, as the day approached, tallow was heated, the ways greased, stops rigged, and the whole thing repacked. Launching day was cold and raw with little wind. The tide came well, as there was a gale

Sheets just started and a nice bow wave — the author's Spray.

in the offing. The bulkhead was cut down in way of the keel passage in case the ways settled; no one wanted any toe-stubbing. There was no check line, as the creek was wide, the vessel small, and what wind there was would drift her back to the dock.

This was an honest saw-off launching. The wedges were driven to raise her, the keel blocks were knocked out, and she bore on the sliding ways. The dogs were tripped, the tide lapped the bulkhead, and the order was given to start the big crosscuts, just sharpened for this occasion. Halfway through came an order to stop; the Master measured each side. Then he said, "Cut her off," and they did. She sat. Edward dropped his end of the saw, faced the vessel, and salaamed mightily, speaking in some strange lingo. A rumble went through the whole structure and she started, slowly at first, then with a rapid increase, a Splash, and much popping up of spewed blocks. A blue cloud appeared at the end of the ways; the tallow had smoked, so it was a proper launching. She was warped in to the dock, the pump was tried, and she was well made fast, for there was wind coming. The cabin stove felt fine, for we had been "keeping fire" now for several days. Tomorrow was Thanksgiving, and to hell with the mess of battered ways for this week. Those that used it had something to take home and warm up with, for all hands were chilled through. Even a small launching can be an exhausting business. The vessel was checked as to water late that night, and next morning the pump was frozen. What matter? She did not need it.

The rest was routine: masting, rigging, trials, and many years of sailing in good weather and bad, many ups and downs. Her construction never let her down. I had her a long time, and she has not had very many owners since. Rumor has it she's still afloat at 43 and is for sale at many, many times her first cost. At 23, when I parted with her, she was quite sound. Now, I don't know. Like many of us getting along, she might well "have considerable dote." I leave the Spray at that.

I've mentioned before doing it like it was,

with simple, honest materials and good workmanship. I think the Spray is a monument to this approach, yet in those days this kind of shipbuilding was the common thing. A vessel twenty years old was considered quite young. All it took was oak, hard pine, some cedar, and some galvanized iron. If she had been built in some other place, maybe other materials would have been used and done just as well. So many things get lost and forgotten; I spend much of my time now trying to pass it on, by talking, writing, designing, and by what I'm able to build, all in very fond memory of those cud-chewing masters of it. There was never a sour face, never a rush, never a false move; the trade was almost a religion with them.

Having become accepted and somewhat adept, I worked off and on between sailing with this same yard for some time, and at other smaller yards in the village. The Master wanted to retire; his boys were not interested in the yard, as is often the case. Finally, the place went to new owners; the old crew drifted off to nearby yards, and some passed on.

The new owners had to start from scratch and appointed a capable local man as manager. A job turned up and I was asked to come back, as I knew the set-up. I suddenly found I was a sawyer; I then realized I knew how. I raised an 80-foot vessel and put on a new shoe, with one other man. Nothing to it; I found I knew just how to do that, too. The railway downhaul broke. I had helped place the big sheave at the outer end some time back, so I "knew how it was" down in nine feet of water. I found myself shinning down a long pike pole in April water with a messenger line to fish through the monster iron block. I got her through, and I didn't like it one bit. Shades of Old Tom. No wonder he was addicted to Rotgut! I guess I had become a shipyard man. So it went, here and there, trying to make a vessel pay summers, for there was something called a Depression around.

I got work in yards down South, not much, for there was not much. Some Nut started a War. This always calls for vessels. Someone heard I could loft. Right quick I was down on my knees lofting the first of a big Government contract under the eye of a past acquaintance. One thing and another, I did it all. I became known as a hot number with an adz, Isaac's adz. I got pretty good at boring alleyways, some big. Big chunks of timber and seemingly impossible shapes fell to me, because I had been trained by men who thought in this medium. After all, some of my teachers had been log canoe builders, or their fathers had. The art of working "chunks" was still around on the Bay.

A planking louse-up developed, and the whole problem was dumped on me. I found myself a planker boss with quite a crew, maybe by default, because no one there had worked with a master of it. I had. The old fellow was gone now, but I think he looked to my efforts, for I often turned to his teachings when things were sticky. I must say that they almost always were right.

Many years later I found myself master shipwright building a sailing vessel in New England, the schooner *Integrity*. I "done the hull of it," as they say, from design on. It was just like of old, the sounds, the sights, the smells, no sour faces, and a happy gleam, though nobody chewed. There was electricity and a warm toilet. The caulkers were the same, only with mystic rites in Portagee, and much taking of snuff. She was "humming tight." I felt the Old Master's presence strongly. I spoke of it to others.

The vessel had some happy years, made a long, successful voyage, was later acquired by lubbers who ruined her, but "The Sea Couldn't Kill Her."

The Master was there all right!

III

Boatbuilding

Being still active with boats, I'm constantly exposed to much discussion about them, and one of the main topics is cost. Current prices in any age seem to have little to do with it; the point is, boats always were expensive. To make the first hollowed-out log took much time and labor that could not be devoted to hunting and fishing. Good things are expensive, and some of us think boats are very good things.

Possibly because boats are supposed to be so very good, we have, over many years, come to the idea they must be made in as difficult and expensive a way as possible. Certainly this was not the original approach, especially in working craft. Good enough to do the job and do it well was what was required. And pride of workmanship was involved to make the boat look as fine as one's resources and her intended use allowed.

Many folks now seem to be trying to think along these lines again. At least there is renewed interest in simple, and thus often traditional, craft. It is said Man has been building boats for 5,000 years, maybe longer. Certainly something has been learned about it in that length of time. Some think this should be pushed aside, for there are all sorts of breakthroughs, new wonder materials, and even newer thinking — all still very young compared to the past development of boats. The new methods of boatbuilding, however, are mostly very much out of reach to the ordinary fellow.

Having worked with everything from cheap skiffs, up through yachts plain and fancy, and Uncle Sam's best in wood, I have long ago come to the conclusion that the traditional craft is by far the most economical and useful in the end, and the most pleasing to the eye. I feel the same way about traditional construction methods, especially if the boat is built by the home builder or the small shop that cannot and should not spend too much money tooling up for just one craft. Many builders get befuddled by "production thinking" in setting up to build a rather simple wooden boat, possibly because they hope orders will come in for many. This rarely happens, and if by chance it does, you simply go on building the same thing, improving where you can, and taking care not to repeat any previous mistakes.

I doubt if there has been much improvement in the design and building of rowing craft since ancient times. Obviously, moving boats by manual labor over the years led to the development of models most suited to that form of propulsion. In connection with the present revival of pleasure rowing, we can do well to study the smart craft of the past. This also applies to traditional sailing craft; the very recent improvements are largely in the availability of better materials: ballast, rope, wire, and sail cloth. Simplicity of rig and ease of repair were always sought after in craft of the past. Those intended

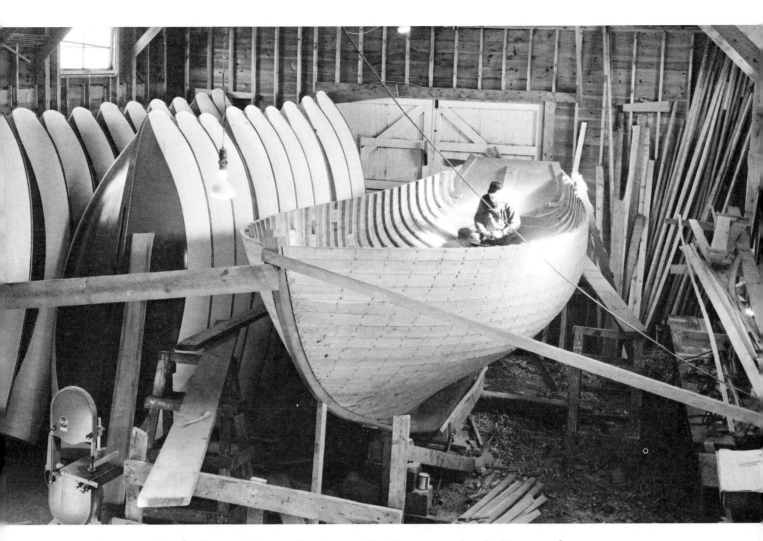

In the boat shop at the Concordia Company, South Dartmouth, Massachusetts. An inventory of twenty Beetle cats is stacked up to meet the demands of a coming sailing season. (Photo by Norman Fortier.)

for speed could sail, for, in some trades at least, to lose the race was to hang!

All this background makes traditional craft most appealing, the more so when you consider how very practical they are, each for her own special use. Needless to say, you should use some judgment in which craft to select. This involves not a little study of the waters she will sail and her intended use, as well as how the type chosen suits available materials. This last applies to small craft or large, and is of much more importance in a boat of some size. Chasing for non-existent stock is most frustrating.

Assuming you have chosen a boat, and are about to build her, either yourself at home or professionally at a yard, once a start is made, you should get on with the job. Many backyard builders figure a long project, even up to five or more years. Some pros start a job and then put it aside for a long period to work at something that brings in ready cash. In both cases, troubles begin. You learn the hard way. Very little timber is really thoroughly dry. A long layoff, and checks develop. The shed or shelter starts to leak unnoticed. A shore or two drops out. Mice or chickens move in. Space is limited,

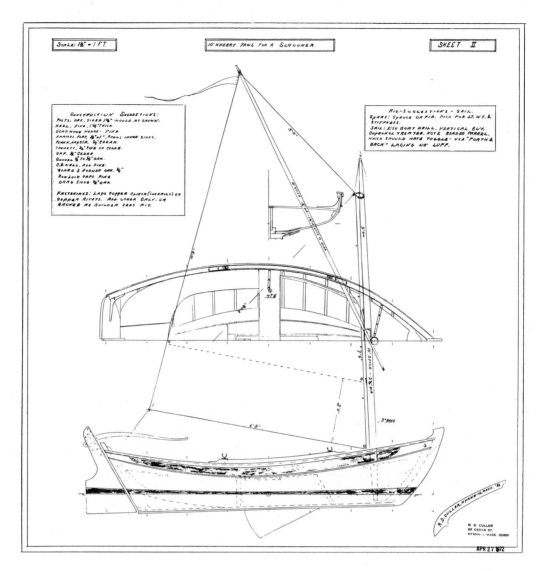

CONSTRUCTION SUGGESTIONS:
POSTS. OAK. SIDED 1⅛" MOULD AS SHOWN.
KEEL, PINE, 1¼" THICK.
DEAD WOOD NEEDS. PINE.
FRAMES FLAT, ⅝"×⅞", RADIUS INNER SIDES.
PLANK, LAPSTR, ¼" CEDAR.
THWARTS, ⅞" PINE OR CEDAR.
CRP. ⅜" CEDAR.
GUNNEL ⅝ TO ¾" OAK.
C.B. WELL, ALL PINE.
'BOARD & RUDDER OAK. ⅝"
ROWLOCK CAPS PINE
DRAG SHOE ½" OAK

FASTENINGS: LAPS COPPER CLINCH (CUTNAILS) OR
COPPER RIVETS. ALL OTHER GALV. OR
BRONZE AS BUILDER SEES FIT.

RIG SUGGESTIONS - SAIL.
SPARS: SPRUCE OR FIR. PICK FOR LT. WT. &
STIFFNESS.
SAIL: 2½ OZ BOAT DRILL, VERTICAL CUT,
OUTHAUL TARRED. NOTE BEADED PARREL,
WHICH SHOULD HAVE TOGGLE - USE "FORTH &
BACK" LACING ON LUFF.

R. D. CULLER
85 CEDAR ST.
HYANNIS. MASS. 02601

APR 27 1972

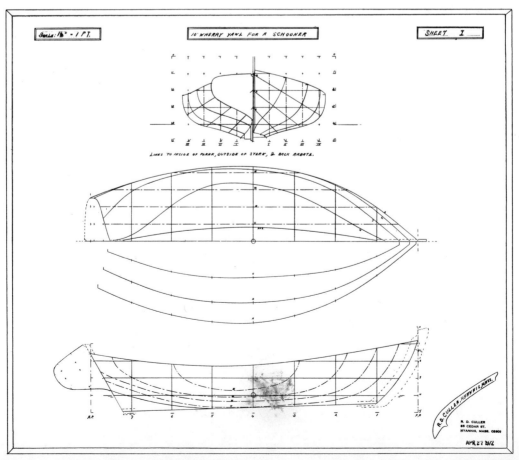

LINES TO INSIDE OF PLANK, OUTSIDE OF STEM, & BACK RABBETS.

R. D. CULLER
85 CEDAR ST.
HYANNIS. MASS. 02601

APR 27 1972

STATION	FP	1	2	3	⊕	5	6	7	AP
SHEER	1-7-2	1-4-5	1-2-1	1-0-0+	0-10-5	0-10-2+	0-10-7+	1-0-3	1-2-5+
BUTT. I		0-5-1+	0-1-4+	0-3-1	0-4-1	0-4-1	0-2-1+	0-1-7	
BUTT. II		1-3-5	0-1-2	0-1-2+	0-2-0+	0-2-0+	0-0-1	0-3-6	
BUTT. III			0-9-7	0-0-6	0-0-4=	0-0-4	0-1-3+	0-3-5+	
BUTT. IV				0-8-1	0-2-2-	0-2-3			
RABATE		0-2-7	S	T	R A I G H	T	0-4-6	0-3-4+	0-0-4+
KEEL BOTTOM		0-3-4+	S	T	R A I G H	T	0-6-2+		
SHEER	0-0-3	0-11-7	1-8-0	2-0-4	2-2-2-	2-1-7	2-0-0	1-8-3	1-3-1
WL 2	0-0-3	0-10-9	1-7-6	2-0-4				1-8-3	TR 1-3-0
WL 3	0-0-3	0-6-7	1-5-2	1-10-7+	2-1-1	2-1-2-	1-10-6	1-5-2	TR 0-4-0
WL 4	0-0-3	0-4-5-	0-9-4	1-4-4	1-5-0	1-7-4	1-0-3	0-2-1	TR 0-0-3
RABATE		0-0-3	0-2-5-	0-4-1	0-4-7	0-4-4-	0-3-1-	NOLL 0-0-3	
KEEL BOTTOM			AS	COMES					
DIAG. A	WL-1 0-0-7	0-11-7+	1-8-5+	2-2-1-	2-4-6	2-4-3	2-1-7+	1-8-4	TR 1-2-2
DIAG. B	WL-4 0-0-7	0-9-2	1-4-5-	1-8-1+	1-9-4+	1-9-2+	1-7-0+	1-2-2-	TR 1-0-0
DIAG. C	WL-3 0-1-1	0-5-1	0-10-4-	0-11-7+	1-0-6	1-0-5+	0-10-6+	0-6-5+	TR 0-3-5

HEIGHTS ABOVE BASE LINE · HALF BREADTHS · DIAGONALS

LINES TO INSIDE OF PLANK & BACK RABATE · OUTSIDE OF STERN.
EXAMPLE: 1-7-1+ = 1 FT. 7 IN. 4/8 + 1/16 — 10' WHERRY YAWL. RDC '72

so the half-finished hull becomes a storehouse for all sorts of junk.

One fellow knocked off for a year, just when his planking was ready to bung. The result was the bung holes shrank and became somewhat egg-shaped. He had to give up bungs and go to putty. Another was ten years at it, then died, and by that time some of his work was starting to rot! Better he had attempted a small sailing skiff and had her done in time to use. You hear occasionally of very large craft built by one man. Many more are started but not finished. You must consider that most of your time can be spent rigging mechanical aids and shifting staging, rather than on actual construction. If this goes on too long, your spirit can weaken.

A fellow can be overcome by equipment that is too expensive and by too much "tooling up." Having a lot of stuff to work with sounds nice, but it takes money, often better used elsewhere; it takes up space, which is often at a premium; and above all it takes maintenance. You can have too much of a good thing. Most traditional craft were built with the simplest equipment, for they are of fairly simple construction as a rule. The usual way was to build outdoors with no shelter at all, or at most a "shade," as they say in the tropics. Nowadays, in certain climates, more shelter is needed, though not as much as many suppose, especially if the building of the craft is a one-shot thing. In the Northeast, many think a fully heated shop is the only possible way, and by heated they mean like our living room. While heat is a must for fiberglass or large amounts of gluing, it's all wrong for the construction of traditional wooden boats. Building a small wooden boat in the modern heated cellar brings on all sorts of troubles. Better a shed of some sort and a drum stove to burn the scrap.

One of my friends built a 36-foot boat in a two-car garage. His method was this: One bay for lumber and tools, the other for the bow half of the boat. The stern half was outdoors, protected by a tarp when needed. He prefabbed parts and pieces during the winter in the cellar, where most of his very modest power equipment was, along with a good workbench. He set her up in very early spring, pushed along during the summer, working forward on bad days and aft on good ones. She was fairly well closed in by fall. He had a stove in the cabin so he could work below during the tough months. Before launching, he had a dry run with his rig to be sure all was right; this also checked out his gin pole setup for getting his masts in and out. He launched in early spring and was sailing the same day, as his preparations were so thorough he did not have to wait for her "to make up," or sit up and pump during the night. She had been swelled carefully with a hose.

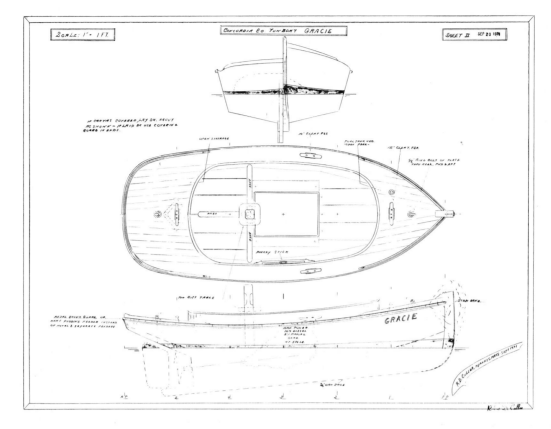

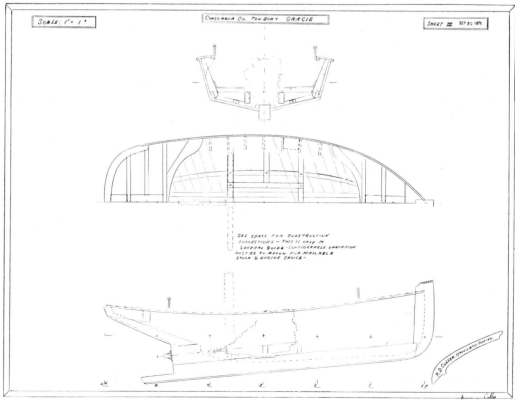

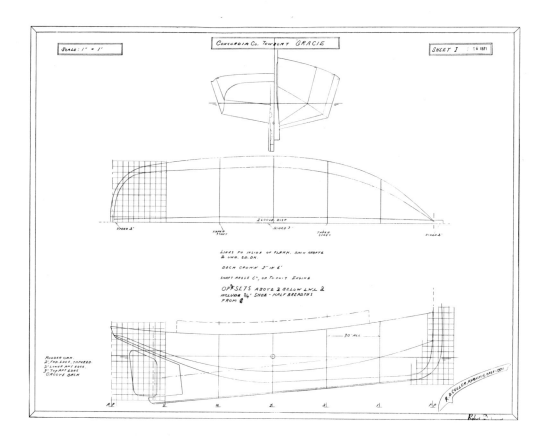

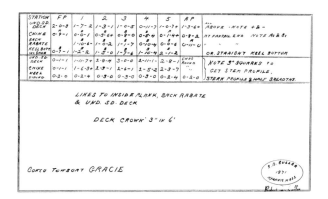

The towboat, Gracie, *taking shape at Concordia.*

Getting out a schooner mast in a Maine boatyard.

The idea is you can make do in many ways with proper planning. Heavy, warm clothes and boots are far cheaper than a heated building. And speaking again of heat in a proper boatshop in winter, I find 40 to 60 degrees the most you want, the lesser for active work with tools, the greater for paint and varnish. Big glue jobs require at least 70 degrees to be successful; if you can't raise that much in winter, wait till spring! You can take a lot of cold when out of the wind, dressed for it, and, say, working out a stem or keel. Oh yes! I've seen it 130 degrees in a Southern boatshop in summer, working on deck, under a roof, and with big floodlights. Some modern shops are kept so hot — about as hot as the attached office — that one soon feels in a stupor. Meanwhile, those "upstairs" rack their brains as to why "production" is falling off and the heating bills are rising. They also wonder why they have so much checked timber and warping.

Turning to floors, or what the craft will be set up on, a stout wood floor is best of all. You can nail to it, lag, cleat, cut holes in it if the need arises, and it's easy on the building crew. If it's a light wooden floor, it's still pretty good, as you can usually block and shore it here and there and get by. Thousands upon thousands of craft have been built on the ground; it's pretty good, be it rocky, muddy, sandy, or just plain along the shore or in your back yard. Tools stand dropping on the ground better than a wooden floor. If it pitches this way and that, so what? That's what a level and plumb are for. You are often stuck with a cement floor. If so, you put up with it and build on a grid. If the builder does not already know it, he will soon find that cement is very hard on the legs and feet. There is nothing to nail to, and if a hand or power tool falls, often that's it for the tool. A lot of things seem to get jarred and fall off in boatbuilding. Falls by workmen are not unknown, and a cement floor seems to be a bad place to take a spill. To set up a new professional boatshop with a cement floor shows a total lack of understanding of wooden boatbuilding, the trade in general, and the welfare of the working crew and equipment. The day comes when a long keel bolt must be got out, or a long stock rudder unshipped. The instigators of the cement floor then see their sins; they have to hire a jackhammer! Later the holes are covered with wooden hatches; they are learning.

There is quite a lot in choosing just what time of year to start a craft, depending on her type, the available working time, location, and what stock you can get and when. A home builder doing a small craft in the North usually works in winter, assuming he has some kind of shelter. A yard, large or small, usually prefers winter, too, and it's apt to be the slackest time. Though many give it no thought now, there is much advantage in using fall-cut timber, usually for the keel and the bigger timbers. In the fall the ground is mostly dry, and timber can be got out of the woods relatively easily. Sap is down, so many think the timber more healthy and less liable to decay, and there is less blue stain in the sapwood, especially in pine. In some places, timber is cut in late fall and winter and trucked out as soon as roads are usable in early summer. While many books on the subject and many elaborately written specifications call for "thoroughly dry stock," in practice dry stock is generally not available for big timber, or for much other timber for that matter. No builder is going to store much big timber for long periods. He has no real idea of the sizes he will need in the future, or even if he will have a boat to build. This all more or less applies to the home builder too, especially for the heavy parts. The fact that most craft are built of green or semi-green timber in the keels, deadwoods, and so forth and that they seem to last speaks well for what the book says is shoddy practice. Personally,

"Launching" the Sharptown Barge from the author's upstairs boat shop. (More photos of the Barge appear on pages 65 and 115.)

I've seen much good timber, including spar timber, that was left over from some job go bad before there was any use for it. It's in the way, is pushed aside, the covering blows off, and soon sun and water do their work. Some may be resawed later into smaller stuff, but most seems to end up as sleepers and props for some new project. If you must build outdoors, and with possibly no more than a tarp to cover some of the work, there is much advantage in laying your stock in the fall, sticking it carefully, and at least covering the top of the lumber and painting the ends. It will dry considerably by the time it's needed.

You have to have a place to lay down, and if space is limited, this can be done "by halves," or even quarters, or, as one well-known Southern

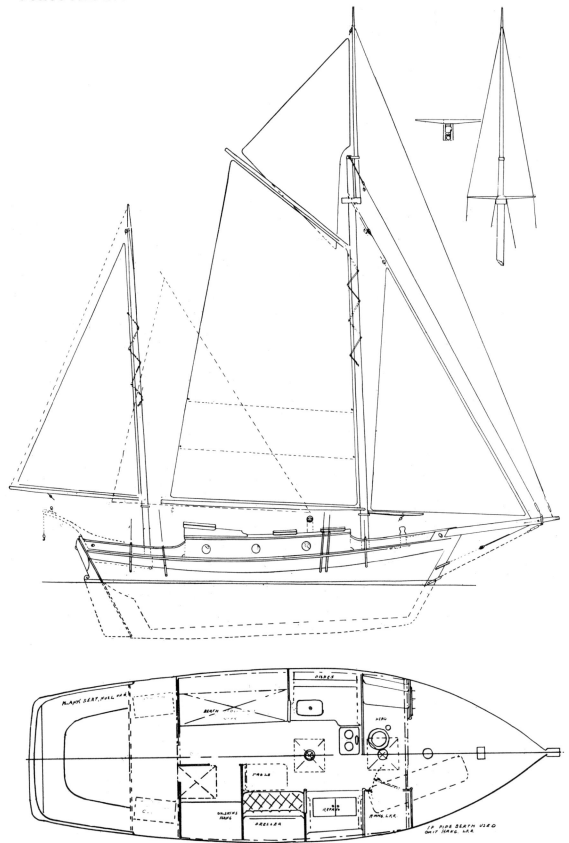

A 34-foot, raised-deck ketch designed for single-handed work.

builder, now retired, always did, by the half-size method, which is suited to some craft. With a sheltered place to make moulds and other parts, you bring the job well along the first winter. Come early spring, set her up and push along during the good months. Even if the craft is only a modest cabin type, it takes plenty of pushing. The idea is to "get her shut in" by fall, and most of the outside stuff done, then set up the stove, even if only temporarily, and do the inside work when the weather is unfit for anything else.

I've seen a very nice lobster boat more or less prefabbed in a cellar during a Maine winter. As soon as the ground was bare, she was set up outside. In a few days, she stood in frame.

Shortly, she was planked, and, so it seemed, as soon as the weather was good, she was at work. Obviously, this was the result of good planning and a skilled man.

To the man who has never done it before, a boatbuilding project looks big and difficult. The more you think about it the worse it seems, when actually the hardest part is making the start. Once you start, one thing follows another in the natural order of boatbuilding, none being really much of a chore. It's just thinking of the whole pile of steps at once that makes the job seem so much of a mountain.

The proper choice of a craft suited to your abilities plus care in planning and careful lofting get a boat off to a good start. Even pros

This small punt will be used as a tender. The boats shown in all these photographs were designed by the author. Unless otherwise noted, they were also built by him, either single-handed at his own boat shop at Hyannis, Massachusetts, or with a gang at the Concordia Company.

have been known to take on a craft that was too much for their setup. And as to lofting, some get carried away and do more than is really needed. "Loft everything but the galley sink." Some designs require much lofting and some do not. In either case, do a thorough job, for it always pays off later.

Lofting on paper is very unsatisfactory, especially if the craft is of some size and the job protracted. Paper does not wear well, and is much affected by changes in humidity. It's surprising how a long length of paper will come and go. For a very small craft that can be laid down and moulds made in a day or two, you can get by using paper. I've found white pine, and in some cases fir, battens the best, made from near the edge of a plank. Oak and cedar battens just don't seem to stay fair long. Sometimes a hard pine one will work well. I might mention that I seldom nail through a batten in lofting, always alongside. Besides being better for the life of the batten, you avoid the slight swell around the nail, if it's a very light batten. As is often the case, the batten is not long enough, so you have to overlap a second batten, one inside, and the other outside the line. The side nailing helps the overlapping situation and makes all lie fair. You partially remove one batten at the lap, mark the line, replace the batten and remove the other, continuing the marking of the line. All experienced loftsmen know this, but the beginner has to learn it from others. For short quick curves, such as body lines, you sometimes try many methods, and break some battens too, in many cases resorting to a bandsaw blade in the end. While building a boat, you should be on the lookout for rippings that will make good battens for the going job or a future boat.

Having tried several colors for a loft floor and worked on several brand new unpainted ones (very good) and many much-worn dark ones, I think very light, dull gray paint the best. Colored pencils and marking pens are handy, especially if there are many lines. These things, not being intended for such work, wear fast, but are worth it. Clinch box nails, when they can be had, are most handy lofting nails. Some of these

A nice flat-bottomed skiff.

come blued, which is no matter. They can be used for fastening light moulds and in setting battens, as the points are flat and thin. They also stay put in taking up lines by the string-of-nails method, that is they don't roll and have thin heads. If clinch box nails are not available, you can use pot nails, lath nails, or something similar.

Many people may be unfamiliar with picking up lines with nails, though it seems that most older builders use the method. Probably, while it's not as old as boats, it's at least as old as manufactured nails. Here's how it works: A piece of mould stock, plywood, or thin plank sufficient to cover the area to be raised is laid over the spot. If more than one piece is needed, it's fitted to the first. Three or more nails are driven against the stock, so it can't shift two ways; the other two ways don't matter, as in placing the stock, one simply crowds it to the nails. When this is set, remove the mould stock. Then place the small picking-up nails, heads on the lofted line, shanks at right angles to it, an inch or more apart. The less curve in the line, the farther apart the nails. All you want is an accurate enough spotting from the nail heads so a batten can be set in the spots they make. When all the area to be moulded is covered with nails, not forgetting such things as sheer height and other needed marks, lower the mould stock almost to the floor, crowd it to the positioning nails, and, taking care not to shift it, lower it right to the floor and kneel on it. Then step over all of the mould stock to press the nail heads into it. Some also tap along the approximate line with a hammer. Then the whole thing is lifted, turned over, and, if small enough, taken to the bench, otherwise laid on the floor. Many of the nails will stick to the mould stock, especially if it's soft, less so to plywood, and no matter; what you want is the marks from the nails. These are battened off in the usual way, marked, and the mould carefully sawed out. With practice and a clean-running bandsaw, you can "split the line" and that's it, or cut slightly wide and bring to the line with a light plane. You then place the mould in position on the floor, and find it fits the lines perfectly.

From the loftman's standpoint, this one's at least, it's better to work from lines to inside of plank. One seldom finds lines produced this way now. Many think they know how to allow for plank thickness and really don't. Even some books on lofting fail really to go into this matter. It's not quite the way it would seem. The usual method of striking arcs of plank thickness in from the body plan station lines, or using a gauge block of the plank thickness doesn't quite give the true picture except near the middle of the craft, though in a very sharp, thin-planked boat, the error is small. Picture a very full-bowed, thick-planked craft, say with the sheer plank cutting a bow station at about 40 degrees. Imagine cutting this plank through vertically with a saw, at right angles to the keel. The face of the cut, "square with the keel," is much wider than the thickness of the actual plank. Or, take it another way: A standard 2 x 4 is 1⅝ inches thick; cut it vertically at 40 degrees and measure the face. You will see right off that considerable error can develop in a buxom craft with a thick skin. A bevel board can be made, based on the proposed plank thickness of the craft, which will show the amount to allow for the amount of bevel.

A heavily raked, curved stern is apt to be the pons asinorum of lofting for many. A close study of the shape and often a doubling up on some lines make it work out. Many naval architects do this doubling up as a matter of course. Certain traditional craft seem always to have had curvature, or "radius," in the stern, and to look the part must be built that way. I doubt, however, if the radius stern has any practical value, only looks. Many sterns that are flat across are quite handsome if otherwise properly shaped, and flatness allows building by flitching up, or using thick stock edge-bolted, plus a nailing frame. Assuming the topwork is kept tight, and the joints are good, I feel this method of construction is possibly less subject to decay than a radius stern that must be made up of many smaller pieces. No doubt many builders won't agree, and I do not wholly condemn the radius stern; sometimes it's worth the trouble. One sometimes sees a rather ugly radius stern; in this case, I think it's a total waste of time and material.

Some round-bilge designs show a minimum of diagonal lines, often not enough. Small matter; you can always strike in more, especially down near the rabbet. This is where things tend not to work out if the craft has much reverse curve and widely spaced lines. This adding of lines sometimes is a help in other than diagonals, say in the ends if the craft is of quick shape. These additions don't always have to go the length of the vessel. You usually have few problems near the middle of a craft. I personally have a great liking for plenty of diagonal lines properly placed. They tend very much to the run of the planking lines in round-bilge boats, which helps very much in lining off for the plank. You can usually tell from the placing of the diagonals on a plan if the designer has a good working knowledge of planking.

A 24-foot outboard launch being built at Concordia and out on her trials. (Her plans appear on the following pages.)

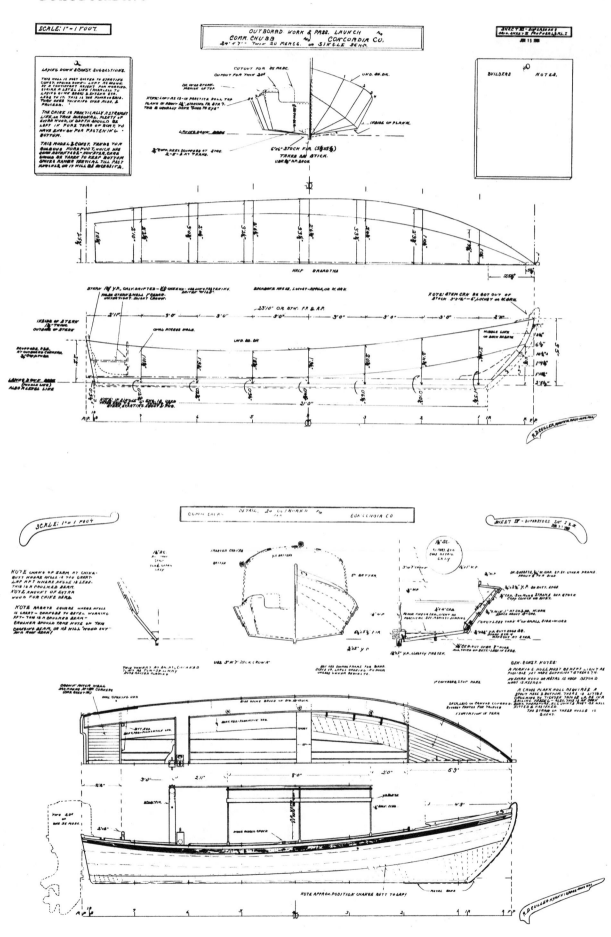

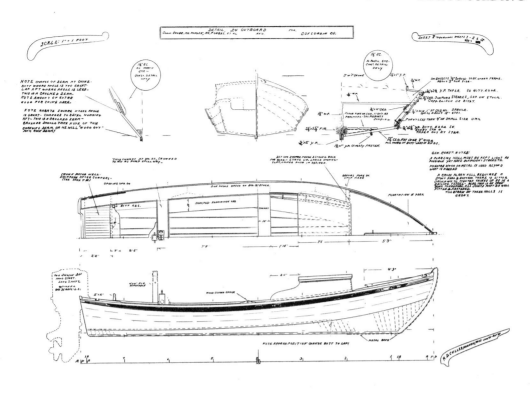

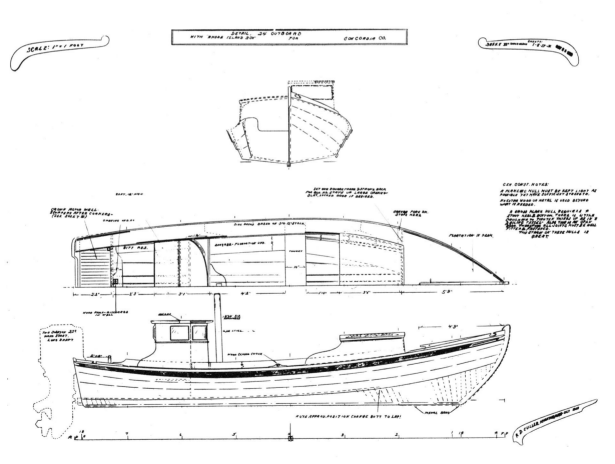

In most craft, especially those of classic model with deep heel and sharp forefoot, you should line out your garboard quite wide in the ends. The object is to gain fast there so as to keep the hook out of the hood ends of following planks. One often hears it said, "plank should follow the waterline as nearly as possible," and that some sort of master-width batten should be used to figure the strake widths at all stations. Possibly this works on a craft with a cigar-shaped hull. This method will probably be accompanied, however, by much edge setting of plank, or fitting the plank by bending it edgeways, "to save stock." Nothing I know of can cause more bother, trouble, fight, and waste of stock than this method, the more so the more shapely the craft. I strongly suggest that when in doubt about lining off for plank, you batten off the whole craft in advance if she's small, so you can see the errors in advance and can make corrections. In larger craft, placing the ribbands along the diagonal lines will give about the same effect. The builder can see his planking run, only in larger panels, and make any small correction as he goes, by sections. In very stout, large, sawn-frame vessels, the harping bands of very stout timber are placed the same way, as nearly as possible along the diagonals, for the same reason. Approached as suggested, planking done this way is by far the easiest, least wasteful of stock, most pleasing to the eye, and best for the boat. In large craft with narrow strakes and with rather long lengths of plank, some edge setting can be done, but the less the better.

Modest errors in lining off seldom show once a carvel-planked craft is joined off and seams are filled and painted, except possibly to the critical eye looking for such things. However, in light, lapstrake craft, the line of the plank can be a most important matter if the boat is to look well. For these craft, I feel it pays to line off completely with battens of about the same width as the laps. Do one side only, of course. Take plenty of time and look from all angles, not always easy in a crowded shop. Make corrections a strake at a time; adjusting one usually calls for tinkering with another. Finally it Looks

Right and that's it. And never — I said never — attempt to plank a lapstrake hull by edge setting!

Most of the "outmoded" methods of the past still work, science to the contrary. Consider, for example, the half model. If you have doubts as to the looks of your craft, you should construct one. Among other things, you will find it an excellent medium on which to practice lining off plank, with the aid of a light batten and pins. After all, many a steel vessel has been built with the aid of a "plating model." While the use of models is frowned on, even laughed at today by some at least, it's well to point out that many of the craft seen now would have been better in many ways if there had been a model used somewhere in their development. Some of the quickie steel jobs around could have well used a plating model. This last is also an aid if you are considering some design in plywood that was not originally intended for it. A little fooling around with cardboard panels will soon show what's what.

Without going into the details of half model making, since they have been well covered by able writers of experience (L. Francis Herreshoff and Howard Chapelle both cover it well, and their works are readily available), it's well to mention that much additional information can be had from a half model with quite reasonable accuracy. Displacement can be worked out rather closely by several methods, all based on the same principle. Various centers can be arrived at. You can see what the craft will look like afloat, using the lifts above the L.W.L. only, and you can appreciate what the fish will see. Besides, a half model is often the only way to get across to a builder unfamiliar with the type just what the craft really looks like, what problems lie ahead, and, above all, if the stern is extremely shapely, just what this is to look like.

If expensive towing tank tests using models are of use to the big-time designer and builder, and they no doubt are, then the use of the cheap half model can be of much help to the small professional builder and backyard shipyard. You don't expect way-out answers from a block of

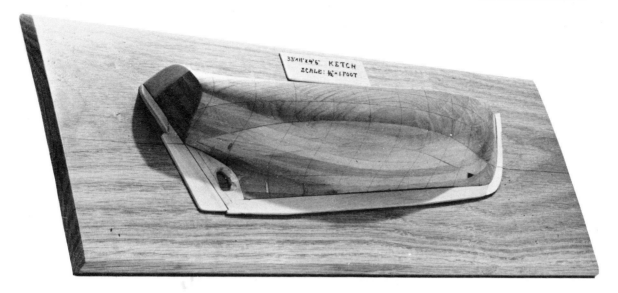

wood, no matter how nicely made, but rather practical guides useful in building ordinary craft.

While it may seem very much the backwoods way, I seldom start a craft without a half model, even a skiff, unless the boat is only a slight variation of some previous design. In larger craft, somewhere along in working up the design, a half model is built, often more than one, or the first one altered. Yes, the model can show you the error of your ways. Besides, it's a fine thing to have around for all the experts to pick apart. After all is done, and this sometimes runs into months and even years, and whether or not the finished craft is a success, the model makes a fine shop decoration, and reminds you of your errors, if any. Usually there are some.

Some amateurs and small boatshop owners like to tinker with design, and that's just fine; excellent craft often come from their efforts. Sometimes, however, a fellow gets a passion for design, learns on his own, or is taught all the very up-to-date approaches, and is good at math so loves all sorts of calculations, but unfortunately has not had the interest or time to learn about boats from a practical standpoint. Any design he turns out lacks something; it's hard to say just what, but one might say it lacks Boat Sense. This fellow is also apt to be a pain in the neck to some builder.

Two of the author's builder's half-models. Above, a 33-foot ketch; below, an 83-foot schooner.

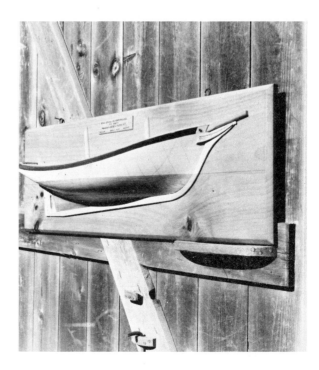

Some years back one of these chaps came to me to learn the real workings of a boatshop. We started from scratch and built him a beach boat. He "worked" along with the builder, and I think he got a lot out of it; we both did, though my neck hurt! Being a whiz at math and the use of the slipstick, he was at first appalled at what seemed slapdash methods of the small shop. We started with picking the lumber and other stock. The fact that cedar is full of pin knots was the first surprise. You so often read about "perfectly clear, dry stock in long lengths" in boat specs. My own experience has been that it's nice reading, but the stock seldom exists. After loading the truck, taking the lumber to mill and unloading, jacking it through the ear-splitting old planer (which, by the way, had no shavings blower; she just spewed to the atmosphere), loading again, transporting to shop and sticking, the budding shipwright allowed as how it was a bit of hard work, and dusty too.

After a terrific battle with the lofting, done by methods more enlightened than others use, a warped grid, and miles of erasing and all the other pitfalls of the know-it-all greenie (the craft, by the way, was a flat-bottomed thing), he finally allowed it was not all in the book. "Taking up" by Noah's method was viewed with extreme doubt; then it all fit exactly. This was a shock in itself. There was an attempt at calculating (by the book) the coming performance of the craft. As no one seemed to know what the prismatic co-efficient of a rowing-sailing beach boat should be, this effort fell on its face. As to balance, it depends on where you put your big butt!

By now we were into drilling properly, tight seams, and all the other routine, along with a couple of cut fingers and other mishaps, such as having to draw a botched fastening, or raise a Nova Scotia Dimple (no offense, it's just a boatbuilder's term) with spit or hot water. Oh yes, he learned to build the shop fire, sweep, and sharpen tools. Some days the shop temperature never got above 35 degrees, but we were too busy and interested to care.

The end result was a nice craft with an an-cient background, so therefore successful in spite of a little science. We both enjoyed it and learned a lot about each other, and I hope something about the art of building small craft. It seems in these little boats we are no more advanced than the old-timers were, and possibly have gone backwards. How far this art of building goes when applied to larger vessels is a moot point. Suffice to say, regardless of your formal training, to design a good schooner you must know something about schooners. Exposure to boats and vessels of your liking is no doubt the best way to train for the future design and building of them.

Many builders of the past, and present too for that matter, have had little or no formal training in the science of it or in higher math. Yet these same men turn out routine work that would seem to require the highest order of calculation. While formal training is no doubt of much advantage, if you can't get it, you pick up the knowledge from some master, who in turn learned it the same way. There is nothing like being exposed to a master shipwright or boatbuilder for long periods. A man learns many things about the trade not covered in writings, and like most other worthwhile pursuits, considerable study is required to fill out his knowledge. Home builders as a rule cannot get much of this exposure to trained men; however, with study, a real will to do it, and all the contact they can get with pros, they are soon on the way. Many amateurs have turned pro, and one is often much impressed with the craft turned out by home builders who really have desire.

Some may think professional builders don't care to discuss the workings of their trade. My experience has been the opposite; they love to gab endlessly about the subject they love, once they are sure of genuine interest. The rare exceptions are those who don't know their trade, and this seems to apply in any trade, the kind who will tell nothing in case the other may use it and get ahead of him. One thing about it, you can't take it with you, so if you have something on the ball, pass it on, so another can create a good boat.

IV
Materials

You may decide to build a certain size and type of craft, a boat well suited to her use, and of course one which you can afford. In choosing a boat to build, it's well to consider what stock and materials are reasonably available. There is no point at all in planning a craft for which you can't get material, or for which you can get material only under great difficulty. Maybe worse yet, it doesn't make sense to plan a boat that will require stuff you are unable to work with readily, due to lack of equipment or skill in the particular material.

We hear about a lot of wonderful new materials; no doubt they are great when used in the right places. Many of them are as yet unsuited to ease of working in a small shop. Some require controlled conditions; others may require out-of-reach equipment. Many folks think wood is now outdated; the fact is, it's the easiest medium for the small-time builder to work in, and is still the most economically practical for one-of-a-kind boats. Besides, it's available.

This last statement may be doubted by many people now, as they know of just three woods: teak, for trimming out fiberglass boats, and, as L. Francis Herreshoff said, two others, one red, and one not. From the beginning, boats were built with what was available. Ships finally made great voyages, and it became possible to import timber. For the most part now, we use wood which comes from many places. Some lumber mills make a point of milling for the marine trade. And it's often quite surprising what you can turn up at a really first-class lumber yard, geared only to shore building trades, and what these yards can get for a boatbuilder.

Many books on boatbuilding go very much into the pros and cons of various woods, where to use each in a hull, and their lasting qualities, which is fine. They fail to point out, however, that many very simple craft can be built with very simple materials, and in most cases be better off for it. A little open boat, constructed with reasonable care, and by nature having plenty of ventilation, does not have to be built of priceless and rare woods supposed to last forever. No wood does anyhow, or anything else for that matter, except possibly granite. This, by the way, makes excellent ballast for some types of craft. It's cheap where it's available, it's non-magnetic, it won't rust, and when the craft is done for, assuming she dies on the beach, you can build a stone wall with it.

Log canoes the world around have been built of local woods. Uncounted numbers of bateaux, dories, scows, skiffs, and other craft have been built of local stuff and continue to be. It's true that transportation is now so readily available, it can be cheaper sometimes to build from "imported" stuff.

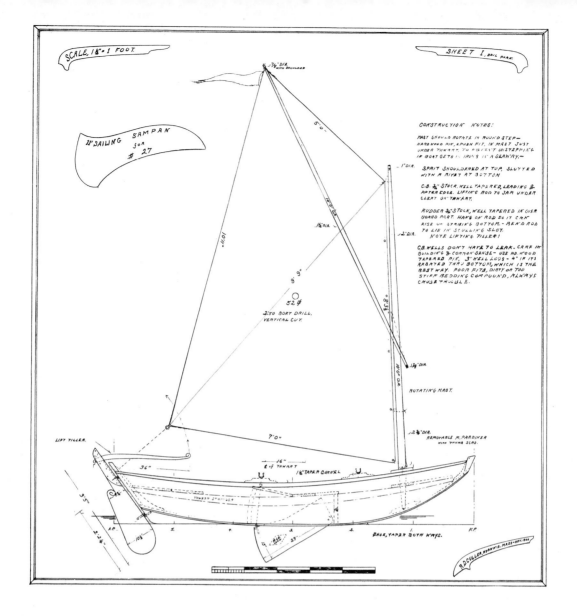

SCALE, 1⅛" = 1 FOOT.

SHEET I, SAIL PLAN.

11' SAILING SAMPAN
for
27

CONSTRUCTION NOTES:

MAST SHOULD ROTATE IN ROUND STEP—
HARDWOOD PIN, SNUG FIT, IN MAST JUST
UNDER THWART, TO PREVENT UNSTEPPING
IF BOAT GETS IN IRONS IN A SEAWAY.—

SPRIT SHOULDERED AT TOP, SLOTTED
WITH A RIVET AT BOTTOM.

C.B. ⅜" STOCK, WELL TAPERED, LEADING &
AFTER EDGE, LIFTING ROD TO JAM UNDER
CLEAT ON THWART.

RUDDER ⅜" STOCK, WELL TAPERED IN OVER
BOARD PART. HANG ON ROD SO IT CAN
RISE ON STRIKING BOTTOM.— BEND ROD
TO LIE IN SCULLING SLOT.
NOTE LIFTING TILLER!

C.B. WELLS DON'T HAVE TO LEAK. CAKE IN
BUILDING & COMMON SENSE— USE NO WOOD
TAPERED PIN, 3" WELL LOGS— 4" IF ITS
RABBETED THRU BOTTOM, WHICH IS THE
BEST WAY. POOR FITS, DIRTY OR TOO
STIFF BEDDING COMPOUND, ALWAYS
CAUSE TROUBLE.

ROTATING MAST.

REMOVABLE M. PARTNER
WITH THUMB SCRS.

LIFT TILLER.

2·50 BOAT DRILL,
VERTICAL CUT.

1⅛" TAPER GUNNEL

SHOE, TAPER BOTH WAYS.

R.D.CULLER HYANNIS, MASS— NOV. 1966

SCALE, 1⅛"=1 FOOT.

11' SAILING SAMPAN
for
27

SHEET III, CONSTRUCTION.

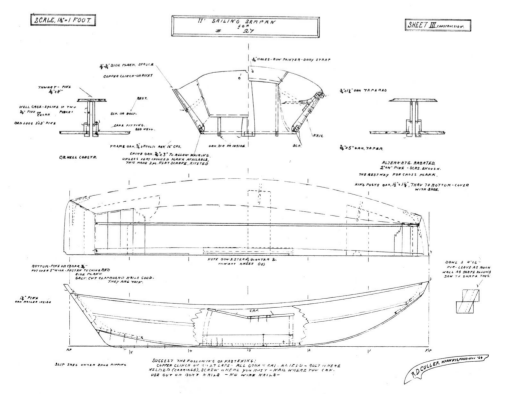

C.B. WELL CONSTR.

ALTERNATE, RABBETED,
2"x4" PINE— SCRD. ENOUGH.
THE BEST WAY FOR CROSS PLANK.

SUGGEST THE FOLLOWING ON FASTENING:
COPPER CLINCH ON ALL LAPS. RIVETS— BOLT IT HERE
NEEDED (CARRIAGES), SCREW WHERE YOU MUST— NAIL WHERE YOU CAN.
USE CUT OR BOAT NAILS — NO WIRE NAILS.

R.D.CULLER HYANNIS, MASS— NOV. '66

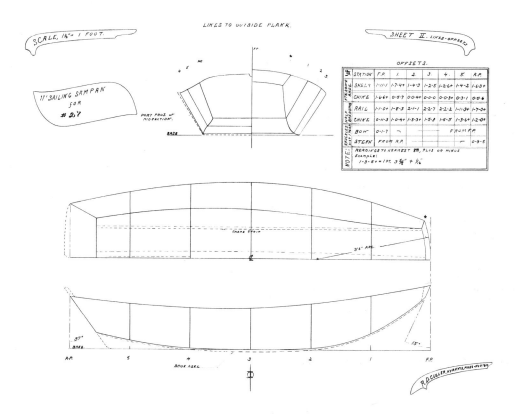

SCALE, 1½" = 1 FOOT.

LINES TO OUTSIDE PLANK.

SHEET II. LINES-OFFSETS.

11' SAILING SAMPAN
FOR
#27

PORT PROJ. OF
MID SECTION.

BASE

OFFSETS.

STATION	F.P.	1	2	3	4	5	A.P.
SHEER	1-11-1	1-7-4+	1-4-3	1-2-5	1-2-6+	1-4-2	1-6-3+
CHINE	1-6-6+	0-5-7	0-0-4+	0-0-0	0-0-3+	0-3-1	0-5-6
RAIL	1-1-0+	1-8-3	2-1-1	2-2-7	2-2-2	1-11-3+	1-7-0+
CHINE	0-11-3	1-0-4+	1-3-3+	1-5-3	1-5-5	1-3-6+	1-2-0+
BOW	0-1-7	~				FROM F.P.	
STERN	FROM A.P.					~	0-9-5

NOTE:
READINGS TO NEAREST 8th, PLUS OR MINUS.
EXAMPLE:
1-3-5+ = 1 FT. 3⅝" + 1/16

CHINE STRIP

3'6" ARC

37"
BASE

15°

A.P.   5   4   3   2   1   F.P.
SHOE KEEL

R.D.CULLER, HYANNIS, MASS.-NOV.'44

A just-for-rowing version of the 11-foot sampan, ready for delivery.

43

Many prejudices, largely unfounded, have grown up about timber that isn't local. It's often said that timber from local sources lasts best in its own area; possibly it does to some extent. However, when you consider the huge number of powerline poles used in the East, nearly all of which seem to come from the West, and the large amount of really good piling which seems also to come from away, both used in situations where lasting really matters, the theory of "local woods only" loses a lot of its meaning. To "the Westward," Maine gray oak is often looked on as inferior, yet uncounted numbers of ships and boats have used it in the past, as well as the present, and made the state famous. The same with West Coast stock; many consider it inferior, yet Oregon pine and a famous Western spruce have been masting, decking, and planking Eastern vessels for a long time.

A government, or other outfit supported by taxpayers, can well build without regard to cost, and a few of the very wealthy indulge their fancy for what they think or have been told is the best. Others, not being able to do so, must use what is available. Probably more craft have gone to pot from lack of care than from lack of the finest lumber. Care of boats and craft is really much misunderstood nowadays. Many are killed by too much swaddling and covering up. Tight upperworks and plenty of ventilation, plus keeping a clean ship, are the first lines of defense. Decay likes dirt and foul air, along with a bit of a drip of fresh water. Other maintenance chores help some: making sure broken places in paint or varnish are attended to; drain holes if any, kept open; metal work attended to; and so on, but they alone cannot replace The Big Three: dryness, air, and cleanliness.

The first fastenings were no doubt lashings of some kind; then came pegs and pins of wood, which developed into the treenail and dowel. There were also devised joints that held themselves together with little aid. All these methods are still in use in many parts of the world. We hear much of monel, bronze, and stainless steel, and just how bad galvanized fastenings are. Personally, I think it's all good in its place,

but when you price much of it in today's economy, you are apt to do some thinking.

A fellow must consider what he can afford, and the type of craft he proposes to build. Buying monel and bronze in thousand-pound lots for a big boat makes the cost mount rapidly. On the other hand, a light lapstrake boat, canoe, or other small craft of rather sophisticated construction is most suited to bronze and copper no matter the cost, for the amount used by the pound will be small. Fastenings on these craft may have to be set flush and therefore will be subject to striking with sandpaper, which is not healthy for galvanizing. All fastenings eventually corrode or become somewhat porous; the smaller they are, the sooner they lose strength. Even in light craft, it's often advisable to use galvanized iron bolts where strain is great, as very small bronze bolts are very weak. This was the practice in many past craft.

The mixing of fastenings as suggested above, has not, in my experience, done any harm in small craft. On the other hand, as soon as some electrical stuff is installed, over and above a flashlight, there is a chance of electrical leaks developing, which hasten the failure of mixed metals, or unmixed ones for that matter. Many will doubt the above statement, yet many of the fine craft of the past — strange to us nowadays — had mixing of metals, yet they lasted. Some are still around, notably the clipper *Cutty Sark*, and the whaler *Charles W. Morgan*. On studying these craft and their construction, one finds he has a lot more to learn. They had no man-made electric currents aboard until fairly recent times. I wonder if this is the real answer. We are now supposed to know a great deal about such things, yet every once in a while some situation turns up that seems to refute the theories.

A stout-built craft, large or small, suited to a lot of nailing, bolting, and drifting, does quite well with galvanized iron fastenings, in fact may be stronger for them. The fastenings are big, so they go a long time without much weakening. You often hear the argument that yes, it was once so when real iron was used, but now it's all steel. Except in rare and special cases, I think

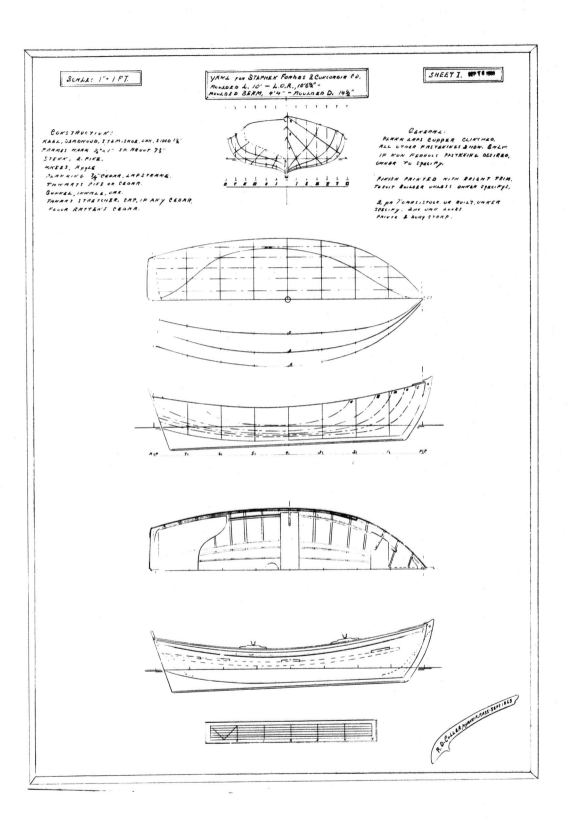

SCALE: 1" = 1 FT.

YAWL for STEPHEN FORBES & CONCORDIA CO.
MOULDED L. 10' — L.O.R., 10'6½" —
MOULDED BEAM, 4'4" — MOULDED D. 14½"

SHEET I.   SEP 76 1933

CONSTRUCTION:
KEEL, DEADWOOD, STEM & SKEG, OAK, SIDED 1½
FRAMES OAK ½" × 1" SP. ABOUT 7½"
STEM, 2. PINE.
KNEES, APPLE
PLANKING ¾" CEDAR, LAPSTRAKE.
THWARTS PINE OR CEDAR.
GUNNEL, INWALE, OAK.
THWART STRETCHER, CAP, IF ANY CEDAR.
FLOOR BATTENS CEDAR.

GENERAL:
PLANK LAPS COPPER CLINCHED.
ALL OTHER FASTENINGS SHOWN. ONLY
IF NON FERROUS FASTENING DESIRED,
OWNER TO SPECIFY.

FINISH PAINTED WITH BRIGHT TRIM.
TO SUIT BUILDER UNLESS OWNER SPECIFYS.

2 PR ¾"OARS STOCK, OR BUILT, OWNER
SPECIFY. 2 PR OAR LOCKS
PAINTR & DINGY STRAP.

R.D.CULLER, MARBLEHEAD, MASS. SEPT 1943

45

little real wrought iron was used after Bessemer got his method of steel making going, and certainly not in the lifetime of most of those vessels still around.

The stock drift bolts, carriage and machine bolts, and boat nails and spikes seem to be of just the same make-up now as in my youth. You used to, and still do, run into occasional poor galvanizing, poor threads, and other lesser defects, just as you can find in more costly fastenings. A batch of poor threads or shallow and out-of-center slots is not uncommon in bronze screws. Usually returning the batch and a little fuss with the supplier straightens things out. Machines get out of whack and inspection misses mistakes sometimes.

Galvanized steel screws have problems of their own. First, they must be tough, and most really are. This means a fairly hard steel and one that is rather subject to rust. The galvanizing is easily damaged in driving, partly because it's difficult to get really clean slots and very sharp threads in making the screws. The larger the screws, the better they seem to be. For any size of fastening, the quality of the galvanizing should be watched. Galvanized screws can be set up far tighter than bronze ones without breaking. Naturally, they are much used in fastening down galvanized iron fittings. Though there is some doubt as to their being long-lasting in certain parts of hull construction, there are many examples around which have lasted, so here again the theories don't always work. I have noticed galvanized fastenings last quite well in properly fitted deck joiner work. In very small sizes, galvanized screws are troublesome; anything below a 1-inch #8 I don't care for.

Every size screw should have a driver bit that fits it, both in width and thickness. In practice, this is never quite so, and much unnecessary slot damage is done. Often, the pilot hole is not quite right. I much favor starting any screw slightly with a hammer before driving, so it takes the line-up of the pilot hole. This saves much jumping off and damage by the bit in starting the drive. This hammer starting is of course commonplace, yet it's often neglected too.

The choice of fastenings depends as much on the type of craft as the size of the pocketbook. The fact that certain types of fastenings may not be available in any area or place has not hindered boatbuilding very much; one can always make do with what is on hand and still produce a good boat. Good workmanship, using what is available, is really the backbone of successful building, rather than setting some unreachable standard and not really achieving it.

Once in a while someone decides to build a boat "regardless of cost." In doing so, many things are lost sight of, and it's been my experience that the craft so produced are seldom successful, as they tend to be very complicated, which in itself makes a bothersome craft to use and maintain. A sound design well suited to its use, and I stress the word *use,* as simple as possible within the limits of its type, always tends to be a good craft, often with a long life, perils of the sea excepted. Such a boat is usually loved and therefore gets care. She is apt to be easy to use, so gets lots of it; a well-used boat tends to last. Like people, boats get doughy and flabby just lying around. A neglected boat will most certainly fall apart, even though she may be built of the very finest material.

V
Tools

Doing things with boats takes, besides money, tools and equipment, but not nearly as much, if you start small, as it might seem. Much is made of good tools for obvious reasons, yet to rush out and load up on many tools, without knowing just what is useful and what is not, can be quite wasteful. In this era of power tools, these are felt to be very necessary. Some are; some are not; some are very specialized. One can say the same of hand tools, I suppose. Boatbuilding tools are considered very specialized too, and to some extent they are, though many not readily bought can be made, for they are simple for the most part.

Starting with some suggestions on hand tools, I say a good broom is the first thing. A new apprentice was always started on a broom; once he learned to sweep properly he was promoted, usually to a scrub broom under a bottom. An orderly and clean shop is a workable place and is safer for men and far less of a fire hazard than a messy, dirty shop. By their nature, boat shops are considerable fire hazards. Yes, a good broom can save a lot; use it often, and always the afternoon of the last day of the working week. Weekends often bring visitors, or the naval architect and his client; a tidy shop speaks well for the builder. Large professional shops using many men must have almost continuous sweeping, and the practiced sweeper does much more than that. He collects uncounted pounds of dropped fas-

tenings, spots trouble in a junction box, and generally knows what's going on. He also has a "gosh box" somewhere, with all the lost pencils, rules, bevels, and other small tools he finds. If something's missing from a man's pockets, a visit to the sweeper will usually turn it up.

As very small children, we take to pounding, and if we like to make things, continue to do so the rest of our lives, which brings up hammers. In my experience at least, the ordinary carpenter's claw hammer has been standard with boatbuilders. For many years I owned just one, bought from a now-extinct mail-order house for 65 cents. It was known as a "second best," which then meant not highly finished. By the price you will know it was bought a long time ago; it's still working and has the original handle. They built well in those days. When I owned just one hammer, I could keep track of it. Now owning six, some of them specialized, I often can't find any; you can have too much of a good thing.

Often, the claw hammer is too light for bolt driving, general thumping, setting wedges, and such, yet the shipwright's pin maul is too much. Most men acquire something stout of the sort that goes by various pet names in various places. Such a tool might be called Thumping Hammer, Tunker, Belaboring Iron, or, as I remember one of strange shape and undetermined original use, Old Thumphead. These tunkers seem to be of no set model, just what's around; I've seen large ball peens, stone masons' hammers, blacksmiths', retired heavy boltsets, and other oddballs in use. A peen hammer of some kind is handy for upsetting bolts. A pin maul is not necessary for the small craft builder.

Hand saws, like hammers, have nothing special about them for boat work. A good saw, taken care of, will last until it's literally filed away, and any saw is only as good as its filing and settings. Besides the standard length of 26 inches, shorter saws are handy for boat work, say 24 and 22 inches. Many of the saws made today don't feel the way they used to; the steel seems different. I have seen and used a recent English saw, which was excellent, and I think came from a well-known tool supply house near Boston. I was much impressed; the price might be impressive too. Few men now file their own saws, yet if one is doing much work, he should learn this skill. And as the saw is the first cutting tool we discuss, it might be said here that all cutting tools must be kept sharp, which means you must learn how. Some wise ones have said: after you learn to sweep, next comes learning to sharpen. I stress this, and will say more about it as we go.

I don't care for a very hard saw. Steel that is tough but soft, so it will file with a good burr (like a scraper) by far cuts the best. Saws made in the past and those still hand-filed usually have a slight downward curve or belly along the teeth fore and aft. New saws seldom do, for the automatic filing machine does not get along with this curve; besides, we are now told this curve is not needed. A good saw has plenty of "gauge," or thickness at the teeth and thinness to the back. It is also tapered some from handle to tip. You don't need many saws; an 8-point, standard length; a 10, which can be shorter; a compass saw; and the usual hacksaw for metal. A hand rip-saw is now seldom needed. If you get the Tool Bug, more will show up. Being a collecting nut, I must have a dozen or more, but the ones I mention get nearly all the use, with the exception of a fine-tooth panel saw or a backsaw for bench work sometimes. As a fellow's interest and skill develop, he will find some favorites

and one or two old types that do a certain thing well.

Good chisels are hard to buy over the counter now, though they are still made. Any hardware man who has his customers' interests at heart has, or can get, the industrial tool catalogues; some are still issued in the United States, and they extend the selection a store can offer. The "tang" chisel and gouge (I include the gouge here, for it's a kind of chisel) must be used for their intended purpose: pushing or paring by hand, or very occasional light tapping. Any cutting that is at all heavy requires the socket type, which comes in butt (short), firmer, and framing, or sometimes called mortise, patterns. I still prefer wooden handles; when one plays out, another can be made. I have not used many plastic handles, and those I have used seemed to bounce back, which is no good. There may be some good ones. Good steel is naturally the important thing, along with nice shape; you acquire an eye for this after awhile. A man does not need many chisels to do a lot of work: $\frac{1}{4}$, $\frac{1}{2}$, $1\frac{1}{4}$, and 2-inch firmer pattern chisels would be a fine assortment. Later you will acquire more. At times butts are handy, and some old semi-retired one with excellent steel will be fitted with a long push handle for paring. For much mortising, such as door making, the chisel must be the exact width of the mortise. A full collection of every kind of wood chisel is quite a pile, and you won't use most of them.

Gouges are worse. I don't know that I've seen all there is here: inside and outside bevels and dozens of radii. Start with a couple and build as needed. If you come across a wide, say 2-inch, very shallow-radius, inside-bevel gouge, grab it. You will always find use for it; in some sticky place other things don't work, but this tool probably will. And a bevel can be changed by grinding; if you come on two alike, one can be changed.

There is that monster, the "slick," common to the old timers and much sought after now by coming boatbuilders, pro or amateur. Slicks can still be had new, but the price knocks a big chunk off one of those bills with U. S. Grant on

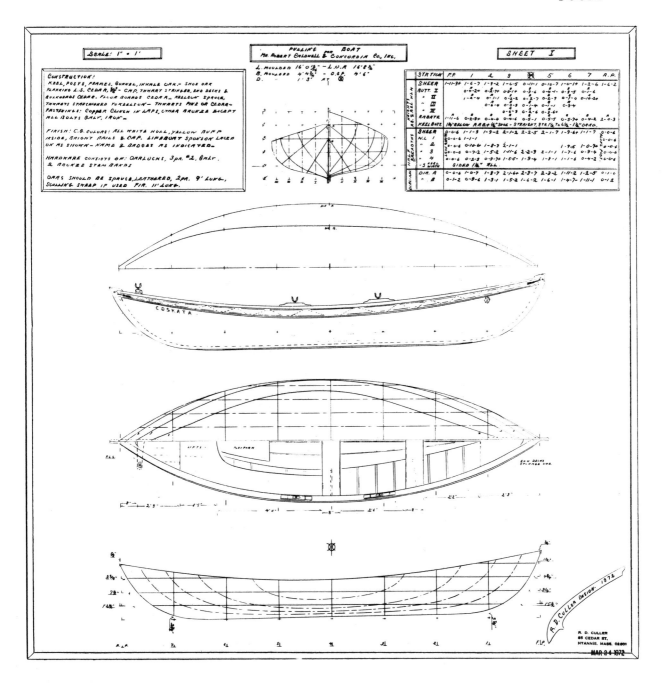

it, so there is much searching for the old. Once in awhile someone I know finds one, which produces more excitement than finding an old Strad. The slick is a nice tool to have, but you can get along without it. In my early days of ship carpentry, the slick was part of a pair of tools. The slick was a chisel about 3 inches wide with a length in proportion; in the pair, the larger tool, about 4 inches wide, was called a "slice." I know of one which was at least 5 inches wide, a huge tool with a standard, D-type shovel handle, offset and all, which made a lot of sense. Its original use was the shaping of very wide, long plank suited to building an oystering skiff of about 26 feet, in place of using the rip saw. I'm told a full set of slicks and slices was as follows, and I've seen only one supposedly full set: the lesser slick; the big slice; a Beavertail, which was a lesser slice ground to considerable radius though flat in section; and one lesser slick with a very slight gouge-like radius. For light boat work, a large, heavy, framing chisel, well ground back and with a long push handle, makes a good substitute for slicks and slices. I base this last statement on having both a slick and a slice and finding the big slice mostly too hearty for light boat work.

Planes, of course, you can't do without, though a big collection is not needed. Wooden planes are now much sought after. There has been some good advice on making your own in the *National Fisherman* and other earlier publications. Most chronic boatbuilders eventually make some. Good iron planes work just fine, but I prefer wooden ones for outboard joining. With the exception of many specialized planes, mostly small, I own just two: a smooth plane and a big jointer that is very old as iron planes go. Except rarely, I use only these few planes: the skew block, iron, smooth plane; occasionally the iron jointer; and various wooden ones with radius bottoms. One exception is spar work, where more of the wooden planes are used. A rabbet plane is needed, either wooden or iron. You can get along quite well at first — years in fact — without a great collection of planes; they seem to come with time.

Most anyone seems to be able to use a plane right off without ever having done it before, though practice develops the skill to a high degree. Using the plane at all angles in all positions is common to boat work and has little in common with bench planing. Some pointers to the new man may help him toward good and easy planing: I, for one, grind my irons to more bevel than some folks do; how much depends on the type of plane and what the steel will stand. I whet often, and always finish up on a leather; this is good practice on any cutting edge for wood. I set the cap iron no more than 1/16th inch from the cutting edge. I make sure that the bed, either wood or iron, which the bit rests on, is clean and free of gum. For some work a very slight radius to the cutting edge is good; considerable radius will help if the plane is used as a "scrub," to hog off stock roughly.

Probably considered in the plane family are spokeshaves, sometimes just called shaves. They seem to come flat, round, or hollow, and once in awhile have some special shape. There are various patterns of shaves, some with fancy adjustments. I've found that if a new one does not seem to act quite right, rounding the back edge of the sole will usually pep things up.

Sometimes a tool not originally intended for boat work will turn out to be just the thing. A box scraper has found its place with me, and with some others who have seen it work and borrowed it. Its body is somewhat like a shave, only somewhat wider fore and aft, with a slight radius athwartships. The single handle is made for two-hand use and is on trunnions so it can be pushed or pulled. Its original use was for planing the marks off packing boxes for reuse. It cuts, rather than scrapes as its name implies. I find nothing handier for joining off the planking of staved, vee-bottom boats, especially in the forefoot and way aft in any tuck which other tools reach only with difficulty. In other words, it's happy on an inside compound curve. This tool works equally well across or with the grain. While not a tool that gives a high finish, it does quite well enough for following up with a jitterbug sander. I highly recommend this tool to any boatbuilder.

I find that I now use hand-turned boring tools very little. Though there are times when nothing does quite as well, power has put hand drills into the background. I've never owned a first-class bit brace, just several old wrecks, each of different pattern. I keep them loaded with various screwdriver bits, which is now about the only way they are used, except sometimes for turning a reamer. A hand drill and an old breast drill are kept handy for the occasional odd hole, when it's not worth the trouble to rig the power drill. I do find small drills, and at times bigger ones, hard to come by in longer-than-usual lengths. Using various sizes of drill rod, and sometimes steel knitting needles for small stuff, drills can, with a bit of practice, be extended by brazing. I think ability in brazing is very valuable to cultivate; it makes you independent when it comes to long bits. I mention again that drills and bits, like other cutting tools, should be kept sharp.

We seem now to have all sorts of measuring devices. I was brought up on the two-foot-four folding rule, large steel tape, and "rule staffs," which are simply accurately cut pieces of wood of definite lengths. In some localities, builders seem to favor the three-foot wooden folding rule. Except in lofting, I seldom use the zigzag rule. The pocket steel tape, unknown or at least uncommon when I started, has eliminated some other measuring tools. The chalk line, plumb bob, and level have their places in boat work; in fact many — nay, most — of the usual hand tools do, and those made just for boat work are few.

The house carpenter's "bevel square" is a hateful thing for boat work. The body is way too thick, and the thumbscrew is always in the way, for most boat bevels are compound (they have to be taken two ways), and the above-mentioned parts "fetch up," so it's hard to get an accurate bevel. The shipwright's bevel is thin of body and thin of blade. It works by friction, usually that of a rivet. Sometimes there is a blade at each end, like a penknife, so that two bevels can be picked up at once. It's not usually available store-bought, but is easily made. Give

it a wooden or metal body, the thinner the better, and a metal blade. Some very big ones are all wood. The making is entirely up to a fellow's artistic ability, what stock he has, and what his experience dictates. I use several, from 2 inches to 2 feet long. This last is handy for lofting and setting transoms. A 6-inch bevel is the right size for much work. One trick to making a bevel is to be sure that the body sides and blade sides are parallel, otherwise an outside reading will not be the same inside. Also, the pivot ends must be an arc, and the rivet hole must be centered to it. Many simple tools such as this, just suited to boatbuilding, can be made, and many always were. As a person's skill develops and the need arises, many tools will just come naturally. Talk with others in the trade will turn up some snazzy ideas. I think each man tends to work out his own stuff, though it may be based very much on what others have worked out in the past.

Besides bevels, there are other tools particularly associated with boatbuilding and shipwrights. Some are of little or no use to the builder of small boats. Returning to pounding, the pin maul is needed when bolts and other fastenings are big enough. I find this tool of little use in boats under 30 feet long, and then only for setting a shore or wedge occasionally. And, if a maul is needed on a bigger craft, I find for most of today's work that it should be on the light side, say 4½ pounds.

The lip adz is a kind of badge of the ship carpenter, and though power tools have replaced it in many operations, it's still the only tool for certain work. Contrary to first appearances, the adz is not at all a difficult tool to learn to use. Having trained a number of men in its use, I find they "catch on" in an hour or so, though the first day sees little improvement in ability. The second day starts differently right off, and there is considerable confidence. On the third day, much useful work is produced, though the effort is tiring. After a week or ten days, the user becomes quite hardened and relaxed, and that's it; you have a useful dubber. Conditioning a brand-new adz takes some work and know-

SHARP MODEL WHLRRY FOR
DR. NICHOLAS FREYDBERG AND
CONCORDIA COMPANY

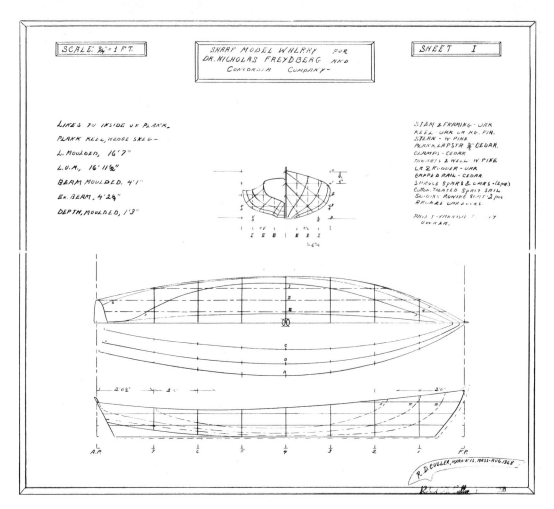

LINES TO INSIDE OF PLANK.

PLANK KEEL, WEDGE SKEG.

L. MOULDED, 16' 7"

L.O.A., 16' 11½"

BEAM MOULDED, 4' 1"

EX. BEAM, 4' 2¼"

DEPTH, MOULDED, 1' 3"

STEM & FRAMING- OAK
KEEL OAK OR NG. FIR.
STERN - W PINE
PLANK LAPSTR ⅜" CEDAR.
CLAMPS - CEDAR
THWARTS & WELL - W PINE
CL. & RUDDER - OAK
CAPPED RAIL - CEDAR
SPRUCE SPARS & OARS (2 PR)
COTTON TREATED SPIRIT SAIL
SLIDING ROWING SEAT - 2 POS
RRLLAKE OARLOCKS.

PHIL J. VARNISH BY
OWNER.

A.P.   7   6   5   4   3   2   1   F.P.

R. D. CULLER, HYANNIS, MASS. AUG. 1968

Robert Culler

SHARP WHERRY FOR
DR FREYDBERG AND
CONCORDIA CO.

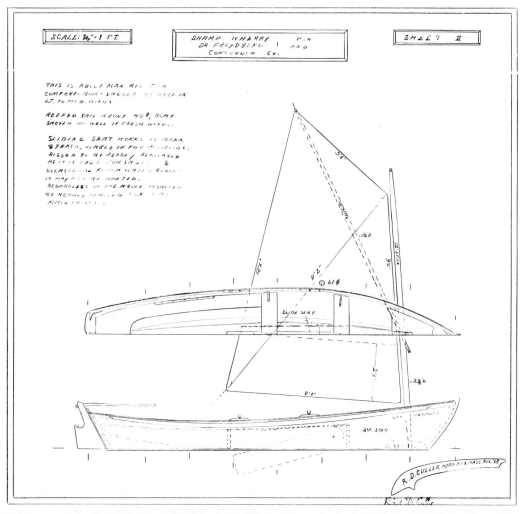

THIS IS ABOUT MAX. RIG FOR
COMFORT- BOAT SHOULD DO WELL IN
LT. TO MED. WINDS

REEFED SAIL ABOUT 40%, BOAT
SHOULD DO WELL IN FRESH WINDS.

SLIDING SEAT WORKS ON PLANK
& TRACK, USABLE IN TWO POSITIONS.
RIGGED TO BE READY, REMARKABLE
AS IT IS FELT FOR SAILS &
OCCASIONAL ROUGH WATER ROWING
IT MAY NOT BE NEEDED.
REGARDLESS OF THE ABOVE IT SHOULD
BE READY RIGGED FOR USE
WHEN TO IS.

SLIDE SEAT

8' 0"

61 φ

R. D. CULLER, HYANNIS, MASS AUG. '68

R. D. C.

how; there is usually much filing, mostly on the back of the blade, and the lips need attention. The bevel of the cutting edge nearly always needs alteration. Hanging the adz, or fitting the handle, is most important. Often the stock handle, if any, is a bit too long. Sometimes a handle has to be made, usually borrowing some old-timer's pattern. Some like 'em thick, others thin, and with more or less crook. Even the experts argue about these points, and the actual hanging, or pitch of the bit, is even more controversial. The angle is adjusted by a wedge in the head, or eye. Being a 3/4-inch man myself, I go at it this way: Assuming I'm satisfied with the handle and its length, I put it in the eye. Taking a measure with a tape from eye to handle end, I sweep the tape from eye to cutting edge, keeping the tape fixed at the handle end. There should be 3/4 of an inch less measure from the cutting edge than from the eye, the bit hanging down toward the handle. Some like 5/8 inch, some as much as 7/8 inch. I've known some pros who used only 1/2 inch. Though I'm not just sure, I think a man's build, the particular shape of the adz head, the length of handle preferred, and maybe some unknown things, all have bearing on a happy "hang." It's said a new adz improves with use; the steel gets better with repeated blows — at least some of us think so — and much tinkering with the cutting edge finally gets it "right." A small, one-hand adz is useful in tight places. A Portagee adz is liked by many, with its strange wooden handle. Or an old-time cooper's adz does well, and a little searching often turns one up. There is also the hollow, or sternpost, adz, sometimes called the canoe adz.

The ship carpenter's broad axe is now seldom seen in use, for, like so many of these tools, the power tools have replaced it. It's handy for some work though, or when some heavy machine is not available.

Long augers are now generally on the electrician's or bellhanger's pattern, though for ease of boring and accurate holes, the barefoot ship auger (with no starting worm) is by far the best. This last can now be had with shanks suit-

ed to power drive. There never seem to be enough bits and augers around of all the different lengths, types, and sizes required. As mentioned, if a man will learn to splice long shanks onto bits, he can be very independent, and save much cash outlay. Also, he suddenly seems to have a lot of friends interested in borrowing. The man in the village who has all the long augers is often sought out!

There are never enough C clamps; own all you can if you are doing any serious boatbuilding. I find for most uses the kind with a sliding upper part, sometimes known as the German pattern, is just fine. A large collection of clamps for all purposes costs quite a lot, but you can readily make some of the special ones for limited use. An example would be lapstrake clamps, either operating by wedge or wooden cam, or by bolts and wing nuts. These usually can't be bought in any case. Most boatbuilding books show some version of them. Wood and metal sliding C clamps can be bought, but they are not difficult to make. They work by cam action and so have limited take-up and therefore limited use. The cabinet or Jorgensen clamp I find to be of little use in boat work, though it's nice to have some around when you run out of C clamps. Bar clamps are needed at times; the kind that fits onto a pipe is not expensive and has the advantage that it can be used on various lengths of pipe. I keep some very short lengths of pipe around, so that when struck with the usual sudden shortage of C clamps, bar clamps can pinch hit. A shot of chain and some wedges are most handy at times for big work, and, along with this chain, an ordinary trucker's load binder can do a lot of useful work on big timbers. The shipwright's tools for big craft were fairly few, and many were based on using wedges, shores, iron dogs, wrain staves, loggers, and other simple gear.

I have played down large numbers of hand tools as necessary to boatbuilding. The right tools, and good ones, kept sharp, are all that is needed. If you like to collect tools and enjoy restoring and occasionally using them, that is to me a separate thing. I do this myself. I have some for which few people know the use, and one I don't know what to do with myself. Doing many kinds of work, I may use a few of these oddballs more than some collectors.

I've mentioned power tools taking over the functions of many of the old shipwright's and boatbuilder's tools. Much is made of power tools, and advertising keeps them in the forefront. Some folks think they can't possibly build a kit pram without a lot of power tools. Certainly a few power tools have taken the pure drudgery out of many phases of boatbuilding. For all of this, it seems to take just as long as it ever did to build a boat, often even more time, for boats are becoming more complicated. Your back seems to ache just as much as in the past. It used to be said that a man who dubbed with the adz and hewed with the axe all his life as a specialized trade, and many did, "was all broken up" at an early age, usually something past 70. Things are easier now. Hand-held power tools are the thing these days, and I find that, as with straight hand tools, there need not be many, if they are the right ones, big enough for the job, and of good quality — meaning industrial grade, which makes them expensive.

Except in cutting large, thin sheets of stuff, I find little use for the hand jig, or saber saw. That's just one man's opinion; most builders won't agree. However many electric drills you intend to own, have one big enough so that the smaller ones won't have to attempt work that is too much for them. There is a lot to be said for variable speed drills for some work. Boat work generally does not require drills that turn very fast. Assuming it's in good shape, any electric tool that tends to overheat is either being overworked, or the local voltage is too low, or the extension cord, if any, is too light.

The hand electric saw has radically changed the getting out of planking as I used to know it, and has changed some other operations too. After the plank was spiled and laid off on the stock, it was lugged to the bandsaw and cut out, and then lugged to the bench for jointing. On thick work, the bevels were done on the saw too, for it was a tilthead, or ship saw. Nowadays,

much of getting out the plank is done right where the stock lies, with the electric saw, and often the jointing is by power too, of which more later. A good electric saw can be accurate if well built and if the operator is practiced. The saw can be moved from place to place and save much jacking about of heavy stock. I consider it a most useful tool, especially for the lone workman. Getting stock of any size through a bandsaw by yourself, even with good rollers, is a tiresome business, with possibly more risk than with the use of the electric saw. The big reciprocating hand electric saws have uses, mostly for alterations in craft already built. I've found little or no use for them in new work.

The electric hand plane, or industrial jointer, is a wonderful tool that is little known to amateurs, though familiar to pros. I'm not impressed by brand names usually, but for electric hand planes, I think Skil is the best. This tool costs big money but it is worth it to any man building a boat bigger than a small, open craft. While not exactly a finishing tool, it can be worked pretty fine with practice. When it comes to the really hard planing, hogging down, and rough fairing, this tool does it all in minutes without fuss and puts the adz into the background. With a second set of knives ground to radius, the electric hand plane makes short work of backing out plank. It's easy to keep sharp using the jigs supplied with it and cares little for direction of grain or tough knots. It is even more impressive for spar making, having upset many of the time-honored methods. For most spars of under 6 inches, it does the whole job without the use of other tools, except in the final finishing. Even with bigger sticks, this tool still can do most of the work. It sizes big timber, too big sometimes to pass through a stationary machine, and seems to do all the things which were at one time just plain hard work. I've outboard joined the wale strakes of a 30-ton schooner with an electric hand plane, to the point where they were ready for sanding. The tool is heavy and should be; using it vertically, about a half day is enough.

A word of warning: all power tools obviously

can be dangerous. The electric hand plane is heavy, and it tends to coast after the switch is off. You tend to want to set it down quickly; have a block of wood handy to set the nose on to keep the still-moving blades from digging into something. Using it vertically, you tend to drop it down to arm's length to rest, knives still turning though the power is off for the moment. This operation has snagged many a pants leg, or worse. Once this danger is understood, I don't think the hand plane is any more risky than other power tools. Most people realize, for example, that the electric saw has kick-back possibilities and that its protective guards sometimes hang up. Or, you can "hang" an electric drill and get terribly wound up. Clamps can fly off under repeated thumping somewhere in the boat. In other words, any risks should be studied and guarded against. Don't hurry.

Sanding machines are plentiful now, as is good paper to go with them. These tools seem well understood. In the day of "flint paper," we did not do so much sanding, relying on sharp planes and scrapers. For small boats, a Jitterbug sander does fine, though as boat size increases, a belt job comes in handy. Disks I seldom use except for metal work, such as hogging down stem bands, rudder fittings, and so forth.

There are of course many other specialized hand power tools, but I find those mentioned are the only ones really needed. If you build one small boat only occasionally, the lower priced power tools will do for awhile, but I think in the end the very best should be bought. Own one or two really good power tools instead of many junky ones. Even the best sometimes gives out, for fairly small motors are doing pretty big work. I never try to stall a tool; slack up and let her turn, for she is fan cooled. Sharp tools cut freely. I suggest anyone owning power tools for the first time learn the art of keeping them sharp. A dull power tool fights back and is a high risk; besides, you become independent of that shop up the street that is not open on Saturdays! These tools like a little pampering at times. Switches get balky, cords fray, and plugs get bent. Look after them. A bit of wax, tallow,

or such on the base makes her push steadily. A gummy blade or knife is always unhappy. If you do any building at all, there will come a time when you will nick a cord, or, as has happened, cut it right off! Most of these tools take a tumble or two sometime in their lives; it's not good for them, so try to guard against falls. I notice more and more that the hired help in professional shops doesn't have much regard for nice machines. Lunch time, quittin' time, pay day. Some say it's The Times. The better the mechanic, the more respect he has for tools.

The principle of economy also applies to the bigger, fixed-position tools; you can get power-tool happy and have too many with too much money tied up in them, and you may find that only a few are worthwhile. First you must consider the size of your power line into the shop. It's a nice idea to own a big, powerful woodworking machine, but can your line take it? Perhaps it is worth running in bigger voltage — sometimes it is, depending on many things. I find that when using 110 volts you are limited to about $\frac{1}{2}$-h.p. motors, which, for many small shops and home builders, is the usual thing. More can be done with 220 volts, and probably somewhat cheaper. It's fine to have a really big production planer, say 6 inches by 30 inches, but you'll find it will require a motor of such size as to require 440 volts. Sometimes what you think is a bargain is a big but old machine with a high cost of moving to your site. It probably will require more power than your line can handle, and, if it's a jointer or planer, it may be an old "square header," which is outlawed insurance-wise in any shops hiring men and is no good for the loner.

It's sometimes said that the table saw is the basic machine for wood working; maybe so for a cabinet shop, but definitely not for boat work. It has its place in cabin joinery and some straight ripping, but after building a boat or two, you will find the table saw does not get as much use as you thought it would, assuming you have the boatbuilder's friend, the bandsaw. I say own a table saw if you can, but not at the expense of more useful tools. I have no particular choice on these saws — tilt blade, tilt table, micro adjusting fence, and what not. They all work quite well enough for boatbuilding if they are stout and if the controls work with reasonable ease.

The bandsaw you can't do without; it will do more than any other machine: rip, crosscut at all angles, and dozens of other things. Its ability to butt cut and back out is constantly used. I suggest owning as large a machine as you think your power can handle, and of the best industrial grade. Put money into your bandsaw, even if you must do without other machines. A home builder can do much work with a 12-inch machine; 14 inches is better, and 16- to 20-inch saws can face up to pretty big work if used with care. These machines all have the tilt table for bevels, which can be unhandy for some big beveling. Only big yards can support the true ship saw, which has the tilting head with the table remaining level, so heavy work does not tend to slide off.

Though it will probably be of no real interest to those building small or moderate sized craft, it's nice to know how these big ship saws work. They are usually 48 inches in the wheels and massive in construction, for wood-working machines need to be rigid. The head usually tilts to 45 degrees, operated by a curved rack and pinion, and the table is slotted to allow the blade to clear as the head tilts. The heavy stock sits on pairs of rollers, at each end of the table and farther away to take the weight along the timber's length. The table rollers can be fitted with hand cranks to take the strain off the sawyer and provide a steady feed. All the rollers are "traverse," that is, they can slew sideways in making a turn or curved cut and pivot the stock at the blade. They also allow the stock to move sideways as the bevel changes. The point is, these saws cut changing bevels, the usual thing in a sawn-frame vessel, as a matter of course. There is another model, in which both wheels swing so that the saw blade pivots around the cutting point. This rig usually tilts 45 degrees both ways, so the stock does not have to be reversed. This is the Rolls Royce of ship saws. The mechanism which keeps the drive belts following the wheels as they move is wonderful to behold.

Now let's come back down out of the clouds to more practical saws for small shops. Good maintenance, sharp blades, and occasional cleaning make any well-built bandsaw give good service. For the amount of work a bandsaw does, it takes modest power, partly because it is a fairly slow-speed machine. As with all power tools, the use of a bandsaw is attended with some risk, though for the amount it's used — more than any other machine in the shop — there seem to be few accidents, and these mostly from cutting oddball stock. When cutting off round stock, or anything which can twist or roll, the stock should be supported by vee or similar blocks. When cutting a short piece with overhang, such as cutting the side bevel on a wooden cleat, the overhang should be supported, usually by inserting the chunk that was cut out. Take your time and use common sense. If you have much odd work, it will pay to make a supporting jig. I've never yet seen a bandsaw blade break and do any harm. Way back, we used to work big ship saws entirely unguarded. There were no insurance inspectors as there was no insurance. An old-time sawyer explained it this way: The instant the blade breaks, it ceases to turn; it can lash, but not cut. He said he "had one wrapped around his neck many a time." He also had a thumb missing. The way these machines are shielded now, I see no risk at all, unless the operator makes a mistake.

In my area at least, tools of any kind are sought after, power tools in particular. Yet by keeping an ear to the ground and looking about, you may be able to pick up a nice machine secondhand, perhaps when some fellow retires or goes out of business. Personally, I prefer some of the older machines, made before die casting of "pot metal," steel stampings, and other lightweight stuff became prevalent. I've never yet seen any reason to build a stationary wood-working machine light, except to sell it cheap. My present bandsaw is a monument to cast iron, is at least forty years old, and shows no wear. It

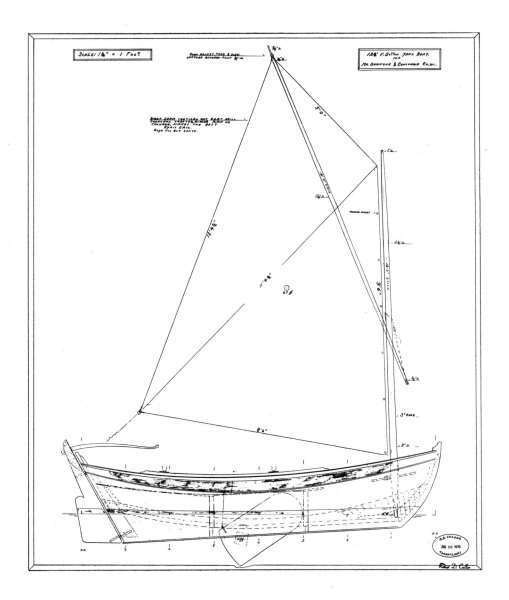

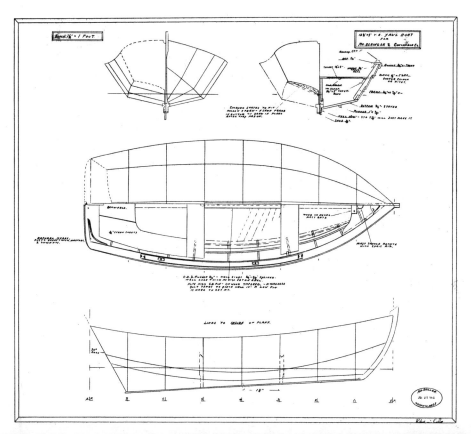

seems capable of going on forever. I wondered about the motor. Not knowing much about electric motors but suspecting some things, I consulted a motor electrician. He put it thus: It's a matter of heat and cost. A motor of a certain horsepower can be made of most any size and be designed to run at several speeds. In practice, there are motors designed for intermittent use, light duty, standard performance, and continuous heavy duty. The windings for these motors vary for the use. For a motor of a given horsepower to last well, it should be big (which means expensive) and should be designed for its use. Then it will run cool. After tutoring, which I still don't fully understand, I have been using, as much as possible, repulsion induction motors that are large for their power. The starting voltage is low, they do much work without heating, and they need very little service, even in what's naturally a dusty business. I think many folks now consider these motors old-fashioned, with their heavy copper starting commutators and their fully-wound armatures. Maybe so, but it seems to me my adviser is right. If anybody has a heavy, old "R. I." he wants to get rid of, let me know; I have a fine 3400 high-speed job that always has sawdust indigestion.

I find a power jointer more useful than a table saw; at least I seem to use it much more. You can get along with a small jointer, but of course you always wish it were bigger. Large yards often have a whopper with 16-inch knives and an 8- or 9-foot table. A 6-inch jointer will do in most cases, or even a 4-incher, though this last is a bit small. This is a dangerous machine and should be treated as such. When dull, it's doubly dangerous. Here again, if you have a choice, take a heavily-built machine. I've known men who worked for years with this tool without realizing it can rabbet to a limited degree. The jointer can also be very handy for some joiner work, in some cases more so than the table saw.

A shaper is even more dangerous, and I think most builders of small craft can get along quite well without it. Except for odd stuff and curved work, I think a moulding head on a table saw is far safer than a shaper and keeps an often idle machine in more employment. I seem to favor the very heavy flywheel-like moulding head.

Every boatbuilder wants a planer, even the backyarder. Alas, this is an expensive machine and takes much power. The more heavily built, the better, for this tool takes considerable strain. Unless you are well heeled and have plenty of room and power, forget the planer. Some professional builders with small shops find it cheaper to farm out the heavy dressing and make do with a small, hand-fed machine for occasional light stock, or else use a hand plane. Of course this is not a happy and independent situation. A really big planer that is capable of producing requires a sawdust blower, ducts, and a big bin, or else you spend much time shoveling away mounds of shavings. If a fellow has the voltage, space, and money, the little 12-inch finishing planer will do a wonderful job, though it's still best to have the mill do the rough dressing. Most mills are equipped for this. I think those who have not actually worked around planers of all sizes may not realize just how big a machine is needed to work heavy stock with any degree of rapidity. Working a small machine on rough-sawn stock, often with overly thick spots produced by a small saw mill, can be a very tedious business. You make pass after pass, each making a light cut, for that's all the rig will take, and there is much jacking around of stock. Besides, the small feed rolls cannot cope with the heavy stuff. It's better to have the work done at a mill and save a little machine for its intended use, finish work.

There is another angle here: assuming you can find a buy on a small planer but your power line won't take it, you can run the planer, and it only, with a gasoline engine, saving up enough dressing work to make it worthwhile to fire up the engine. This can be a bothersome chore in winter when the machine has been idle for awhile. Here, a big air-cooled engine might be best, with no water problems and necessity for draining in cold weather. Even so, any gas engine that has been asleep awhile in winter can be fussy to start. A gas engine seems to take about twice as much rated power as an electric motor to run the same machine. A governor is needed on a gas engine; it must turn at close to its rated speed; overload it and it stalls.

A wood-turning lathe is handy at times for belaying pins, stanchions, bull's eyes, and so forth, but you can well do without it. Building a wood lathe is not a difficult thing if it's found one is needed; the few metal parts are not difficult to come by, and the rest is made of timber. The wood-working lathe is a non-precision machine, unlike the metal lathe. Nowadays, the idea of making such a tool might dismay many people, yet in the past many yards had lathes built without benefit of machine supply houses. In fact, many a small lathe was built at sea in whalers and other ships, some in the pursuit of hobbies. One old-time sea captain, who later gained fame as a single-hander, built his own bandsaw at sea and later took it ashore and used it in the building of a small steamer, if the reports about this are correct.

There are several other wood-working machines, mostly specialized, or suited to big mills, or in some cases, to very big yards. They are of no use to the kind of boatbuilding we discuss here. I say again, have no more than earn their keep, and have good ones if possible. They all take maintenance, power to run, and must, for your own good and theirs, be kept sharp. A dull tool of any kind has no place in boat work. Good fits, reasonable speed in getting things done, and safety, all dictate sharp tools.

In this age of the motorization of everything, including tooth brushes, we tend to lose sight of some of the basics. Boatbuilding tools should not be motorized gadgets. If a power tool will save a lot of time, by all means use it. Hand tools certainly still have their place. What is needed is a basic assortment of high-quality hand and power tools. Really good tools always have high resale value.

Perhaps the most basic principle of acquiring and using tools is simply not to expect a tool to do a job it was never intended for. When you rationalize this principle away in a moment of haste, you generally regret it. As one of my long-time friends in boating has pointed out many times, "A lightweight, high-speed steam roller just can't do the job!"

VI

Flat Bottoms

I have mentioned choosing a type of boat appropriate to the intended use several times, and also the importance of working within your abilities. Hence, we start with the simplest form, the flat-bottomed craft. Many people do not understand flat ones and condemn them. Probably the aversion to them comes from their looks; they can be just plain ugly, but need not be so. Flat-bottomed boats have been with us for a long time; there must be good reasons for the durability of the type.

It's been said by others that a flat-bottomed skiff is easy to build but hard to design. This seems to be mostly because in the process of designing one, there are only three important lines to work with, which severely limits what a designer can do. Over the years and through the efforts of many seamen and builders, certain limits and rules have been worked out. They are not very scientific, but they work. If these rules are not violated too much in seeking the impossible, a good workable craft results, and she will be good looking, too, for her kind.

Howard Chapelle's book, *American Small Sailing Craft,* spells out in detail what makes a good flat-bottomed boat. I cannot hope to improve on his pointers, but to try to drive home the worth of the flat-bottomed boat, and how she should be shaped, will repeat in my own way what the experts of the past have worked out by trial and error.

Whether for rowing, or sailing, or power, the flat-bottomed skiff should not be too wide. She can, under most circumstances in fact, be rather long and slim. The freeboard should be rather low, by today's standards. A wide, high craft becomes unmanageable except in the lightest weather. She must not sit deep in the water when not loaded. The idea, now popular, that "a boat must be high, wide, and deep, so she will be safe" is particularly bad in flat-bottomed craft. It's her shape that makes a boat able, not the height of her sides or vast initial stability. Some flare to the sides is always good; for certain uses, very great flare makes sense. I have heard many excuses for not using good flare in recent years, and the fact that one of the ways of getting an able and good looking design is by the use of flare makes these excuses hard to understand. A boat without flare is like a ship painter's pontoon, and about as handy underway. If the advantages of flare are pointed out, the reply may be, "Plenty of power will take care of things," which it does not.

A "Good Little Skiff," built at the Mystic Seaport, Mystic, Connecticut. (Photo by Russell A. Fowler, Mystic Seaport.)

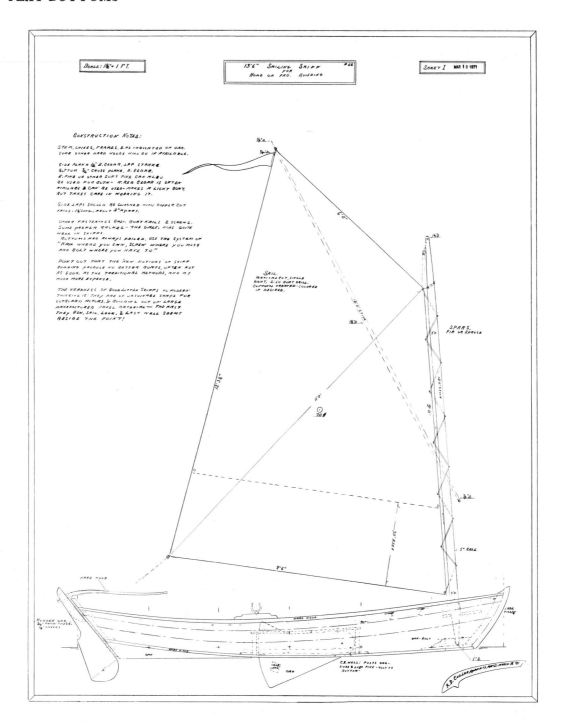

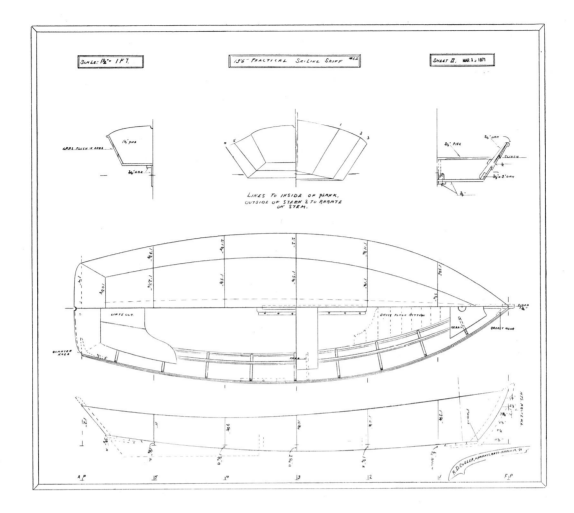

Most of the bad design in flat-bottomed boats seems to stem from trying to get too much out of a simple, and in many ways limited, boat: usually headroom and capacity on a short length. It now seems the accepted fact that a short boat is a cheap boat, rather than the real truth that displacement, complicated construction and fittings, and much power to drive an ill-shaped hull, whether by oars, sail, or motor, are the big cost makers. Some pros do boats of bad design against their better judgment; they may need the work, and the client is adamant. I've done it myself, and always say never again. A handsome craft is often relatively easy to build, and her shape is apt to make her quite durable.

Over the years, the method of building flat-bottomed boats has become more or less stand-ardized, with local variations to suit exact types and available materials. Lately, there have been attempts to change the methods, often to suit new materials. Yet most troubles with recent craft have been caused by not building them the way they used to be built, probably through not understanding why it was done that way. Flat-bottomed craft don't take kindly to Gilding the Lily. Honest, careful workmanship in the tradition of these boats is all that's required, along with a good design. Beyond this, you simply run into complications for no good reason.

The cross-planked bottom is now frowned on as being crude, as much from misunderstanding of just how it works and how it is built as anything else. If a cross-planked bottom is properly done, you never have chine troubles with it, as there is little 'thwartship pressure to force off the chines. Moreover, its swelling, being mostly fore and aft, is a help in preventing a boat's natural tendency to hog. Of two flat-bottomed craft of about the same model, one cross-planked and the other fore-and-aft planked with bottom framing, the cross-planked boat is apt to be the stiffer hull. Possibly the bottom bucking the hogging tendency has a lot to do with it. She is less cluttered in the bottom too, and she is lighter, for there are no frames. While fore-and-aft bottom plank is standard in dories and works well, it's been my observation that a very wide bottom planked by this method often pushes open at the chine, be it the dory style with the bottom landing inside the side plank, or the skiff style with the bottom lapping the sides. A dory's bottom, particularly on a Swamp-scott dory, is a rather small part of her whole structure, which minimizes any disadvantage of fore-and-aft planking.

Cross plank is laid in three ways. There is ordinary "tight-lay" with no caulking, and with wicking or marline on the side plank, clear of the chine, for the bottom plank to land on; I prefer marline of a good grade and even lay. There is totally caulked bottom and chines, using outgauge as for any caulked plank; this method may be best if the craft is hauled out of the water much. And there is the splined bottom for special use, say for a boat that is mostly on shore and is afloat only for short periods. This last, though not much used, is quite easy to make using the standard power table saw. A bottom can be built somewhat lighter using splines.

In some places and with certain stock, the tight-lay bottom is not always driven up to show a tight joint, but some opening is left for swelling. Some woods swell very much. Usually, in leaving this swelling space, some sort of gauge is used. One old way was to use the thin, brass blade of a ship carpenter's bevel. The back of a thin hand saw, without taper, was also much used. Nowadays, a thin piece of sheet metal, without bumps or wrinkles, works just fine. How much do you allow for each kind of wood? I really don't know. Assuming the wood is reason-

ably dry, Maryland loblolly pine seems to take kindly to the thin saw back. Local cedar I set right up, and so far, as long as the planks are under six inches wide, have never had a bottom coper; that is, bulge the plank and leak at the chine. Our local cedar is soft and compresses a lot. Southern cedar is harder and slower to "make up." Cypress, which we don't see much of now, swells a lot and shrinks accordingly. At one time, lots of skiffs were built of cypress; it's very durable, even though it takes up a lot of water. At the end of the season, some of the old boats were very "sobbed" and were a chore to haul up, though if of good model the extra weight affected their rowing very little. Whether using the tight-lay, caulked, or splined method, it's essential that the plank edges be joined true, without humps or hollows, otherwise the bottom often won't make up tight. This is no chore with a properly set power joiner and not much more so with a hand jointer plane. On a caulked seam, either tool will make the outgauge also.

Flat-bottomed boats should always use a chine timber; oak is best if it can be had, though other wood that holds fastenings and bends reasonably well will do. Sometimes it must do; you build with what is available. Usually these bottoms are nailed. This is really the place for boatnails, though ring nails can be used, and bronze at that, if you want to pay for it. There's really no point in bronze, as skiffs, some of very large size, have been boatnailed and lasted for years and years. The fastenings should, of course, be bored for, and on a tight-lay bottom should be raked, so as to jam one plank against the next. If the boat has a good flare, which rakes the nails yet another way, her bottom cannot be taken off without destroying it. With a hardwood keel plank, nicely tapered of course, and possibly with a couple of parallel, tapered skids, this construction makes a very tough bottom. The skids, as well as the keel plank, should be hardwood, either screwed from inside out, or clinched if you see fit. Skids or chafing strips should *never* be bent around the bottom of the chine, as is so often seen. Put on that way, they make a great oblong hoop in the water, and

The long, slim Sharptown Barge. (More pictures of her appear on pages 29 and 115.)

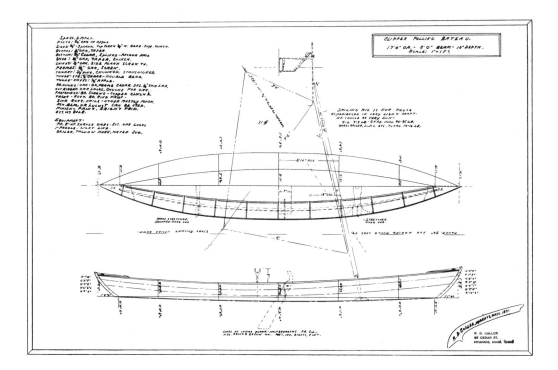

The Otter, *the author's own 17-1/2-foot fast bateau.*

cause the craft to be very dull, under either oars, sail, or power. Usually flat-bottomed craft have some sort of skeg to help directional stability. In rare cases, two parallel skegs are used, and once in awhile a lesser bow skeg or foregripe is added.

Most flat-bottomed boats are built with rather heavy side planks, set on edge and caulked, unless one wide plank is available. A pair of wide skiff planks, cut out near the center of a big pine or cypress tree wide enough so each will make a complete side, is seldom seen today. My own preference, unless the boat is some sort of heavy work scow, is to use rather light plank, say ½-inch for a 16-foot boat, and lap the planks, using two, three, or sometimes more planks if the craft is large. I think lapped sides are strong, light, and good looking in a nice model boat. You can use the full lap, dory lap, or some variation, though I prefer the full lap. This requires clinching, and dory nails can be used if available. For the small amount of metal required, I prefer to use copper cut nails. I see little point in using copper rivets, as clinched cut nails seem, from much experience with them, to do just as well in these boats and are simpler for one man to handle. Lapstrake planking is now much misunderstood. Many think lapping is a waste of time in flatty-type boats. I think it makes a superior and lasting skiff.

Along this line, it's now thought that flat-bottomed boats are best built of plywood. I'm sure a good one can be built, but most of the plywood skiffs you see are rather limber even when new, and tend to have chine troubles. The "engineering" is often poor, even though the material and fits may be fine. The point is that plywood requires far more framing to produce a good boat than most people suppose. The lavish use of glue and bedding compounds cannot overcome the lack of framing for long. I notice that so many of these craft bell and pant in the bottom, and often to some extent in the sides. Many transoms flex also, especially with an outboard motor, and most plywood skiffs seem to be built for outboards. Rudders and even centerboards are seen that flex like cardboard. Such plywood

skiffs needlessly give the flat-bottomed boat a bad name.

For many uses, nothing does quite so well as the flat bottom, cost and ease of building aside. Handiness on the beach, ease of hauling up with plank and rollers, even with considerable size and weight, and shoal draft often overshadow other needs. With proper design, a flat-bottomed skiff can row extremely well, not quite as well as more complicated models, but outstandingly compared to most rowing craft accepted nowadays. For best results, you want a rather long, narrow bottom, and otherwise fine lines, and not unduly heavy construction. I mention weight again, for you should keep in mind that the type is heavier than, say, a round-bottomed craft of similar capacity. In designing for good pulling under oars, some care and planning is necessary. Use poor oars of the wrong length, and the boat already has a strike against her.

These skiffs can be very good sailers too; they are usually useful boats. If you design for it, a very fast boat is possible. Most flat-bottomed craft, however, are not good drifters in very light airs, though some are better than others. A Swampscott dory, properly rigged, largely overcomes this weakness; probably the round sides and very narrow bottom help. This lack of ability in very light airs has been one of the reasons for designing away from the true flat bottom by using some deadrise or an arc bottom, of which more later.

A true flatty can be designed that both rows and sails well, but trying to design for rowing, sailing, *and* power with good results all around just does not seem to work out. The run is apt to be too flat for good rowing or sailing, or not flat enough for good results under power. The flat-bottomed boat that is designed for power, however, takes very kindly to both inboard and outboard motors, within certain limits. Properly shaped, these flatties can be very fast, especially with outboard motors, and, let's face it, if really fast they can hammer and pound fearfully. Yet for sheltered waters and with some common sense in handling, they can be most satisfactory.

While the care and maintenance of flat-bot-

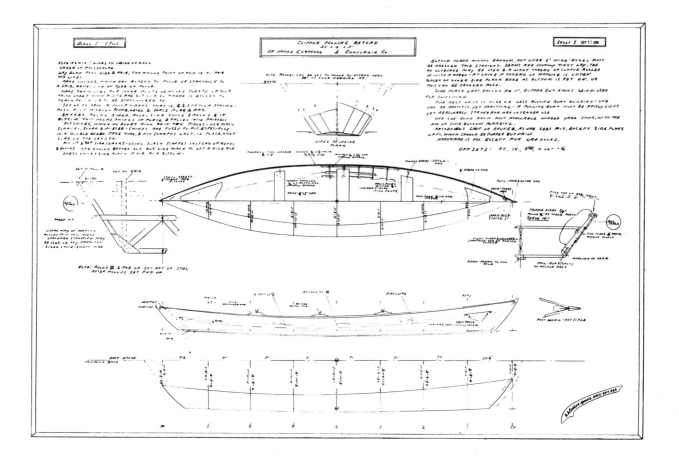

tomed boats is simple and most of it needs no dwelling on, there are some points that seem to have been forgotten. The inside bottom of flatty skiffs is usually painted, and I doubt that the paint does much good. The bottom gets lots of wear and tear with people tramping on sand and shells, so the paint does not last, looks messy, and has a tendency to scale off. It's better for the wood to treat it with boiled oil and turps, with a bit of pine tar added. The mixture drives into dry wood; it's all the better if it's put on hot. If put on a new boat, this stuff can, with proper application, fully penetrate the bottom. It turns dark in time but never looks really messy and is easy to keep. Once the bottom is thoroughly soaked, an annual treatment is very easy and cheap.

This oil treatment, once standard in the bottoms of log canoes and open bateaux on the Chesapeake, helps very much in slowing the shrinking to which these cross-plank bottoms are prone when hauled out for long periods. This drying out, largely preventable, has been the

cause of much condemnation of this kind of construction. Of course, there are some folks looking for the totally maintenance-free boat. Such things are said to be around, and my observations of them have been: You acquire one, run it to death, and get another, meanwhile putting up with a production craft that fills the bill somewhat but is intended to suit all people and all places and all conditions, and so suits none really well. And for some reason, few such craft can be called very good looking. If this is what boating means to many people, so be it, but they are missing out on much that makes just messing around in boats worthwhile.

The annual drying out is not nearly as bad as it seems and can, as said, be prevented to a great extent. Some woods tend to dry out more than others, but with a little help, swell tight again quite readily. Often a new owner will spoil his bottom right off the second season; he has an uncontrollable urge to stuff the dried-out seams full of something. He does not stop to think that if it was once tight, it will swell up again, which it does against his stuffing, often forcing the plank off. By now he's fussing at the builder, who explains it all again and usually points out, "Now you have learned it the hard way."

Assuming laying a skiff up for the winter, she goes in a barn, shed, or garage — never in a heated cellar or any heated building. If the building has a dirt floor, so much the better. Block up the boat or set her on horses, never upside down except when bottom work is going on. Be sure the craft is clean, having been well washed inside and out with fresh water and a strong soogy and then well rinsed. She will dry off very nicely once the salt is removed. A dust cover can be put over her, especially if birds use the shed too. Sometime in the middle of winter, a charge of oil and turps can be applied to the bottom inside, put on very hot with lots of turps, as it will be going on chilly wood. Assuming the bottom outside is clean, a brushing, sanding, or both, if needed, and a thin coat of copper paint at this time are also good. Come spring, you will find there has been little or no drying out, that is, if you fit out fairly early. If you wait till the March winds have had their go, there will be some drying out, but nothing some water won't cure after she's all painted. If you store outdoors, still keep her upright and use a tight tarp with ridgepole and stay pieces, and with ventilated ends. March winds get in more work on a boat stored outside, so the winter treatment, weather allowing, is a big help.

As to swelling up a craft that needs it, remember that warm water swells wood much faster than does cold water. Water at near freezing temperature has little swelling ability. Most of us now have hoses, though lugging some water, if done right, is not much of a chore. Old clean rags, sacks, canvas, or just plain worn-out longjohns should be spread on the bottom to help the water work and keep it in the ends. Don't expect to hurry it. There can be a not uncommon disaster; some guy does all the above, turns the hose on full as it seems the water runs right through her, then rushes off to work. Some woods have a way of going along for a spell and then taking up rather quickly. The day turns

Two basic flat-bottomed types: a skiff and a sampan.

69

The author's dory.

warm, the sun beats down, and about three p.m., she takes up considerably. The blasting hose fills her right up, breaks the horses down, and the craft tumbles, often hurting herself with maybe a ton of water in her.

Another way some folks swell a boat is to put her in and let the sea do it, which in some ways is fine. If she's in shoal water and takes the bottom at low tide, chances are she'll fill with both water and sand. Then she "comes together" on a mess in her seams. Three or four seasons of this, and she refuses to make up. She needs a new bottom; the seams are sand-hollowed. Seams full of sand eventually wear hollow due to the slight working of the craft, to a point where they will never be tight. If the boat is re-bottomed, the builder will end up with about a half a bushel of sand on his shop floor. Some people avoid the sand problems by anchoring the skiff in deep water and letting her fill right up, certainly a better practice, but with some drawbacks. If the boat is in an exposed location, she could wash the sternsheets or foredeck out from the constant surging of considerable weight of water. And with the present-day dirty harbors in many places, the boat can be plastered with gunk and oil inside and out. The proper way is certainly the easy way in the end.

My method for my Swampscott dory, based on her location and method of storing, is geared to cooperating with Nature as much as possible.

Though the craft is small, she stores outdoors under a proper cover. I start work as soon in March as that month allows. Roll the cover partly back to go at it, cold fingers, drippy nose, and all, covering again each night, or sooner, rather hastily for sudden falling weather to protect the work completed. This is no different from doing the bigger craft in boatyards. I get it done eventually, usually about the end of the month. Comes a day to pull the cover off for good and do the rails; by then it's April. The Swampscott has dried out very little, and tomorrow it rains. The plug is put in partially and Nature does the rest. Finally a good spell, she's launched and moored, for all is ready, and, being tight, she often goes for a sail the same day. Her season is long, about seven months, as the Cape Cod fall is protracted. Her bottom is copper-painted at least once in mid-season, sometimes twice, depending on how "weedy" the summer is. The dory is a smart sailer and I like to keep her so. I notice that as the season advances, she sails faster and faster compared to many craft; near the end of it, she's extremely fast. It pays to keep a clean bottom.

The above maintenance points pretty much apply to other than flat-bottomed cross-planked craft, and now we can discuss some of these others and why they may be of more advantage to own, for some uses and some places, than the true flatty.

VII
File Bottoms

File bottoms were probably so named because they looked somewhat like a cant-saw file in bottom section; later they were called vee-bottomed boats or, on the Chesapeake, "deadrises." Deadrise is the rise of floor in craft, so the "deadrises" had some, as opposed to the flat-bottomed boat, which had none. Just how and why the vee-bottom developed seems quite apparent, and there were two different approaches. One was an effort to simplify round-bottomed construction and utilize materials not well suited to it. The other was an attempt to improve the usefulness and ability of true flat-bottomed craft.

The significant changes from a flat-bottomed boat to a file bottom are: an increase in displacement when needed, sometimes a better run when heavily loaded, slightly more depth of hull, and a somewhat stronger craft if she must be large. It has often been said that the use of deadrise is to eliminate pounding in a head sea. With proper design and intelligent handling and sailing, in my experience at least, this terrible pounding in either type is far less than some folks think, and often non-existent in ordinary weather. All craft, large or small and of various types and shapes, find at times a sea and wind condition in which they are unhappy. I have been quite comfortable sailing along well at sea in a modestly small cruising craft while a large steamer nearby was rolling most dismally; conditions of the moment did not fit her. A sudden let-up in wind with some sea running does cause pounding in many shoal craft of angular construction; they are sitting upright instead of at a nice sailing angle. Nearly any sailing craft is not at her best in such conditions, though some are better than others.

There was a period in yachting when racing rules, speed at any cost in summer weather, and just wanting to follow the style of the moment caused the development of a type, round-bottomed to be sure, that was a fierce pounder. Some of these boats had such flattish sections that their design shortened the life of many a hull. In some ways we seem to be going back to this style again in both sail and power. This same thinking has done some strange things to the vee-bottomed boat, which, like the flatty, has had a long and skilled development as a working craft. Rough and ready "rules" have long been worked out, which, if followed, tend to produce a good boat. Much departure from these traditional craft, and the design begins to get out of hand. The notion that if a little helps, a lot will do much more is often tried here. Give her a lot of deadrise so you can get headroom, stow ballast low and make her able, and reduce pounding. What actually happens is the development of a short, deep run and a pot belly. Such craft are usually dull sailers and not attractive to the knowing eye. Often moulded frames with reverse curve are used aft to improve the run;

The 36-foot, file-bottomed sharpie, Old Glory, *about ready to go overboard. (Her plans and more photos appear on pages 102 through 105.)*

there is full fore-and-aft planking and even curved sides and other complications. Then the whole principle of the vee-bottom is lost, and you have a difficult craft to build — often more so than a true round-bottom. The "secret" of the file bottom is: Don't use too much deadrise amidships.

The deep-vee powerboat was considered quite a breakthrough, and I suppose it is for some uses. One thing for sure, it's a type that needs a lot of power. I note, now that the first flush is off, a trend back to shallow vee for some conditions. All types have their drawbacks.

The file bottom is considered a good boat for the home builder, as well as for the small professional shop trying to meet competition, because it's "easy to build;" it can be rather easy if the above-mentioned complications are left out. Except in high-performance planing power craft, these complications offer no real return for the work and cost involved, and even in very fast motor craft, that little extra gained is seldom needed.

The simple approach to building a file bottom is only a modest variation from flat-bottomed skiff construction in that you can use the well-tried, cross-plank, "herringbone" bottom. This is very strong, tough, and easy to repair. The only real trick in building it is — as in all boat carpentry — to get good fits, well fastened. It's often pointed out that the slight washboard effect on these bottoms slows a boat down. My own experience in rowing and sailing these craft is that if it does, it's not noticeable. Some folks

think that the herringbone pattern is a benefit in a fast craft that planes — "lets her break out of it and get on top." One can argue the point; my own feeling on it, based on designing and building this type, is that the cross-planking does help.

With the herringbone bottom construction, a stout keel is a must, along with a couple of sister keelsons, for there is no bottom framing unless the craft is of some size. On larger boats, two or more strongbacks are used; they are not true frames, as they rest on the keelsons, chines, and, of course, on the main keel, being well bolted to all. This method is well described in good books on boatbuilding, and clearly illustrated. In small beach boats of this construction, I place the sister keelsons outside on the bottom to act as chafing strips, bilge keel, and additional lateral resistance. Properly placed the same way on fast planing motor craft, they act as skis, and I find add much to the boat's performance. On sailing craft or non-planing motor boats, I place them in the usual inside position. In either case, they should be very well fastened.

In general, these craft, like the true flat-bottomed skiff, take only common sense and common care in their upkeep. Kept clean, well painted, properly stored and ventilated, they have a long life, even with much use, and seem to go on as long as any other type of construction, often outlasting more complicated hulls. However, I do notice one exception. Very fast planing boats — and this seems to apply to all types of construction — are often driven without

mercy. Such driving shortens a boat's life, and I sometimes think might shorten the operator's life too — possibly suddenly.

For the home builder, the traditional dead-rise boat built the way she originally was, and of a design suited to her mode of propulsion, is a most satisfactory and economical craft. Rather than say, "It's easy to build," I will say it's "un-difficult," if there is such a word. Nothing really good is totally easy. Many amateurs, and some pros, want to build in plywood, but they don't consider the model. Once they do it, they become educated. Plywood can make a good vee-bottomed boat, but *she must be designed for it.* In other words, she must not have what are compound curves for the plywood. Some folks still think they can bend this stuff both ways at once, and, as the boat appears to have straight sections, why not? They soon learn that all is not as it seems. That's what the "developed surface" is about. A fellow interested in this phase of design can soon get the hang of it out of the books, or he can use the barnyard method: Chop out models till a piece of light sheet metal will lie snug without a fight. Don't use cardboard; it's too easy to cheat with; it will bend a little both ways. Remember that this boat requires framing, and that good fits are essential. Many plywood vee-bottoms show the same construction weaknesses as do their flat-bottomed sisters, and for the same reasons.

A plywood, vee-bottomed boat designed for large sheets, as opposed to plywood plank, shows convex sections in places, usually forward, and

that is perfectly proper for a design intended for this construction. I really see no objection at all to a plywood vee-bottomed boat, if you can get the kind of craft you want in looks, durability, economy, and reasonable ease of building.

I've found these qualities far easier to come by, however, just building with plank. Good plywood is expensive. Unless marine mahogany is used — finished both sides, not just clear both sides — you will spend a great deal of time in getting a good finish on the work. Fir is troublesome to make look right and then does not seem to hold the finish. Outdoor grade construction stuff has voids that can cause leaks and usually do; these leaks can, in many cases, be impossible to stop without a major operation. Large sheets of any material are awkward for a loner to work with. You should really have tools made for cutting plywood; it helps in the final finishing. The lofting and moulding of the frames is more trouble than making the traditional plank sides and herringbone bottom. With plywood, you cannot get a fine, sharp forefoot, if that is what's wanted, or a shapely stern. Many designers fall down badly on getting a nice stern on a vee-bottomed boat, at least without a lot of complication. A nice stern can often be had, and a study of many old-time craft in books, pictures, and plans will show it can be done. I feel far less limited using plank than plywood in the design and building of simple boats.

For some brutal uses, where any craft would be considered expendable, I consider plywood

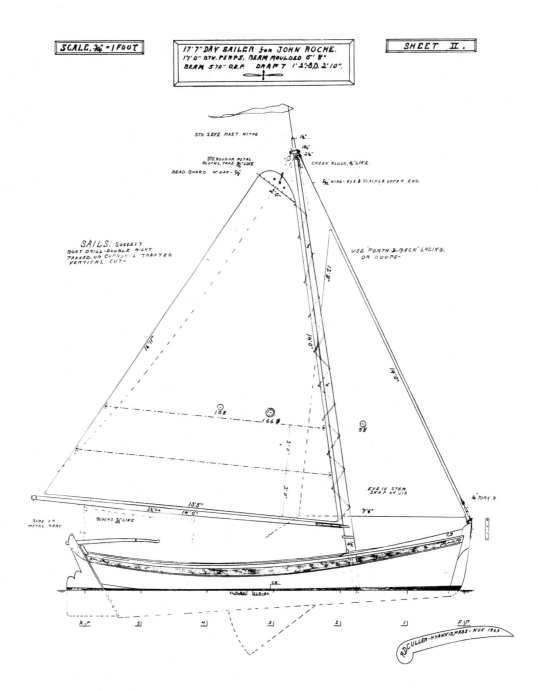

SCALE, 3/4" = 1 FOOT

17'7" DAY SAILER for JOHN ROCHE.
17'0" BTW. PERPS. BEAM MOULDED 5' 8"
BEAM 5'10" O.S.P.   DRAFT 1' 2"-B.D. 2'10".

SHEET II.

STD. 2 EYE MAST WITHE

STD. WOOD OR METAL
BLOCKS, TAKE 5/16" LINE
CHEEK BLOCK, 1/2" LINE.

HEAD BOARD W. OAK - 5/16"

5/16" WIRE- EYE & SHACKLE UPPER END.

SAILS: SUGGEST
BOAT DRILL - DOUBLE WIGHT,
TANNED, OR CUPRONOL TREATED
VERTICAL CUT -

USE "FORTH & BACK" LACING,
OR HOOPS -

108

166#

58

EYE IN STEM
SNAP ON JIB

1/4" TURN B.

RODS CO.
METAL TRAV.

BLOCKS 3/16" LINE

2 1/4" DIA
14'0"

13'5"

7'6"

CB

CLR-B.L. CLR-BD.

A.P.   5   4   3   2   1   F.P

R.D.CULLER - HYANNIS, MASS - NOV 1963

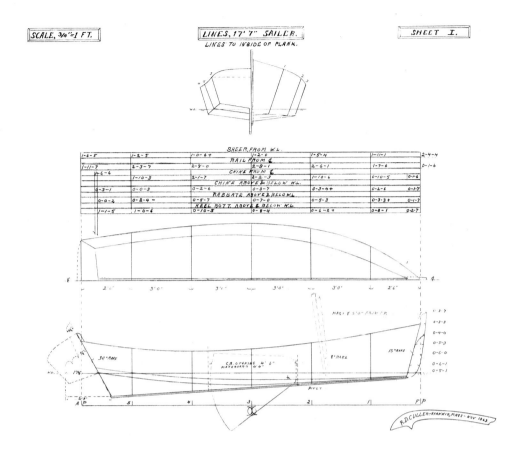

SCALE, 3/4"=1 FT.   LINES, 17' 7" SAILER.   SHEET I.
LINES TO INSIDE OF PLANK.

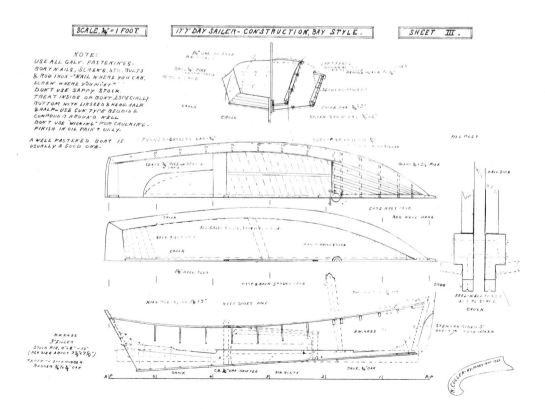

SCALE, 3/4" = 1 FOOT   17'7" DAY SAILER - CONSTRUCTION, BAY STYLE.   SHEET III.

NOTE:
USE ALL GALV. FASTENINGS-
BOAT NAILS, SCREWS, STD. BOLTS
& ROD IRON - "NAIL WHERE YOU CAN,
SCREW WHERE YOU MUST"
DON'T USE SAPPY STOCK.
TREAT INSIDE OF BOAT, ESPECIALLY
BOTTOM WITH LINSEED & KERO. HALF
& HALF - USE GUN TYPE BEDDING
COMPOUND AROUND WELL
DON'T USE "WICKING" FOR CAULKING.
FINISH IN OIL PAINT ONLY.

A WELL FASTENED BOAT IS
USUALLY A GOOD ONE.

superior. It will take a fearful beating up to a point, when the whole craft sort of goes to pieces more or less at once, and it's time to replace the boat.

For the right use and model, the file bottom takes kindly to the sharp stern. This is true even in a rather fast power boat of easy-driving shape. This hull form is not much understood nowadays, but the originators of the type knew all about it and, once engines became available, used the sharp stern with success. The long, lean, flat-run double-ender, or, more properly, sharp-stern deadrise, can be quite a performer with very modest power. For rowing and sailing, this type works well too, and often a very handsome craft can be turned out. The round, or fantail, stern can also be used with certain models, and, if properly done, can be very good looking.

Just why we see so many ugly and clumsy vee-bottomed boats today is hard to understand. I have heard it stated that good looking boats are a thing of the past, that no one can take time anymore, and shoddy shapes and workmanship must be accepted. Wooden boats, the few that are made, must be built with all sorts of short-cuts. Steel boats that are wrinkled tin boxes are standard. Cement and glass are expected to look inferior and so on. I differ. Most anyone can tell the nice looking from the ugly, whether or not he knows anything about a boat. A builder who can and will turn out an attractive craft will always have a few interested clients who will beat a path to his door, and, surprisingly, many are willing to pay what they think is a little extra for such work. In the end, paying the extra is apt to be the cheapest way out, for good boats last. This principle seems to apply in whatever material a careful builder chooses. If his boats are good, people soon know it.

It is my opinion, backed by the products of many past builders, that the file bottom can be a most handsome craft. She can be designed to suit, using many bow profiles, many sterns, and many tricks of fitting and trim without becoming overly complicated. Why make a homely craft, when, with a little head work and imagination, you can make her really attractive?

Some of the "tricks" of making any boat look well might be of interest. Naturally you start with a shapely design, though it might be a very simple one, and you stick to it. Fair curves in any boat work are most important; humps and hollows never can look well. A good looking sheer seems to catch the eye first off. Boat shops seem always to be crowded, so that you can't back off and look at a sheer batten. Different craft take different approaches. Double enders, very full craft, and long, lean ones all have different sheer problems. The ideal situation, seldom found, is a boat well out in a field so you can get off from her. If a shed roof can be clambered up on, or even a tree climbed, you often see things not apparent from the ground. The usual situation, however, is a crowded shop. When sheering a craft in cramped quarters, I put on the batten, fuss with it, fuss some more, and then go to dinner or knock off, depending on the time of day. Another look in an hour or the next day often shows up "hidden" shapes. If, by chance, the sheer batten will not be in the way for some time, I just leave it there; sometimes, several days later, I see fit to change it a bit. Never hurry battening a sheer any more than you have to. After much experience with this sort of thing, you tend to hit it in short order without much fuss. I never cut down a stern or a stempost to exact height while setting up. Some folks do — and lessen their chances if they have to jockey the sheer much. One-quarter or one-half an inch to play with in the ends is sometimes a lifesaver in getting a nice sheer.

An occasional bead and taper on things does wonders in giving a boat eye appeal. Many parts can be made quite attractive very simply by using judgment and imagination. We have all seen wooden cleats, some crude and some quite handsome. They both take the same amount of material and almost the same amount of labor. The handsome ones work better. Clean building, with a few nice touches, often makes the boat. If she is clean and fair, she will be good looking even though of plain finish. Without fairness, something is missing, and no amount of high finish will make the boat pretty. More likely, it will make her look worse.

A 30-foot outboard cruiser, showing the herring-bone construction of her bottom. On her trials she made 24 knots. Her plans are on the next two pages.

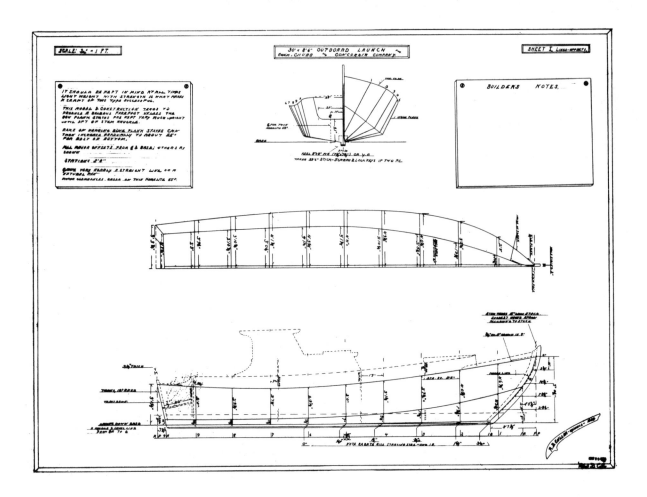

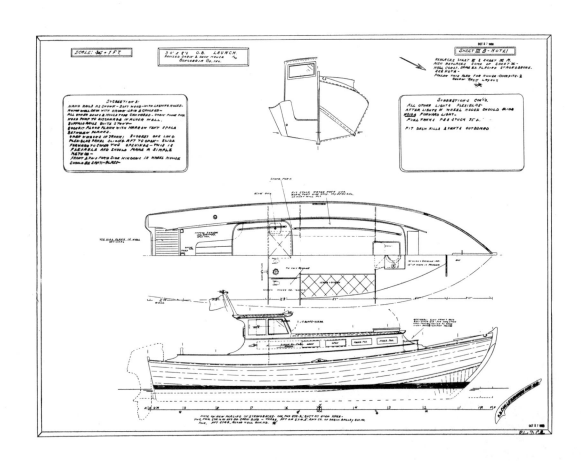

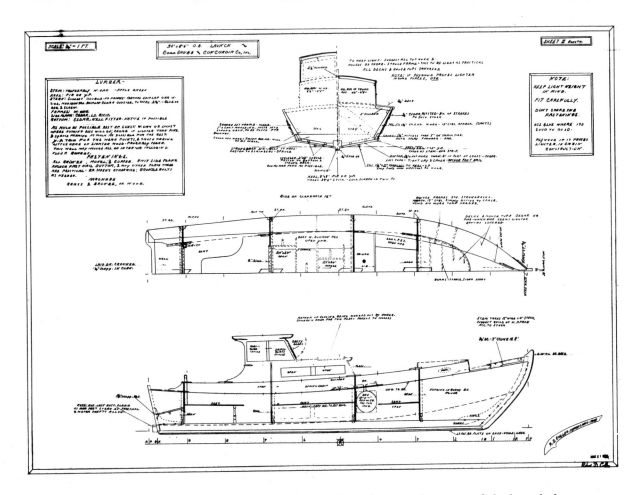

A certain touch to any part of a boat's structure is a help in making her look fine as a whole. There is no simple, step-by-step way of showing such touches to any extent on plans, or of really describing them either. Just keep the niceties in mind, have sharp tools, and use your imagination. Each builder's craft will show his mark even though several may build boats of the same design, and this is as it should be. Boats built by individuals are not at all like the usual mass-produced items that flood us, all alike even to the mould marks. Each boat the work of a man who likes what he's doing — this is boat building!

I have little more to add about the lore of chine boats, either flat or vee-bottomed. They may fit your use and pocketbook along with your available skills and building equipment, or you may hate the sight of them and prefer to shoot for higher things. A transition type might be mentioned here, though I think for the most part she is quite specialized and complicated. This is the craft with a round bilge forward turning into a chine aft. Many of these craft

have been quite successful, though from an economical standpoint they leave much to be desired, at least in the building. If a certain performance is required for a certain use, they pay off. The type has been used many times for rather larger motor yachts and was much used in some classes of wooden military craft. These last were built because it was thought they were needed; cost did not enter into it. Usually these craft had bent frames and were padded out aft to form a chine. I suppose they could be considered semi-planing boats, when they were not overloaded. Most war boats seem overloaded most of the time. There were other complicated approaches: full-chine boats with fully bent frames, webs over stringers, and all packed with wood, just like a wooden airplane wing. These were 40-ton boats, and to turn out one a day complete, with men who had little boatbuilding experience, was a feat. Some of these craft are still around, so the design and building must have been sound in their way. I think no amateur and few professionals will be tackling such craft these days, so I leave them at that.

VIII

Lapstrake

The round-bottomed hull may well have been Man's earliest type of boat, being the natural shape of a log. Of course it has progressed from the log to almost every possible variation (and some nearly impossible ones). Since the log — and it's still with us in many parts of the world — about everything has been used at one time or another for covering a frame. Skins, cloth, woven work, reeds, wood in many forms, paper and many materials now long forgotten have been used to make boats watertight. Relatively recently, we have seen fiberglass and cement added to the list. When you think about it, some ancient craft, dating back to Moses and before, were not very different in principle from modern craft. A woven hull covered with some kind of waterproofing, such as asphalt, is not so far removed from a hull of woven glass cloth covered with a man-made stickum. You can be sure of one thing: the old timers used what was available. It was either that or stay landbound!

One of the finest coverings for the frames of small to moderate sized boats is lapstrake planking, well worked out by the Norsemen and not improved on since. Just why and how it developed is well put down in books by those who have made a study of ancient sea ways. I will only point out why I think it's still the finest way of planking certain craft. Lapstrake planking has been used in much larger craft in the past than many now realize. Old photos of

Scandinavian and British harbors show many fine lapstrake craft, cutters, paddle tugs, luggers, and coasters.

Many boats used on our coasts in the past were lapstrake, or clinker-built, as it is sometimes called. Boats used for surf work were nearly always of this build. These boats often had to take a pounding on a beach, even with the most expert handling. They could not be too heavy, and lapstrake makes a light boat for her size and strength. Lapstrake was also much used for ships' boats, as the construction stands being out of water for extended periods. If lapstrake boats do leak after a long time out, it's usually not much, and they have a way of taking up quickly. A carvel, or smooth-planked, boat used on the beach can get a bad pounding and spew her caulking, and she is then leaking beyond coping with. A lapstrake boat can take considerable straining and still not leak to the point of being useless.

A small craft which must be reasonably light, one that hauls up a lot, surf or beach boats, some small, fast, motor craft, and, in my opinion, some types larger than we now accept for this method should be lapstrake. Even if a person has an aversion to lapstrake, unfounded or not, he must admit it does offer something, or why would they copy it in glass, metal, and soon, I suppose, in cement? Aside from giving a boat a certain style, it has been long known that laps

A small yawl boat set up in the author's shop. She is being battened out for lapstrake plank.

make for dryness if the boat's model is otherwise good; they are a sort of battery of little spray rails. It's also been said that laps tend to give a fast boat more speed, whether a planing model or a "displacement" craft. This is a point to be argued. Some old timers used to say that if you had two boats built to the same lines, one smooth, the other lapped, the lapstrake was apt to be the faster, but not always. What went on here? Was it a weight difference or the way the water went around the hull? My own feeling is that, assuming a craft of good design, a lot of it may have to do with the lining off of the strakes to suit the flow lines of the hull. This lining off, whether or not it has anything to do with the speed and ability of the boat, is one of the fine points of lapstrake building.

It's now said that the building of lapstrake craft is a most difficult process. I find it by far

the easiest way to build most round-bottomed boats. I say most, for some models are not very well suited to lapstrake. The best general shape, to me at least, follows somewhat the lines of a small Norse longship, without the dragon head of course. She should have a long, easy hull with a thin forefoot, and a thin heel if she's double-ended, though she can be quite full on the rails. Some slight reverse in the garboards I find of advantage, though not necessary. A turn of bilge that is an increasing curve as it comes up from the dead flat to the rail — a somewhat flaring side in other words — is desirable. If she has a square stern, she should have some reverse next to the deadwood. The model can vary in shape and size, yet there should be a definite Norse cast to her. A nice, flowing sheer is essential. Other shapes work well if of nice model, though a bulbous craft does not. A bulbous boat is not

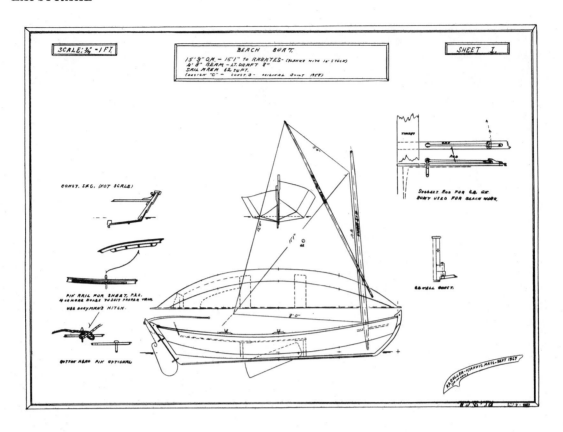

The beachboat, all set up and rigged.

much good built by any planking method.

When lofting lapstrake craft, or any small, shoal craft for that matter, I like to use sufficient diagonal and buttock lines. Waterlines, especially the lower ones, are of little use in accurate lofting of rather flat, shoal boats. Be sure to mark the moulds with the diagonals; these give a good guide to the lining off of plank, as touched on before.

In lapstrake construction, keels, posts, and sterns and their kneeing are no different from those of a smooth-planked boat. Depending on the size, type, model, and available stock, the keel can be scantling with a cut rabbet, or can be made with an apron and lower keel, or batten as it's sometimes called. Or, a plank keel with a worked rabbet can be built, as in a wherry. The deadwood can be in the form of a planked box, as on a Jersey Seabright skiff, if a wide, plank keel is used, or can be in the form of a shaped wedge with a rabbet. I prefer the wedge, made out of Eastern pine. Work a little reverse into it if the craft's other sections show some. I think all the above are more trouble than the true scantling keel, though if the design requires it, the plank keel in some form must be used. This last is very handy to set a centerboard well in. When using a scantling keel, rather than swelling it to accommodate a centerboard well, I prefer to use the offset well, finding it less work, and very strong. An offset centerboard does not affect the sailing of the boat at all, though some folks are prone to think otherwise.

You see many methods of setting up. Upside down is common for small craft, and if they are very small, this is probably the best. Don't fit the last or sheer plank until she is righted, though. I have not yet learned how to get a good sheer upside down. The method of setting up depends on the layout of the shop, but for most boats I think I prefer what I call the Norse set-up. The boat is built right side up on shored keel posts, with shores from the moulds to an overhead timber running along the centerline of the boat. The post and stern shore to this timber also. The floor under the craft is nearly clear, which is most handy. The overhead shores battering inboard are little in the way, and, with a nail or two here and there, are handy to store battens on or hang tools from. I hear complaints about having to squat to work on the bottom plank; I find a stool or shoal box helps here. The fact that shores can be used handily from the floor is a big help, and you avoid crawling under an upside-downer at times to see what's going wrong. This Norse method is very rigid, and as work progresses, the craft is never totally adrift from the set-up; when she is framed and the moulds are removed, she's first shored from overhead to the top of the keel, and as she's now fully planked, a couple of bilge shores on each side steady things just fine. I use enough keel shores so they can be shifted when in the way of interior work.

The mould stations should be established in designing the craft, and if they are not, as perhaps when using a design other than your own, they should be established and lofted to. Their spacing should be divisible by the amount of the frame spacing; in other words, 2-foot moulds fit 6- or 8-inch frame spacing. This is overlooked by some designers. If the craft is not moulded to inside of plank, the difference must be allowed for. I think a person doing his own designing should learn to do it to inside of plank, no more difficult than building a boat that has been designed to outside of plank.

In designing your own boat, lapstrake or not, allow plenty of deadwood in posts outside of the rabbet. If it's too much, you can always cut it down; too little, and you get that stubbed-in effect that can spoil an otherwise fine, sharp entrance. Keel and post siding can be far less than many people suppose in light, sharp, lapstrake craft. My rule of thumb is: Twice the thickness of the planking, plus the thickness of the stem bolts, plus $\frac{1}{8}$-inch. Thus with $\frac{3}{8}$-inch planking and $\frac{1}{4}$-inch bolts, keel and post would side about 1-$\frac{1}{8}$ inches. I often "fetch the bolts" in final rabbet trimming and knick the chisel! This proportion gives a fine, thin forefoot, and, with the usual wide beard or back rabbet here, it's quite strong. I think many forefoots today turn out stubby on account of not using this kind of proportion. Often the mistake starts in the lofting and is carried along.

In lining off — and some of this will apply to carvel planking as well — first decide the number of strakes. It is better to have one too many than be one shy. Some experimenting with short blocks of wood can be a guide, using the mid-mould to see just what is needed. The width of the stock will be a guide too. Some craft can take fairly wide plank, though the stock available may not allow it. By playing with the blocks, establish what lap you will use, and what plank thickness. I find that on classic craft of more or less easy model, 10 to 20 feet long, ¾-inch lap and ⅜-inch plank work well for the most part. Use thinner plank on a small, light boat. If the plank are narrow and the boat well framed, you can build a craft of quite some length using ⅜-inch plank, say in cedar or some other lively wood. I prefer as much flat grain as possible; edge grain, though the finest kind for decking, tends to split more easily than flat grain.

Rip out battens from any soft wood that does not kink after sawing and of a length to reach around the boat. If the stock is too short for that, I simply splice, using long, slash scarfs fastened with tacks or clinch nails. Battens can also be lapped, though the bump is sometimes hard to see around and get fair. I think splices are worth the slight trouble, especially for a small craft. The battens can be quite thin, but should be the width of the laps. You only have to batten off one side of the boat; use the more convenient side. I use the side next to the saw and workbench. Batten the sheer first, and the garboard next, keeping the ends well up, as mentioned before. Then put in the rest of the battens, one for each strake edge, being guided by the diagonals. Then stand off and study it from all angles. Little errors will at once become apparent and should be corrected one batten at a time. Shifting one may call for shifting another a second time. I usually do not attempt to have the hood ends forward all the same width, letting those above the garboard be wider than those near the sheer as a rule. Take your

time. The object is to have the boat all fair and pleasing to the eye.

Bear in mind, if the craft is a nice, easy model, that which would be the shutter in a carvel planked boat should have very little shape, only taper, in a lapstrake boat. What you are doing, starting with the garboard, is throwing the ends up and reducing the hook in the plank. The hook will increase again somewhat as the sheer is reached, the amount depending on the uprightness of the top plank and on the amount of sheer.

I say again, never attempt to edge-set lapstrake plank. There will be at times a slight unavoidable edge-set when a plank springs as it is sawn out, which it sometimes will with certain stock. This spring will haul back in place with little trouble, as the plank was laid out to the correct shape. Usually the plank are sawn out in pairs, tacked together, so you just line off one. Before you take off the battens, mark them top and bottom at post, moulds, and stern. These are the marks to spile to, and also "browse off" to when beveling one plank for the next to meet.

When spiling plank, naturally you start with the garboard. As it lies to the moulds, it is spiled just as is any plank which might lie to the frames. The garboard, once on, takes little browsing off, many times none at all, if there is some reverse in the sections. Now here is the rub. The next plank does not lie to the moulds, but laps the garboard. Its upper edge touches the mould, or its middle sometimes touches the mould at the turn of the bilge. The spiling batten must lie the same as the plank to get a true shape. I simply tack small wedges on each mould to simulate the lie of the plank, making sure that the wedges are no thicker than the plank which was put on and browsed off, and that their points fetch the upper mark of the plank being spiled. The batten now takes a proper lie. Naturally, no wedges are needed at post or stern, as the planks flush out here.

I feel planking in single lengths can be carried too far, and more can be lost than gained by it. Besides requiring wide stock, single lengths tend to produce cross-grain plank in the

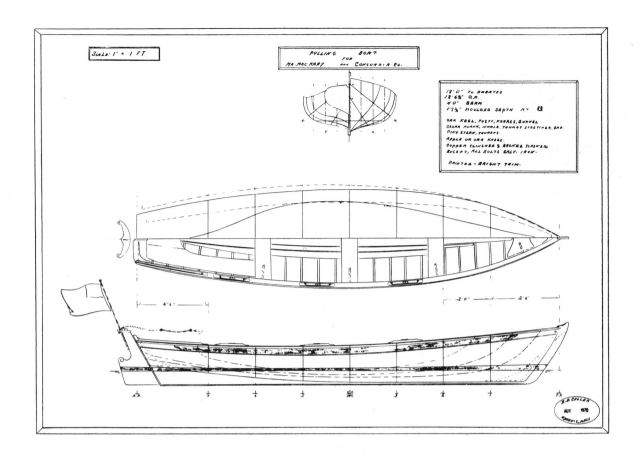

*The 18-1/2-foot pulling boat, before and
after delivery.*

A pair of smart wherries.

ends. Well-made butts are, in my opinion, far less objectionable than plank prone to split. The usual butt block is all right in a boat not intended for lightness, and which has a lot of joinerwork inside; in such a craft they do not look out of place. A light pulling boat is another matter, and in her the slash scarf should be used. These can be made either on the bench or on the boat.

This is the way I like to do it. If I can locate a butt on a frame, so much the better. I try to have the butt come in a clear part of the plank, allowing for the stagger of other butts of course. It's no fun making a butt with a hard knot in it! My rule is to make the scarf length the same as the plank width. I cut the scarfs on the bench; with sharp tools, it's simple, once you have done a couple. I join them on the boat, thinking there is less work and less chance of error that way. I use Weldwood glue and fit blocks that cover the scarf, separated from it by wax paper, with all the clamps there is room for. When the scarf is set, I clinch it up with copper tacks. Glue and gluing are subject to much argument. I use Weldwood because it's simple and strong. Some folks say it's no good because it won't stand boiling. If you are going to boil your boat, don't use it! Good fits and plenty of pressure are necessary. I confess I know nothing of gap-filling glues; the kind of work they seem to encourage I have no interest in. When properly made and sanded off, and with the boat painted, the scarfs I describe are often next to impossible to see.

Let's turn to fastening the laps. The dory lap, with galvanized clinch nails, is seldom seen except in dories. Copper rivets are used for fastening laps and are, of course, good. Working single-handed, however, these are sort of a chore. You don't have enough hands, so you resort to some method of holding the bucking iron, such as strapping it to your leg, or hanging it from a line around your neck, letting body pressure hold it to the work. None of this is very speedy, especially when putting in frames hot. For small craft, I like the copper cut nail, clinched, and have not seen any weakness in this method.

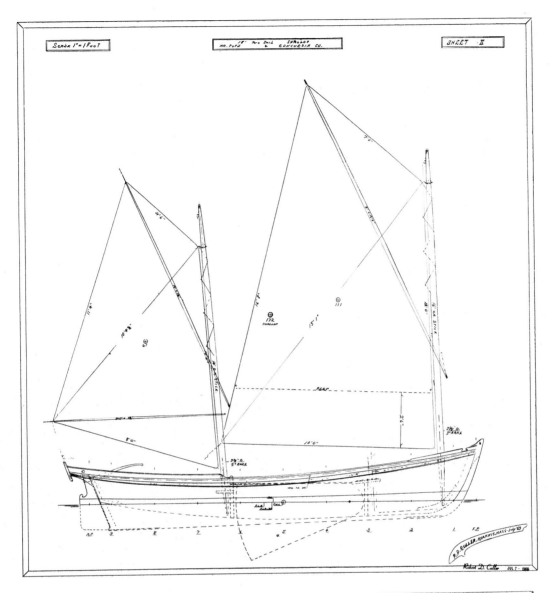

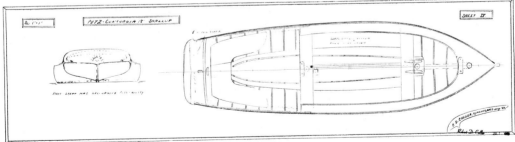

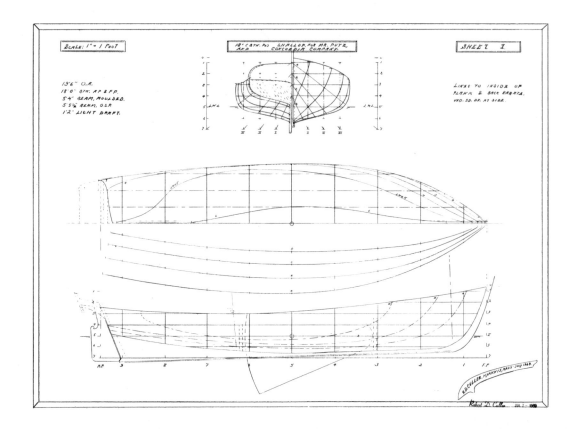

SCALE: 1" = 1 FOOT

19'6" (BTN. Po.) SHALLOP FOR MR. PUTZ,
AND CONCORDIA COMPANY.

SHEET I

19'6" O.A.
18'0" BTN. AP & FP.
5'4" BEAM, MOULDED
5'5⅜" BEAM, O.S.A.
1'2" LIGHT DRAFT.

LINES TO INSIDE OF
PLANK & BACK RABATA.
VRD. 3D. DR. AT SIDE.

R.D. CULLER, H. HAWIS, MASS. July 1969

Robert D. Culler   JUL 7 1969

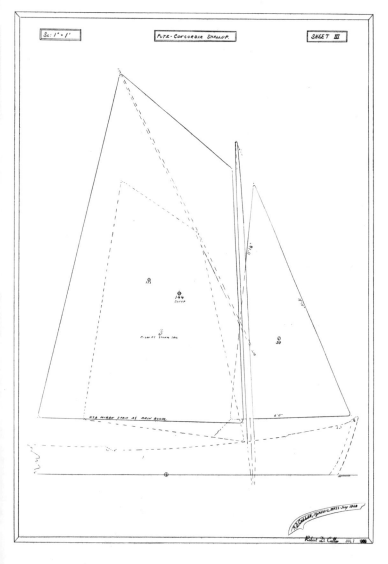

Sc: 1" = 1'

PUTZ-CONCORDIA SHALLOP.

SHEET III

R.D. CULLER, MARBLEHEAD, MASS. July 1969

Robert D. Culler   JULY 1969

A model of the 19-1/2-foot shallop. The model was made by George Putz, for whom the author designed the boat. Though the model was carvel planked, the boat can also be built lapstrake. (Photo by George Putz.)

It's best to clinch across the grain of the plank in soft wood. I find in hard wood, even though hot and wet with steam, you should clinch with the grain to get a good bury of the nail point. On a craft of some size, say over 20 feet, possibly it's best to use rivets. A bigger boat usually calls for a helper at times anyway. The main objection to galvanized iron clinch nails in a light craft is that the heads are not sunk and the clinched ends are never deeper than flush and so are subject to striking with sandpaper, which soon goes through the galvanizing, and rust streaks result. Even so, a boat built this way seems to last a long time. Certainly a light boat of classic model should have copper, either clinched or riveted, as the builder sees fit.

Laps should never be glued. Gluing does not allow the plank to "slip" in changes of wet and dry, and so will either buckle or split the garboard, or some other plank. The time-honored way was a dry fit. Many builders just must put something in between; if so, use a bedding compound, like Dolphinite, thinned with kerosene to the consistency of thin paint. It won't do any good, but if it's thin enough, it will do little harm, assuming you do not get chips and dirt in it to prevent getting a tight lap. All these sticky things play out after a while, and some, when done for, seem to leave a sort of dry ash. Much better wood to wood! There have been attempts to "improve" on the fastening of lapstrake craft by using glue-like sealers, short screws, and other short cuts. In the end, they don't work.

Once a builder tries lapstrake planking on a craft of a shape suited to it, he will find it's not the most difficult way of planking boats. You line off, spile, saw out, fit, and fasten, and browse off for the next one. This may sound like a lot. As compared to smooth plank, you do some things about the same way, some differently, and some not at all. Except for the garboard and hood ends, you work no caulking seam, there is no backing out of plank, no fret to get a good edge-to-edge fit, and usually no sinking of fastenings in a very light boat and only the screws to sink in a stouter one. Nor is there any outboard joining in the true sense; I've never met anyone who said he enjoyed this particular operation! And there is no caulking, paying, filling of seams to amount to anything, and not many fastening holes to fill. Even the framing and preparation for it go faster with less work on a lapstrake boat. True, you batten off to get the planking run on one side with light stuff, but there are no stout ribands on both sides to bend frame to, no sticking the frame to hold it with nails and sometimes screws till plank comes to it, and no removing all this temporary stuff as you go. You simply frame to the already-planked hull, one at a time, fastening while hot. The lapstrake frame is also lighter and easier to work with, takes only one clamp at the sheer, and is easy to crowd to the inside of the already-planked hull. Once in and fastened, it's done, complete in itself, finished — unless it broke and you didn't notice in time! I leave lapstrake at that.

IX

Carvel Planking

Carvel or smooth plank is no doubt the most common way of building a round-bottomed boat, and, as a method, has a lot going for it. There are of course various ways of getting a smooth skin on a boat besides a single thickness of plank, edge-to-edge-caulked; all are more expensive than the common carvel method, and are for specialized uses and types of boat. Right now "strip-built" is popular; I think the shape of the craft has a lot to do with where and when to use strip planking. The common idea is that strip building is rather cheap, easy, and rapid. The idea is that you can work to a standard taper and use light strips, either beveled, or hollow and round, done on a shaper. This is fine if you own or can borrow a shaper, but one that can really produce all day long is not a cheap machine.

I feel a sort of spindle-shaped hull is best suited to strip building. A classic hull, especially if of a very shapely model, will soon develop a bad "hook" in the strips, making for much sometimes impractical edge-setting. Then the principle of the master taper strip can fly out the window. My remarks on the lining off of regular plank point very much to just what goes on. All this setting tends to spread the hull and pull the plank away from the moulds. I sometimes think, for some hulls at least, a set of *outside* moulds would be better, not forgetting to have many rolls of wax paper on hand to keep the

plank from sticking to them, for strip building relies on some sort of stickum, glue, or gunk along with edge nailing. Jointing off in this mess once the hull is planked is a sticky business and often prone to dulling tools rapidly. If the craft when finished is to show her skin inside, there is much work here to make her presentable; she's often glue-smeared and ridgy.

Just how strip building developed, and where, we can only surmise. Probably it was born Down East when lumbering was in its heyday and strips were free for the lugging off. Winters were long, the old ripsaw was sharp, galvanized wire commons were cheap, and a man needed a new boat. There was no fuss, no complication. Work with what you have; it made sense, and another boat could be built the same way when the first wore out. By the way, a few of these old craft still exist. My own feeling, though, is that strip building, if done well, using expensive stock, much glue, and bronze nails, and involving some of the complications above mentioned, is not the easy or cheap way to build a boat. And it is totally unsuited to some shapes of hull.

Then there is double plank, and even triple plank, the latter having two of the skins on the diagonal. For special use, such as in a light racing craft, or wherever much strength with light weight is needed, these methods are worth their trouble. Some lifeboats used to be built this

One of a pair of yawl boats for the replica of the schooner yacht America. (This boat's plans appear on the following page.)

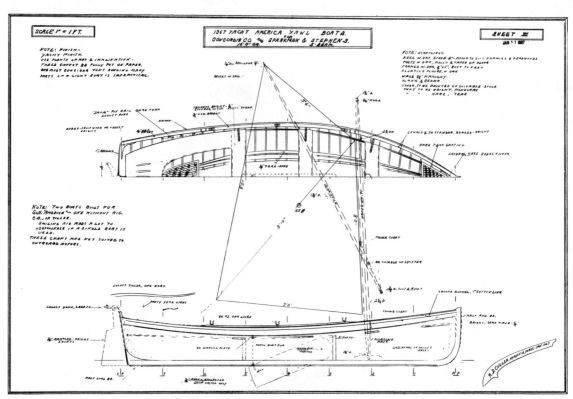

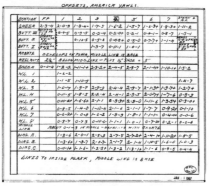

OFFSETS, AMERICA YAWLS.

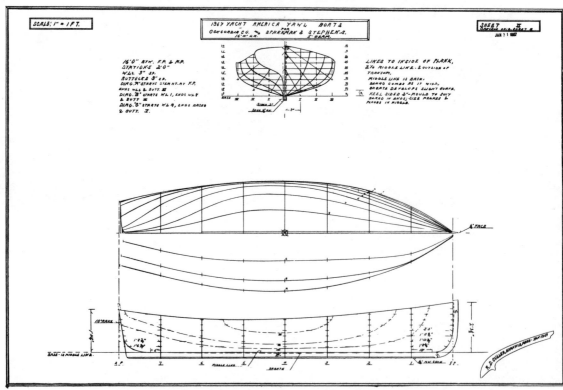

way and will stay tight out of water, even for long periods. Multiple planking is expensive and time consuming. In the Great War, many small wooden craft were built, using many planking methods. Some members of this splinter fleet are still around and in commercial service. Some were made into yachts, and to my way of thinking did not make good ones. As to lasting, the single-plankers seem to have lasted about as well as the craft with more than one skin.

This leaves us with the old standby, the single-planked, caulked-seam method of boatbuilding, on which millions of words have been written. Why say more? I won't say much, just a few things, long known but often overlooked.

I have seen carvel plank as light as ⅜ inch in fancy dinghies, but I think lapstrake for such craft is better. Some craft plank with ⅝ inch, which I think is still too light for a long life. With ¾-inch plank and heavier, carvel planking comes into its own. In figuring plank thickness in these small dimensions, you should consider the amount of backing out and dressing off required for the particular design. On the other hand, you should not put stout plank on too light a frame; problems in fastening and holding the shape develop if the frame is too light. And whether the craft has bent or sawn frames, there is a need for three or four sawn frames right aft, as no amount of stout plank will pull true frames that don't quite make the curve there. In other words, right aft, especially topside, things tend to flatten in.

While it's not often that sizable craft are backyard jobs, because a big vessel is just too much unless the home builder is dedicated, I really like vessels that require plank of 1 ¾ inches and up, with thicker wale strakes and garboards. The latter should be preferably of hard, or semi-hard wood, say fir or hard pine, and she should have an oak bottom. Or, she can be all oak if she's salted. A professional caulker can really button up such a hull. He uses a choker of cotton, followed by sufficient oakum, and the garboards are caulked complete, but are not hawsed back until all the rest of the vessel is done, including the covering boards. You can hear her tighten up day by day, as the caulking progresses. The day the garboards are hawsed back — the last operation in the caulking — the hull rings like a bell. If the thick garboards and wale strakes are edge-bolted, so much the better. The smells are there, the sounds are there. To use the words of a well-known statesman, there have been blood, sweat, and tears (and once in a while bankruptcy). This, bored reader, is wooden shipbuilding. Few now have a chance at it. If you ever do get a chance, take it up!

I think that those folks who recommend or sell some of the new compounds said to do away with caulking know nothing about wooden boat and shipbuilding. Caulking, by one who knows his job, is what stiffens and ties all the structure together. Before the days of steel strapping, large wooden vessels were packed solid between the frames, especially in the bottom and at the turn of the bilge. The frames were caulked and pitched both sides, then planked and ceiled; planking and ceiling were both caulked, as were all the decks, and there were often three. All this was to tighten up the whole structure, and help it keep its shape for a while. By no efforts and skill of men could every joint be perfect, and this was the way — the only way — a large vessel could be given sufficient strength. Yes, a carvel-planked, single-skin hull should be caulked in the traditional manner, be it a light boat, with a fine thread of cotton put in with a small caulking wheel, or be it a big craft with coarser methods.

No seam compounds I know of last indefinitely. Some of the newer cure-all ones certainly don't last in proportion to their cost. Those in use a hundred or more years ago are still good; some of these are readily available and others are a bit of trouble to get today. Mostly they go unnoticed, as they are not packed in cans with a picture of a boat on them. White lead and whiting make an excellent and lasting seam and fastening-hole filler for carvel-planked boats, especially those of rather stout model. This stuff is too hard for use in laid decks, and is not the same as store-bought white lead putty. Put dry

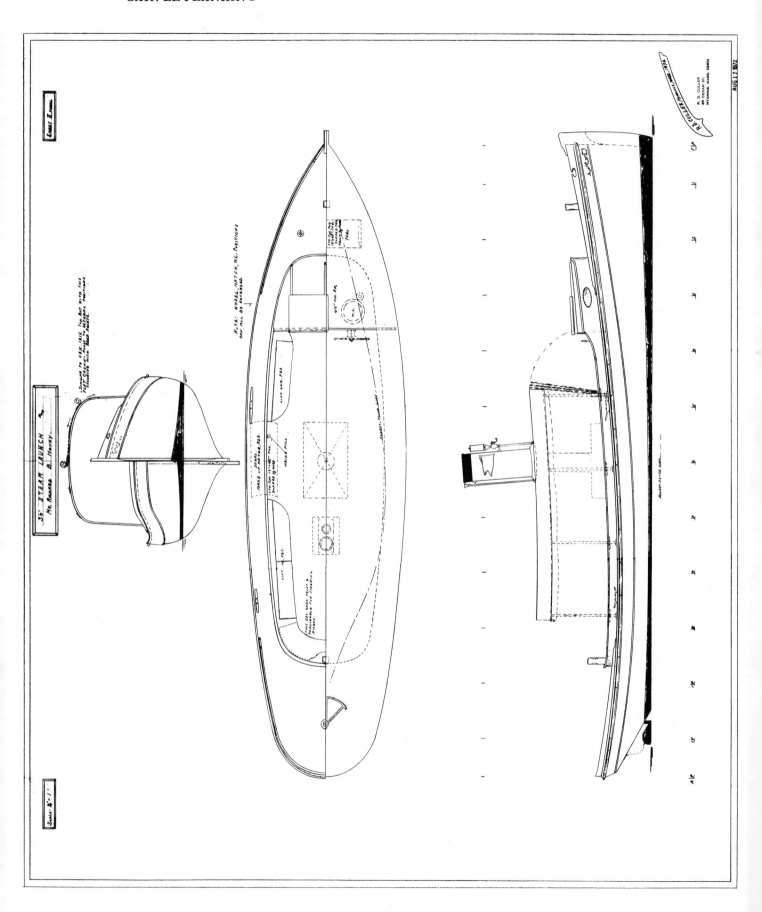

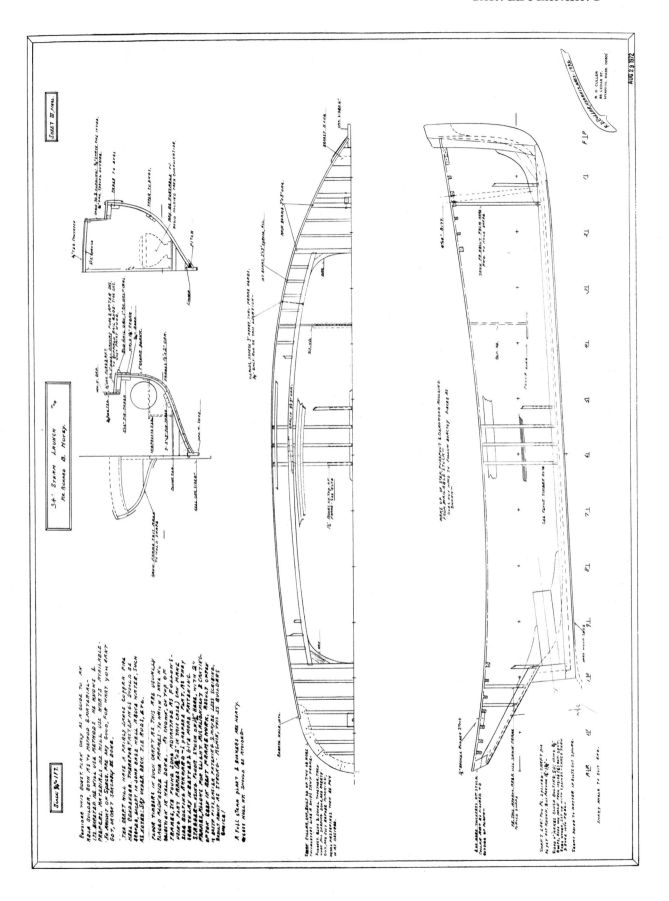

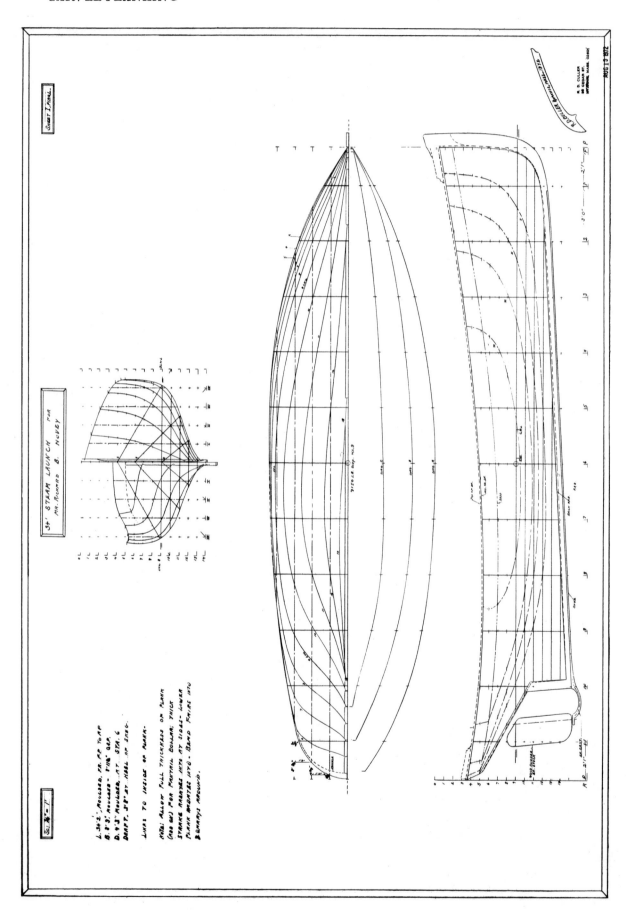

	STATION	FP	1	2	3	4	5	⑥	7	8	9	10	11	AP
HEIGHTS ABOVE & BELOW LWL	SHEER	4-4-0	3-11-4	3-5-5	3-0-0	2-7-4	2-3-6	2-0-6	1-10-6	1-8-7	1-10-2-	2-0-2+	2-4-2	2-8-2
	DECK		DECK IS 1" THICK, SO				READS	THAT	MUCH	ON	ABOVE- NO NEED	TO	FAIR.	
	BUTT. I		0-11-6	0-8-2	1-1-1	1-3-5	1-5-6	1-7-3	1-7-7	1-5-6+	0-10-7+	0-1-0	1-3-7	1-11-6 AT KNUCKLE
	" II			0-5-2	0-5-6	0-10-2	1-1-3-	1-2-7	1-2-5	0-11-6	0-5-2	0-5-0	1-5-6	1-10-3+ " "
	" III				0-5-2	0-4-1	0-8-2	0-10-4	0-10-2	0-7-1+	0-1-0	0-10-0		1-6-2 " "
	" IV					0-10-7	0-1-2	0-2-4+	0-2-3	0-3-1				
	RAB.	2-0-0	1-3-3	1-6-5	1-8-5	STRAIGHT— NOTE-THIS IS BACK RABATE					2-8-3			
	KEEL BOTT	0-10-2	1-8-1	1-11-3+	STRAIGHT— INCLUDES SHOE.						3-0-5			
HALF BREADTHS	SHEER	0-2-0	1-5-1	2-10-0	3-8-6	4-2-6+	4-5-1	4-5-2	4-4-0	4-2-0	3-10-4	3-5-1-	2-9-5	
	DECK	0-2-0			AS	GOES								
	WL 1													
	" 2		1-4-6											
	" 3		1-4-2	2-8-4	3-8-5									
	" 4		1-3-4	2-8-7	3-8-2	4-2-5+								
	" 5		1-2-5	2-7-7	3-7-6	4-2-3+	4-5-1	4-5-2				3-5-0	2-8-7	
	" 6		1-1-4	2-6-1	3-6-4+	4-1-6	4-4-6	4-5-2	4-4-5	4-2-4	3-10-6	3-4-7	2-0-2-	
	" 7		0-11-6+	2-3-5	3-4-2	4-0-3+	4-4-0	4-4-6+	4-4-5	4-2-4+	3-10-2	3-2-4		
	" 8		0-9-5	2-0-2	3-0-6	3-9-5	4-2-5	4-3-6	4-3-4	4-1-3	3-7-6	2-2-6+		
	LWL 9		0-7-2	1-7-4	2-7-5	3-4-6-	3-11-0	4-1-4+	4-1-0	3-10-2	3-1-4	0-9-6		
	WL 10		0-4-6	1-2-0	1-11-6+	2-8-6	3-4-6	3-7-5	3-7-2	3-2-3	1-9-4	0-2-2		
	" 11		0-2-3	0-8-0	1-1-4	1-8-0	2-3-4	2-7-0	2-7-0	2-0-1	0-10-4			
	" 12			0-2-1	1-7-6	0-7-6	0-11-5+	1-3-0	1-4-1	1-0-4	0-6-1			
	" 13						0-1-6	0-3-4+	0-5-1+	0-5-3	0-3-2			
	RAB.		OUTER RABATE 2" ALL THE WAY-											
	KEEL BOTT	2" ON KEEL- START TAPER FR. STA 1½ TO STEM- FINISH ½" ON STEM FACE- TOTALS FOR 1" STEM BAND.												
DIAGONALS	DIA. A		1-5-1+	2-9-1	3-8-1+	4-3-5	4-8-3	4-10-1-	4-9-3	4-7-0	4-1-5	3-4-2	2-0-1	
	" B		1-2-6	2-2-2	2-9-5	3-2-1	3-5-2	3-7-0	3-6-5	3-3-4+	2-8-6+	1-9-2-		
	" C		0-8-1	1-1-6+	1-5-7	1-8-4	1-10-1	1-11-2	1-11-6	1-10-1	1-3-7	0-6-1		

R. D. CULLER
85 CEDAR ST.
HYANNIS MASS. 02601

LINES TO INSIDE OF PLANK & COLLAR, & TO BACK RABATE.
FIGURES IN FEET, INCHES, & EIGHTHS, + OR - ; EX., 1-8-2 = 1' 8¼".
—OFFSETS FOR RICHARD B. HOVEY 34' STEAM LAUNCH—

R.D. CULLER 1972 HYANNIS MASS.
AUG 16 1972

whiting on a board, like flour when kneading bread, and work up a wad of white lead ground in oil until it can be handled. Don't get it crumbly. I suppose this mix might be 90 per cent white lead. I've known it to last for 40 years.

Underwater, a similar mix, using pine tar and whiting instead of the lead, lasts and lasts. Pine tar is still available if you hunt a bit for it. Black asphalt paper shingle stickum works just fine too; it has a way of "settling in," even in an overhead seam. This is fine in a new craft; there is less to flush off when she sets herself. This shingle stickum is fairly cheap, easy to use, and very durable. There are other things to use, but why get complicated when the above will do the job?

Carvel plank usually suggests bunging or wood-plugging the fastenings. This is fine if the plank is thick enough; if it's not, bungs are trouble. I feel many craft that are now bunged in the interest of having the best are not in the end the best. They may be too light for bunging. A rough rule of thumb is that bungs should be set about as deep as their diameter, and should not cut the plank through more than a third of its thickness, preferably a bit less. There is no use in cutting a plank half in two, as is often seen. Bungs that fit too tight compress in driving, and this leads to puffing out later. Bungs are set in all sorts of stuff, depending on whether the plank will have a bright or paint finish: glue, red lead, any old paint, varnish, and way back when I learned about this, often in shellac for bright work. Nowadays, it's thought shellac is no good; somehow it seemed to work. Take your choice.

Much fuss is often made over carvel planking, yet it is rather simple. With proper planning, attention to lining off, the right amount of backing out or dubbing flat if she's a sawn-frame vessel, and care in taking the bevels, all goes along without bother, assuming, of course, that the frame is of proper size, well ribbanded, and fair. I've worked on many large craft with very stout plank, and very little use was made of "C" clamps. Often there was no place to put them; the ceiling crew was pushing well ahead of the plankers, and clamps were of much more use to them. Putting the heavy plank in place was nearly all done with shores, wedges, wrain bolts and staves, loggers, chains, and common sense, along with the standard planking dog. Experience on large craft certainly does simplify your outlook on smaller boats.

X

Engines, Oars, and Sails

Boats are made to go. I'll take up first what in some ways is the simplest form of propulsion—the engine. Raised eyebrows? Engines are bought as units, either new or second-hand. It's just a matter of money; I don't know of a man who has built his own engine for his boat, unless, in rare cases, she's a steam launch. Internal combustion engines are manufactured and are made very precisely nowadays.

I'm still approached now and then by people who want an old-time, slow-speed engine, new of course. They just like the idea, and so do I. With three or four exceptions, however, there are none now made, and, on explaining these exceptions, the subject is soon dropped, for most folks want self-starting, and may not realize that certain two-cycle engines still made don't take kindly to clutches, reverse gears, and fancy instrument panels. We settle for a high-decibel automotive job — yes, automobiles are where they all come from until you get into big rigs. Diesel, of course, is the best of all, and for good reason, though no one has yet built a quiet one that I know of.

In planning a powerboat, it should be kept in mind that the machinery will be a very large part of her cost and also of her maintenance. This applies to outboards, and with the very complicated installations of all kinds that you see nowadays, power craft can be quite a drain on the wallet. They don't run for free; every mile costs, and usually the faster the mile the more it costs.

Some few folks can build a cheap boat, and, being whiz mechanics, can work from a junk pile and have a very usable rig, though it may not meet presently accepted standards or even the law in some cases. Besides, the lash-up is not insurable. Yet most of these inventive craft seem to give very good service, just because the operator knows very well what he's doing.

High speed is always expensive; if there is a real need for it, it is, of course, quite worthwhile. Much consideration should be given to whether or not speed is really needed or practical for the intended waters. There is a saying around my area that great speed is practical mostly in the early mornings only; afternoon winds usually make the water very lumpy. Many people don't like to get up early. There is a lot to be said of a non-planing boat of small power and very easily driven model, yet now such boats are seldom seen, probably because the idea of using the great length required just appalls. A person trying out one of these long ones for the first time is astounded at their easy way of going and at what fine seaboats they are. They make a most economical type of power craft, and, though long, are not big boats, having a modest displacement. The displacement is where the cost is, both the cost of building the boat and the cost of the power to drive her.

There are all sorts of plans of fast, long, narrow craft to study. One of the finest examples was the wooden subchaser of World War I. Her record stands, and for her day she had extraordinary endurance and range. North Atlantic weather separates the pots from the ships. That the principle works in both smaller and larger sizes is shown by the motor crab skiffs in Chesapeake Bay and by the liner *United States.* If you wonder about the *United States* being narrow, take this liner's dimensions and divide by nine. The result is close to a 100-foot steam torpedo boat of Captain Nat Herreshoff's design. The speed record of the *United States* speaks for itself.

Outboard motor boats are, of course, everywhere, and in the smaller sizes make a lot of sense. Boats can be simple, and the taking care of the motors the same, if you don't overdo the motor. Some of the huge washing machines still called outboards make me wonder, and I speak here with some slight experience, having designed successful outboard boats up to 30-feet long, all twin-screw. They work just fine and fill the present desire for fast boats.

I personally don't care for fast boats, though they are very useful and fun at times. They are not at all economical by the hour, though not so bad by the mile when the weather is light. The cost of powering the fast boats I've designed is high, even though these boats use half the power of most outboards and yet have plenty of speed. Maintenance of the power plants is reasonably easy but by no means cheap, and the engines, by their nature, do not live long.

Someone is always suggesting outdrive, which sounds good. I have no idea how many of these are in use. The number in boatyards in a laid-up-and-taken-down condition in mid-season puts their durability in doubt. I assume a bronze lower unit is impossible because of cost and weight; the durability of the potmetal ones speaks for itself.

We hear of new types of power plants just around the corner that will revolutionize motor craft. I'm sure they will, when they come. Since my earliest exposure to boating, these wonder engines have been lurking behind that corner; a few have peeked out and then drawn in their horns again. The gas turbine is now with us, but it can only be bought by the taxpayer for his Government. The cost may come down later on. A machine which, from the drawings, looks somewhat like the inside of some auto oil pumps

An outboard skiff, showing off.

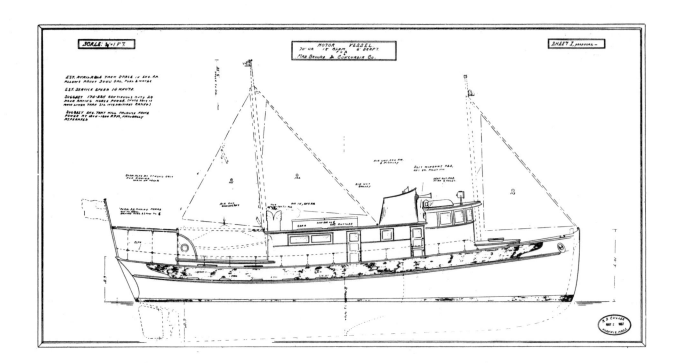

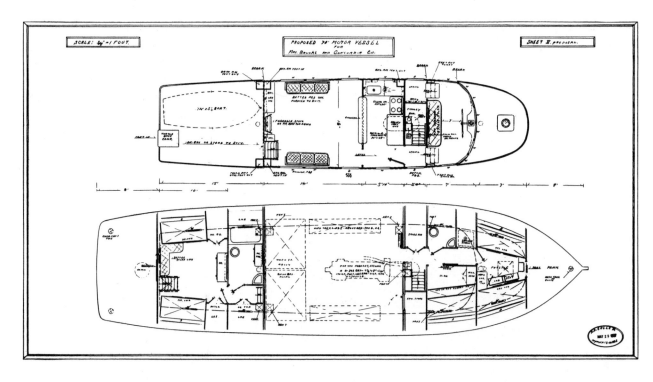

is about to take over the automotive industry, and, doubtless, boats, lawn mowers, et. al. We'll wait and see; there may be great things coming for boats.

There is another kind of engine, the steam engine, considered by many motorboat men merely the plaything of nuts. Yet, if you are exposed to the right type of steam engine, you've had it. Steam enginitis is very catching. Those who work with steam are not so much concerned with its lack of pollution — though they always make a point of it — as with the sounds and smells, and just watching an open-crank engine go. Some fellows who do this stuff are so dedicated they build the whole thing, hull, engine, and boiler, while others stick to the machinery and acquire the hull. A proper "steam hull" is classic and much sought after, and if she still has a steam wheel on her, so much the better. A steam propeller, by the way, often has a pitch twice its diameter, and to see a tiny engine, overshadowed by a hulking boiler, simply run away with that hunk of bronze is a sight to behold. Steam jargon is different too: double simples, tandem compounds, in-lines, Wards, Navy K's, Stephenson links. It's awful; don't go near it or you are hooked. I like the smell of soft coal myself!

A more complicated yet cheaper form of propulsion than engines is oars, and I think we should include sculling oars and paddles. The complication is that you cannot buy really good oars off the shelf; it is far, far easier to buy a good engine. I've expounded on oars before, do so now, and will, no doubt, in the future. A good boat requires good oars, and as her type varies, so, to some extent, should the model and construction of her oars. Until you have tried a good pair of oars, it's impossible to realize what you have been missing. Fortunately, good oars are not difficult to make, for those who like a little woodworking, and the stock to make them is easy to come by.

Most oars are made way too short nowadays; they should be at least twice the beam of the boat, often more, and it's difficult to find any long enough in a store. When you do, they are

frightening — great logs of wood, often with poor grain. So you grab the shortest, which are lighter, but good for little except stirring a great vat of jam.

You can purchase a stock pair of oars if they are of sufficient length and then work them down. These are never quite right, however; as well as having too much wood in the wrong places, which you can work off, there is not enough of it in others. Greatly oversized surplus lifeboat oars have enough wood so they can be worked down successfully; there is a lot of trimming, but they are often cheap. They are apt to be of heavy wood, and though they may well suit a dory or other working craft when taken down, the stock is unsuited to light, smart craft.

Many lumber yards stock construction spruce, and if you know a yard crew who happens to be the kind who lets you pick — leaving the pile as neat as it was, naturally — some very nice stuff can often be found. A place that has a big turnover is good; if you don't find it this week, go back next. The stock is often wet or damp, so it must be taken home and stored carefully to dry. No matter, it's fairly cheap, so get enough, say longer and wider than your oars require, so you can use the best parts.

Ash has been the standard for working oars for a long time. Good fir also does well for workboat oars, though it has more weight than, say, spruce or some other woods. Sitka spruce is just fine for light oars, if you can get it and want to pay the price. Depending on the use, many other woods can be used, and just because they are not used now is no reason why they can't be. I have a canoe double paddle which is 75 or more years old and seems to be made of Eastern pine; it's in fine shape and lively.

Built of solid stock, an oar or paddle can be very wasteful of stock. Gluing up, which has been done for a long time, makes it quite easy to build up a suitable oar out of stock of almost any dimensions, saving much material and a little labor. Oar and paddle making, while by no means difficult, is not a fast, machine process, if the oars are to be any good. You make a big pile of shavings, which is, I think, pleasant work.

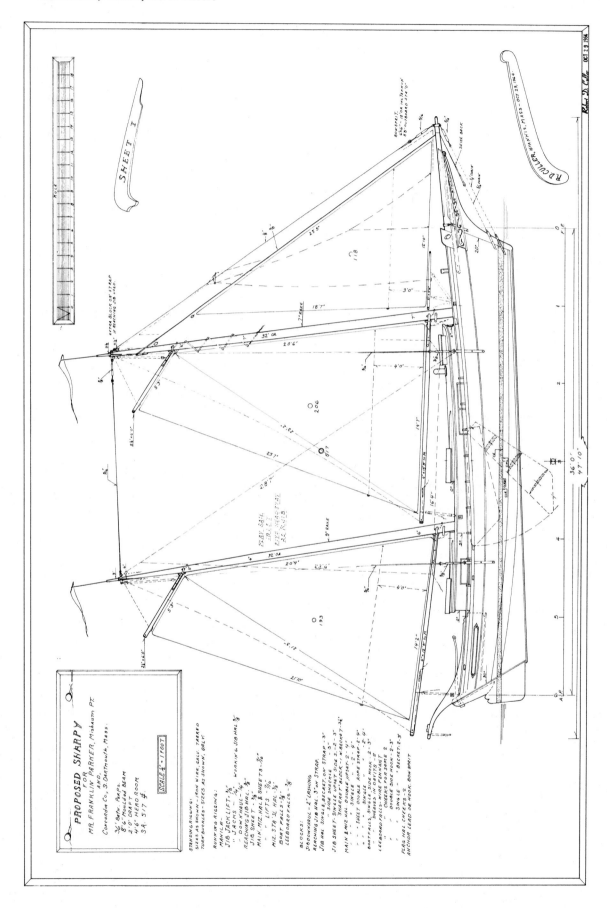

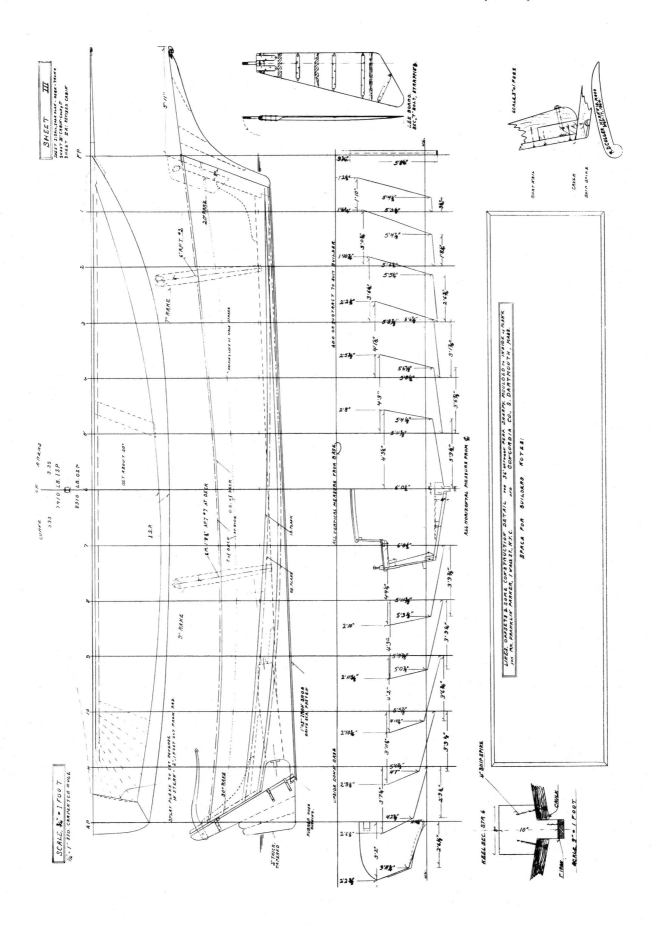

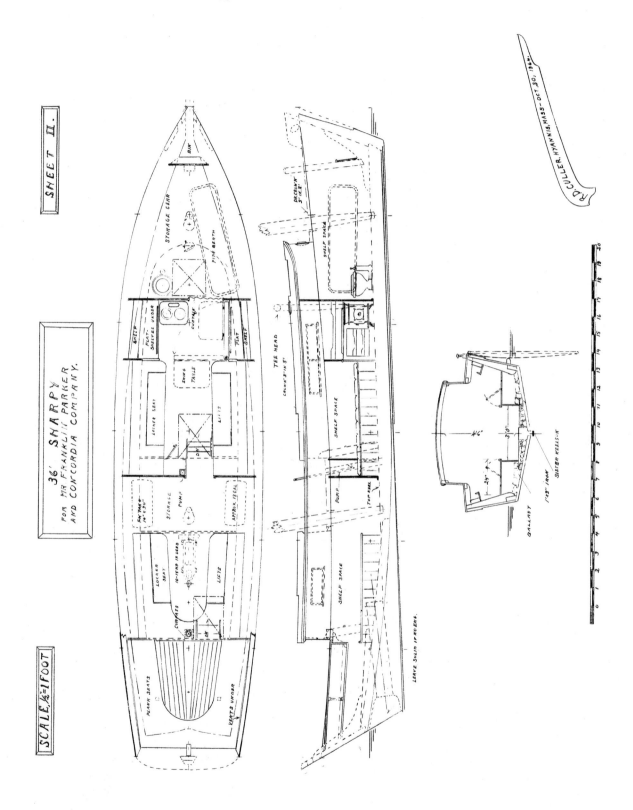

SHEET II.

36' SHARPY
FOR MR FRANKLIN PARKER
AND CONCORDIA COMPANY.

SCALE ½"=1FOOT

R.D. CULLER, HYANNIS, MASS.—OCT. 30, 1964.

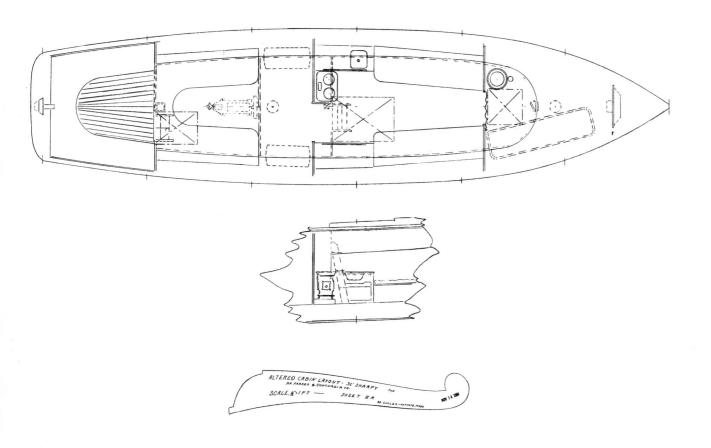

ALTERED CABIN LAYOUT · 30' SHARPY

FOR

R. PARKER & CONCORDIA CO.

SCALE ½"=1 FT — SHEET II A

R.D. CULLER · HYANNIS, MASS

NOV 14 1964

Some details of the sharpie. (More photos of her appear on pages 72 and 73.)

Proportions for one oar are shown in the accompanying drawing. I feel these are not, and never can be, absolute. The boat, the wood, the physique of the oarsman, the waters to be traveled, and your plain artistic ability and imagination all play a part in just how an oar should be built. Here are some guides I've found to work. To begin with, children often row, and should be encouraged to do so; right away, you are apt to think of a set of small sized oars, but unless the boat is tiny, too, these don't work. A properly shaped oar, made out of the right material and of the proper length for the boat, is so well balanced that any active child can handle it with ease and usually with delight, as the craft responds for him as it should. We need to keep children out of boats of poor model with oars like clubs. One of my Down East friends describes such craft by saying, "They're so bad you can't row 'em, you just sort of pry 'em along."

People's hands being about the same size, the grips on the oar should be about the same length regardless of the oar's length. We are not speaking of big single-banked lifeboats where you use two hands to an oar. A length of 5 inches is about right for the grip. Never use a keg shape, as in a stock oar, but give the grip a diameter of about 1¼ inches at the inboard end tapering to about an inch next to the swelled part of the oar, just the opposite taper to what you might think. A very light oar for a slight boat and small hands can be a bit smaller. This is easy to make; you just whittle and feel until you're happy with it. Whatever the finish chosen for the oar, the grip should be left bare. Give it a smooth finish, and palm grease will do the rest.

The inboard part of the oar, between the grip and the oarlock or thole should be large. The idea is to keep the weight, such as it is, inboard. The balance point should be only a little outboard of the leather. Most oars are very blade heavy. Just how you shape this inboard part is, I think, a matter of fancy, so long as you have enough wood for balance. I like eight-square or four-square, but an oversize cylinder is workable. The Turks and other Mediterranean people use a big, nicely shaped swelling.

The oar outboard of the lock should be very light and nicely shaped. There should be a fairly rapid taper to the neck, or thin part at the start of the blade. The loom should start turning to oval right after clearing the leather, with the long part of the oval horizontal when taking the stroke, putting the more wood in the direction of strain. The thin dimension of the oval can be quite small, sometimes an inch or less.

The blade should be narrow, with a nice taper to the widest part, never more than 4 inches, even for a 9-foot or longer oar, and slightly less for shorter oars. A ridge should be formed on each side of the blade, extending from the wide part of the oval and not quite dying out at the blade tip. Much hollow should be worked on each side of the ridges. This combination of ridge and hollow lightens the blade very much, gives it sufficient strength, and, for some reason, makes the oar almost self feathering. Just how the tip of the blade is finished seems a matter of taste. I like a very flattened roof-like angle, relieved in the edges so the blade looks to have no thickness at all, except in the center ridge, which is not touched. This shallow point is nice to shove off with. Some Mediterranean oars have a hollow half-moon in the ends; I suppose this might have advantages in shoving off. The oars of some pilot yawls of the past had almost circular blade ends. Maybe more investigation is needed on this fine point.

Softwood oars require leathers, and store-bought leathers now are way too short, about 7 inches. They should be at least 12 inches; I prefer 14 inches myself. Usually, sufficient material can be had from a worker in leather goods, or if a fellow is going to make several pairs, a tanned hide can be bought. Leathers should be kept lubricated, as should the oarlocks and sockets. I like tallow best, though vaseline will do. A rowing craft should have a container of such stuff aboard. Cow horns not being available to everyone nowadays, I like to make a thing that looks somewhat like an old-time rigger's tallow horn, of wood, with a plug and lanyard, and keep the goo handy in that. This is part of a

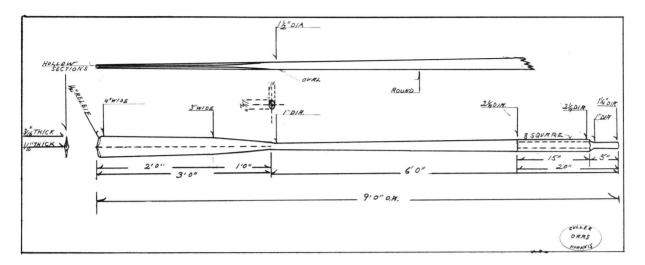

well-run pulling boat's gear. Ash or hardwood oars do well without leathers if they are kept greased. Grease seems to work well on thole pins too, though plenty is needed, especially in wet weather.

Who uses tholes now? Not many, yet they work just fine and are traditional to dories. The slight thump of the tholes on a quiet morning is pleasant. Except in one way, they are no different to use than locks. The exception is the simply-learned trick of jumping the oar out when coming alongside, to prevent a broken pin or oar. Otherwise, if you can't use tholes, you have not really learned to row. Oarlocks, either of bronze or galvanized iron, are apt to have a poor finish inside. Some work with a file soon fixes this, and though filing cuts the galvanizing off, it's no matter, as the galvanizing soon goes on the inside of the lock anyhow. Use, with lubrication, will keep things in order. On sizeable boats, oarlocks are often too small, usually number ones; I would sooner use number twos that are a bit slack than number ones that are too small. There are not as many oarlock patterns available now as there used to be. I like what is called the Boston pattern, a ribbed lock with a small side-eye for the lanyard. The lanyard or chain that goes through the socket is a two-handed abomination. Tholes require lanyards through the holes, and these are awkward

too, if not rigged right. You need nicely shaped tholes with slightly tapered bottom ends and sunk lanyard holes. Reeve the lanyard from one thole through its hole and up through the second hole to its thole. Use a wood toggle or metal thimble in the bight that hangs down. With the tholes lying inboard, run your hand under them, grab the lanyard, give an outboard toss of the hand and a pull on the lanyard — a natural movement — and the tholes pop in at once. I have never seen this method used, except on my own boats. I'm sure it's nothing new.

Many old craft had some form of wooden oarlocks. Those I've used all work, and like lubrication. If they suit your particular type of boat, there is no reason at all for not using them. It's sort of nice to make your own gear and fittings; they are easily replaced or repaired, often enhance the right boat for them, and, of course, allow a bit of artistic license and imagination.

Some discussion of rowing might be in order. The rowing of shells and sculls is a thing in itself, and there are experts on it, which I am not. The boats we consider here are different. I feel a sliding-seat craft can be unhandy around saltwater if the area is exposed, and I sometimes think spoon-like oars are not worthwhile unless the craft has a sliding-seat rig. I'm no doubt open to some critics here. I have noticed that those trained in shells and sculls who have done

A yawl boat in Oregon waters.

little or no rowing in other craft darn near kill themselves in an attempt to pull a dory in any wind, even one of rather sharp model. It's a different kettle of fish. Those who have rowed only dinghies, boxy skiffs, and most of the stock craft, with poor oars, too, find that they too have something to learn about using a proper rowing craft. The short dory stroke, so often seen when pros pull them, does work. A more sophisticated stroke, if in any wind at all, does not get the best out of a dory, even a Swampscott, and is tiring. I find a smart boat, say a Whitehall or similar easy-moving craft, pulls best in light weather using what I think of as the old yacht hand's stroke — not too much forward reach and a good long pull aft, letting the elbows kick out on the recovery, with the body upright, and a precise, quick feather with the oars just clear of the water. The old-timers seemed to clear the water by about 1/16 inch, they were so skillful. Many of these watermen used what I choose to call the Battery boatman style of rowing, with their hands one ahead of the other instead of side by side so the grip was in the center of the boat for both hands. Some craft take very kindly to this, and there is less weight of oar on the hands. Try it; once mastered, this technique will move a boat very well, and it's not tiring.

I think variations of stroke in rowing are worth cultivating; they suit different boats, and a change of stroke can be restful on a long pull. It's sort of like the wise old dog, trotting down the road on far-off business, usually going somewhat on the bias, and every now and then changing tacks, no doubt to change the load on his muscles and rest them up. I feel a lot about rowing has been somewhat forgotten and that we must be willing to experiment and re-learn to get the most out of it.

A pulling boat of good model can be a lovely and satisfying thing, even though she may be somewhat plain. Good oars she must have to respond, and if they are nice to look at and maybe have some decoration, they add much besides their efficiency. Usually, if you get interested in pulling boats, you want a smarter boat, or one for more specialized use, and this is good. Having such craft is economical, you get close to the water, life is not complicated, and I think the exercise from rowing does no harm to one in any sort of health at all. In fact, it may do a lot of good, mentally if not otherwise.

To my way of thinking sail propulsion is the least simple of all the methods of making a boat move through the water. It is not that the rigs themselves, particularly in the smaller, classic

108

craft, are complicated, difficult to use, or expensive. The complications come from the wide range of possibilities with sail, the many hulls that can be developed for it, and the wide variety of sizes of craft that can use it. A tiny skiff can be made to sail quite well, within her limits. Sail has been used on craft nearly 500 feet long. The variations in rig to cover such a range of sizes are many. Moreover, rigs are influenced by the trade and the local conditions in which they are used. The gear to control all the rigs that have been developed is extensive and, in many cases, elaborate, if the craft is large. Probably no one man has ever become adept at using all rigs, though any trained seaman in sail would not be totally at a loss with an entirely strange rig. He would soon catch on, as all rigs have things in common — the use of the wind and supporting and handling sail with rope and wire. The smaller the craft, the simpler her rig should be.

Sailing, at least under half-way decent conditions, is probably the most pleasant way of moving about on the water, and the mastery of handling several different alongshore sailing craft is not learned overnight. Sailing is not at all difficult, but it takes time, experience, and study. All of it is enjoyable, though some heavy-weather experiences don't seem so at the time. You tend to learn fast in rough weather, or give it up. True deep-water sailing is a trade in itself. Some may doubt this. Many a coaster of long experience and good record is uneasy, however, when well offshore. Sea buoys, dirty gray-green water, and the sounding lead he understands well. The true deepwater man in the great days of sail, on the other hand, had a great fear of the land. His vessel was not designed and built to find herself suddenly with a strange coast close aboard, and once she made her port, it was not so good either, for there were land sharks about to prey on her crew, stores, and gear. The deepwater ship was a true daughter of the sea. The coaster, able as he was, always had some shore dirt clinging to him. Most of us have to be content with just that.

XI

The Sprit Rig

Rigs being so many and so varied it's well to start with the smallest and simplest. Pulling boats and dinghies, though mainly for oars, can well use a sail, which will much increase the pleasure and range of these boats. Most such craft can use centerboards to advantage, though a board is not needed if the sail is only for reaching and running. The beach boat types are, as a rule, well adapted for sailing. Naturally, a small, open boat, often having a model with little sail-carrying power, must have a simple rig, one that is easy to use, light of canvas and spars, and with the latter reasonably short. The rig should be easily struck and set up, for it's not permanently placed. The common dory spritsail, properly cut and rigged, is the most efficient and practical of all small, open-boat sails. Do I hear great shouts of doubt? Try it and find out. I repeat, it must be well-shaped and cut. Such sails are shown in Howard I. Chapelle's *American Small Sailing Craft.* Anyone can have such a sail with the aid, if need be, of an interested sailmaker.

The spritsail, in its simplest form, has a minimum of rigging. There is a snotter to hold up the sprit. It's just a bit of line, though the way it is rigged is all-important. There are a few robands, or else a lace line, to keep the sail to the mast, and a sheet. The sail should by all means be loose-footed with no boom. The sheeting point is critical, but not at all difficult to de-termine. That's all there is to it. No sail has less, and the spritsail has the maximum sail area for the least spar length. Any of the other practical small craft rigs require as much or more gear and longer spars for the same amount of sail.

The rig can be taken in rapidly in the event of weather making. If need be, once the knack is learned, the whole thing can be thrown over-board to leeward, still spreeted out, on a slack but fast sheet (don't lose the end!) and ridden to as a sort of sea anchor until such time as it's convenient to drag it aboard, and furl it. A very handy thing to know, yet the knowledge of this trick has nearly been lost.

A somewhat larger craft, say from 16 to 20 feet in length, still of a model that rows well, can have more of a rig. Such boats being longer than dinghies, and usually somewhat sharper, are often very smart sailers and will be used under sail except in calms or just for the plain fun of rowing. Here the sprit rig still works best in most cases, and its handiest form, if considerable sail area is wanted, is the old working boat two-sail rig.

This rig is most versatile and is suited to all kinds of conditions and strengths of wind. The full two-sail rig is the light weather or pleasure rig and its area is suitable for light to moderate conditions. There is a foremast step and a mizzen step, usually in combination with mast gates

in the thwarts so the spars can be easily handled in a bit of a lop. There is a third step between the first two; this takes the foremast when the foresail is used alone. This makes the working rig and is suited to moderate to fresh winds. Usually the sail is cut high enough in the foot so the mast rake can be changed a bit to achieve good balance. Often the foresail has a reef so that it's usable in a stronger wind than just fresh. In the event of having to work in a strong wind, the little mizzen is stepped in the middle hole, often with considerable rake.

All this makes a very workable and seaman-like rig, one that is able to adapt to all sorts of uses. The rig is light and reasonably cheap with very little upkeep. The whole rig is struck un-less the boat is sailing, except for occasional short stops, such as beaching to clam. If the boat hauls up and the rig can be put in shelter, fine. If she's moored and the rig is left aboard, it should be well lashed to the thwarts; then she can stand much thrashing in bad weather. I find that when leaving the rig lashed in the boat, a sail cover is very worthwhile.

I think cotton sails are far easier to handle in these small boats than sails of any man-made fibers yet developed; these are just too slippery and fluttery for easy use in small boats. If Cup-rinol treated, a cotton sail lasts as long as any other. Plain ordinary boat drill used to be the standard for these sails. They do well with a vertical cut and should be roped on at least three sides. This is very much 18th Century thinking and for good reason; this kind of boating is from that era. It is boating that in-volves the attractive and economical boat, one that has many uses, that will teach much sea-manship and be a pleasure for many years. Peo-ple seem to be seeking this kind of boating, yet it is hard to discover in today's yachting mag-azines.

A 15-1/2-foot, sprit-rigged beachboat photo-graphed from the author's Swampscott dory.

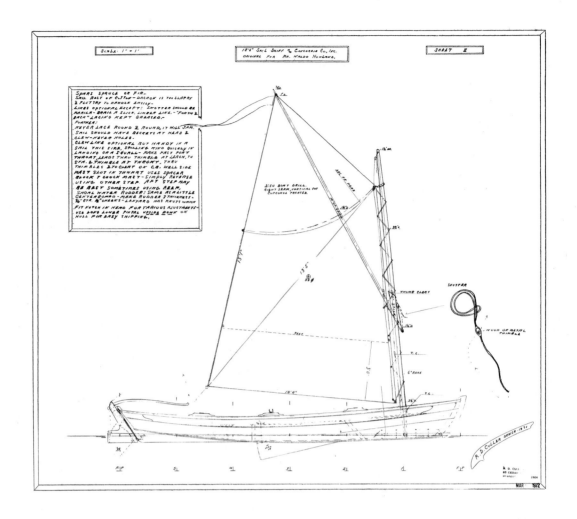

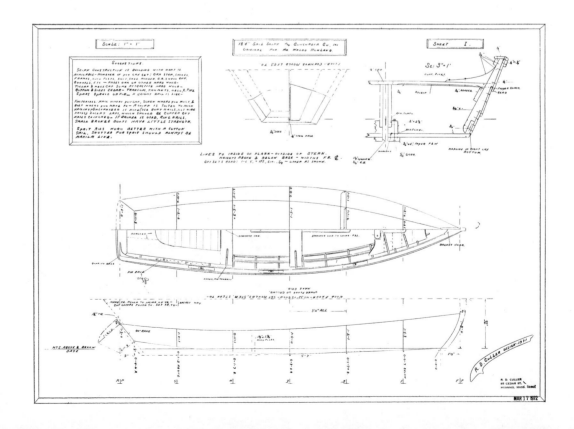

The 18-1/2-foot sailing skiff tethered and furled up. Waldo Howland, the long-time owner and manager of the Concordia Company, uses this one in tropical waters.

The average craft of the size and type we are discussing with a two-sail rig has about 100 square feet of sail. Spars for these rigs are small and light. I'm often asked just how and where you get a wooden spar. The answer is at a lumber yard, unless you are so fortunate to be able to go out in the woods, which is more fun. Sprits for these rigs are about the same length as the mast they work with, and vary from about 1⅛ inches to 1½ inches in diameter. A reasonably clear 2 x 4, split, makes a couple of sprits to be shaped up. Spruce or fir does quite well. Masts go from 2½ inches to 3¼ inches in diameter, and a 4 x 4 of the same stuff does the job. Sometimes these little sticks are glued up out of thinner stuff, but with the availability of 2 x 's and 4 x 's, it's not worth the trouble. A spritsail mast should not have much taper until near the head; sprits themselves have a taper each way from the middle.

The fittings for these rigs are of wood, and easily made. The few fittings needed have had long development and work far better than fittings that can be bought. These latter seem designed to fit all small boats, and so fit none just right. This is more backward thinking, but the wood and rope stuff is efficient, cheap, looks the part, and, as one of my friends has so often pointed out, "It can all be repaired if something goes wrong at 7 o'clock on a Sunday morn, when all the marinas are closed."

There is a shoulder on the sprit's upper end to engage the becket in the peak of the sail. The spindle beyond the shoulder should be 4 or 5 inches long. This maybe can't be called a fitting; it's whittled on the spar. In the lower end of the sprit there is a slot to take the snotter; a rivet should be driven through just above the slot to prevent splitting. The mast has a round, tapered heel, since a sprit mast must rotate, or the snotter, robands, and all will bind. The foremast needs two or three small thumb cleats for reefing. Each mast has a fair-sized hole about an inch from the head. It's been said that a hole

The design of this yawl boat was a joint effort by the author and Murray G. Peterson, a Down East naval architect who shared the author's traditional approach to boats.

takes no maintenance! If the boat carries the two-sail rig, she will require a fairlead on or near each rail, of wood, naturally, for the fore sheets, which must be double to work around the mizzen. A single-sail boat, or one using the bad-weather mizzen, uses a single sheet.

Mizzens in use as such need some sort of spar to make them sheet properly; some folks use booms, others, short clubs. I like the sprit boom, much used in the past on many craft, notably on Captain Nat Herreshoff's early boats and on Commodore Ralph Munroe's sharpies. This boom is rigged with the inboard end above the foot of the loose-footed sail so it's clear of the helmsman's head; it makes the sail set flat, as a mizzen should, and the sail can sheet to the center of the boat without twist. It's sort of like

sheeting a barn door; the sail's draft can be adjusted nicely. The principle is the same as that used on New Haven sharpies and Chesapeake small craft sails in regard to taking care of the foot. A sharp-headed sail of the sharpie cut can be used as a mizzen on an otherwise sprit-rigged craft, and though this rig saves one spar, the mast has to be quite long to get sufficient sail area, a general failing of any sharp-headed sail.

If the tack of the foresail is set very low in the boat with a high-cut clew, she carries sail better. Many folks don't want the rig low, saying they can't see ahead; you can, better than you first think. It's important in sailing small boats to keep the center of effort low. Some of the rigs now seen on small stock boats demonstrate that this principle has been forgotten, and if you sail in the racing classes you have to go along with tall rigs.

The best way to rig a spritsail on a mast is to use a laceline. The lacing can be some slippery line, rather small, kept greased with tallow, and *not* passed round and round the mast, for then it will jam. Pass it back and forth, forth and back, and it will never jam. The laceline can be quite slack. A single-part throat halyard is best, with a cleat for it on the mast so it can rotate with the spar. I make fast the tail of the halyard to the throat of the sail so it goes aloft as the sail is hoisted, leaving no line to coil, and just slack enough to belay. A mast loop or toggle with wooden parrel beads should be secured to the sail's throat to keep it to the mast, for the sprit tends to push it away.

I find a foremast from 12 to 14 feet long with sail and sprit rolled up on it to be not at all difficult to step and stow, if the spars are well chosen and shaped. A 16-foot mast is about the reasonable limit and will be suitable for a 20- to 22-foot boat with a two-sail rig. In bigger two-sail boats, or in a sizable boat using a single sail, another kind of small craft sail becomes more practical: the standing lug. We can take this one up later, with all its simplicities.

A sprit foresail of 60 to 70 square feet in area should have a reef, one about two feet deep. Many folks ask just how you reef a loose-footed

The Sharptown Barge under sail. (More pictures of the Barge appear on pages 29 and 65.)

sail. It's done just the same as one with a boom, with the added advantage that you can't make the mistake of tying the reefpoints around the boom! Assuming the sail to be lowered, pass the tack lashing, stretch the foot taut with the sheet and keep it so, pass the clew lashing between clew and reef cringles, set up just snug, and tie the points. That's it, and it's simpler than with a boom in the way. Incidentally, the lace-line needs no taking up when reefing; I don't know why, but the old timers who worked it out knew their stuff!

Some folks nowadays think reefing is too much work or "sissy." Some designers go along with this attitude and turn out grossly under-canvassed craft. Yet the owner will go through all sorts of antics struggling with many light sails, their purchase, stowage, and upkeep, to make his under-canvassed boat go. In a properly rigged craft, you are exposed a much shorter

time to the more risky parts of the boat in reefing than you are when tussling with light sails that are out of hand. If you race, you put up with the going thing, be it sensible by your lights or not.

We have mentioned a snotter several times; all it does is keep the heel of the sprit up. If it's not right, the sail won't set properly. There are several methods of rigging the snotter, some quite complicated for the big working sails of the past. For small craft, my favorite snotter rig does just fine. I have seen it nowhere else than on craft I have to do with, though, being simple and practical, it was worked out long ago, I'm sure. Take a piece of line of proper size, say 5/16 inch for the size craft we are considering. Make a long eye splice sufficient for the eye to pass around the mast and about 3 inches more. Seize in tightly a wooden or brass thimble next to the splice. Then pass the whole rig around

Sprit rigs on a wherry and on a little double-ender.

the mast, putting the single end and thimble through the long eye. The thimble should now be on the forward side of the mast and a couple of inches below where the doubled line passes through the eye. Naturally this rig wants to slide down the mast; one of the before-mentioned thumb cleats is needed to hold it up. The best position for the cleat can be determined by trial with the sail spread on the ground. The cleat goes thumb upwards on the aft side of the mast. It can be shifted later if not right.

To set the sail, ship the sprit in the peak, take a turn through the slot in the lower end of the sprit with the single end of the snotter, then reeve it up through the thimble, then haul it down. You have a nice little tackle. Peak the sail up well, for things do stretch. Never sail with the peak too low. Hitch the end of the snotter in the sprit slot. There should be little strain on the end of the snotter under a press of sail, so the snotter can be let go immediately if need be. Some methods of rigging a snotter make it difficult, sometimes impossible, to let it go in a hurry.

Sheets are simply lengths of line, single-part for sails of the size we are describing. The old standard belay was a slippery hitch on a half pin under a thwart. A half pin, sticking below a thwart or pin rail does not get foul of things, and if a slippery hitch is used, a twitch of the sheet frees it instantly. For snotters and sheets I still prefer manila line. The other stuff is slippery, though it's all right in other parts of the rig, not that there is much more.

Sometimes, if your place of getting underway and coming to is awkward, a single brail can be very handy on the foresail. It can kill part of the sail's drive without slacking the sheet or touching the sprit, and it tends to quiet flogging. A slippery line that won't kink when wet should be used for a brail. Rig it this way: spread the sail on the ground or floor with the sprit rigged. Strike an arc with a piece of string from peak to throat, carrying it out to the leech, and mark the spot. Here sew or seize a small brass thimble to stand vertically on the leech, just like a reef cringle. Similarly secure three

more thimbles to one side of the luff, one at the throat, another about half way down, and one at the tack. It does not matter which side these take, so long as they are all on the same side. Fix one end of the brail to the throat on the opposite side from the thimble there, reeve out through the leech cringle, back through the thimble at the throat, and down along the luff through the middle and tack thimbles. Have enough slack to come back, and some more, to a cleat on the side of the centerboard well or some other handy place that suits. To brail in the sail, simply slack the sheet and haul on the brail, slacking more sheet as needed. A brail is a handy rig, though now seldom seen. The one I have described is no different in principle, though much simpler, than the big brails with many leads used on large barge sails or ships' spankers. I find the brail a most useful bit of gear on a loose-footed spritsail, and it in no way interferes with the usual method of furling, which is rolling the sail up on the sprit and securing with the now-loose snotter. A sail rolled up with the sprit does not blow loose.

All this Old World gear always raises eyebrows. It can't possibly work or be "efficient." It does, however, and if the boat is any shakes of a model at all and the rig tuned, as any must be to perform well, she gives a good account of herself in modern company and sometimes takes over, a wolf among sheep. Then the eyebrows do some twitching! Try it.

An old-time boatyard owner, now retired and somewhat of a sage, tells an interesting story that illustrates some basic differences between "modern" craft and the simple boats we have been describing. The story is totally true: A man, wife, and children with picnic baskets arrive at the waterside for a day's sail in their ultra-modern boat; she's no bigger than a dory, but she has everything. Her owner stores his boat at the yard; the craft is nearly new. The family is put aboard by launch. There is a flurry of sail bags and there is much rigging up, as these craft require. After some delay, comes considerable waving; the launch finally spots this signalling and goes alongside. Seems something is wrong

with the tiny wire halyard which reeves inside the hollow metal mast; the trouble is aloft. The launch tows the boat to the club dock to see what can be done. No one there really knows what's up, so they send for the rigger from the yard, which is nearby, and he shows up. The boat is jockeyed alongside, wife and children having been put ashore, and the rigger balances shakily atop a piling and reaches with long-nose pliers. No dice; he needs help. His helper is sent for, arrives and they struggle. Still no soap; something more is wrong than they can reach. So they take her to the yard crane and hang a man from a bos'n's chair, for the craft is too frail for going aloft on. This requires the yard launch to tow the boat to the crane and a man to operate it. She's put in position, the great boom is swung over her, the big block lowered, and a chair hooked on. By now it's dinner time and all hands knock off. The Yacht Owner and family sit glumly on the caplog with picnic basket, which has suffered some from the hot sun. They munch from it. The children start to bicker. (Can't blame 'em.)

Finally, the yard gang straggles back, we assume well fed, and go at it again. The crane is a hand-winder. Little Joe is the operator; he's a hot man on a crank and puts the rigger over his work with some dispatch, bucket of tools and all. There is more struggle, sort of like pulling teeth from a sky hook, and it goes on quite awhile. The helper sends things up and down on a gantline; the crew know their trade. At last word comes from aloft, after the helper has done much more pulling from under the deck, "Can't budge it. Got to take the mast out and unreeve the whole thing." They do, laying the mast out on horses ashore. Its innards are removed to reveal some sort of kinked thingamajig. Have to make a new one, which they do with dispatch, as the yard has the latest tools for putting fittings on this light wire and a bin of the doodads. Then the re-reeving starts. A mouse with a string on his tail, chased by a cat, might have taken a pilot line through. There is neither cat nor mouse handy. Finally someone turns up with a plumber's fish, and the job is accomplished. It's now mid-afternoon. The proud owner decides to go home; his wife has been dictating to him; the children are at each other's throats. The boat is buttoned up before quitting time and put out on her mooring with care and dispatch by the yard towboat and her man.

Some days later the owner appears and inquires as to his craft's health. He's assured she's fine, at the moment, and is presented with the bill for her recent sickness. Seventy-eight bucks! (This was in the cheap days.) The Yachtsman goes straight up! He lands, running, and heads for the Sage's office. He howls and screams. The Sage looks sad, but there is an interesting light

Dory spritsails — variations on a theme. This is the author's Swamp-scott, which has seven different sail combinations. In the lower right photo, the mast has been stepped aft a little and the foresail (made by the author) is setting nicely, though reefed. She's ready for a breeze.

in his eye. He is wise; he is patient; he explains the bill, item by item: rigger and helper teetering on top of piling, so much time; towboat and man twice; rigger and helper for most of the day; crane charge and the cranker's time; wire and fittings (the least of it); someone to run the plumber down and get his fish. The poor Sage has to charge his time somewhere. Besides, the plumber was hard to find; he was under a tank in the bowels of some vessel, it was hot down there, and he was somewhat irritable and had to be talked into lending the fish. The Sage has a way about him; the owner is now willing to admit, yes, the time must have all been there, but, God, all for a 14-foot boat?

This gives the Sage the opening he's been waiting for; after forty years of boating, he's very knowledgeable about these things. "Mr. So and So, simple wooden craft, yes, of nice model, can be very smart. The simple sprit rig, a plain hole, and a bit of line are so cheap. And these are things you can repair yourself in a few minutes. Something that can readily be rowed if need be (no towboat and man), and something attractive to the eye. It's all so much more fun and you get at the sandwiches before they spoil, and so on, and so on. Maybe another type would be better; come sailing in my Yankee sloopboat sometime."

The fellow does, and gets hooked. The Sage builds him a handsome classic craft, for a good price, but she's a lovely thing. She's smart, docile, can sail herself, and is a witch at working in tight places. The owner preens a bit, for many take notice, even those who don't understand her. If you do or not, no matter; she's good to look at. She was designed by some Cuss from Cape Cod who is noted for his set ways when it comes to boats and tobacco.

I leave the sprit-rigged ones right here.

XII

Other Rigs, Including the Ketch

In continuing to discuss open craft, which in many ways are the most fun, it may be well to mention another rig which seems to be almost forgotten, yet which is well suited to a boat a bit too big for the sprit rig. This is the standing lug. Like so many working rigs, the standing lug will spread considerable area of sail, yet without the necessity of long spars and lots of gear. With a properly cut sail, the rig has a lot of drive to it.

Unless the boat is big enough for a two-sail rig, and a mizzen is used, the standing lug is loose-footed with no boom. A mizzen lug sail usually needs a boom for proper sheeting, as does a sprit mizzen. The lug requires a somewhat longer mast than does a spritsail, as there is a halyard, single-part for most boats, or with more parts if the sail is large. The sail requires no method of keeping it to the mast; it sets alongside the spar and stands on its own merits. Rigged right, stand it does! The tack only requires a lashing to the mast and a thumb cleat to keep it from riding up. The sheet can be single, or double if the boat is two-sail, and can have as many parts as you feel you need, in practice the less the better. The head is spread by a yard, which should be well peaked up, and this crosses the mast at a point about a third of its length from the fore end. There should be a small-line serving on the yard where it crosses the mast, to take the chafe. This should be kept greased, in which case it will have a very long life.

There are several ways of keeping the yard to the mast. The simplest is a strap or parrel passing around the mast with a wood toggle to engage an eye. It should have a loose fit. It may have parrel beads in a sizable craft; usually they are not needed. The object of the toggle is so you can easily remove the yard from the mast. Setting the tack adrift makes the whole sail portable; it can be put in a long sail bag if left on board, or can be taken ashore. I like to rig a few permanent sail stops right on the yard so the sail can have a proper stow before removing.

The mast can be left standing, or can be lowered if it is small enough and there is a gate. A lug mast can be longer than that for a sprit rig and still lower fairly easily, as it has no sail and sprit stowed on it. Often the halyard is set up to the stemhead to steady things at a mooring if the mast is left up. Unstayed masts in small craft are quite able to stand for themselves, with the exception that now most harbors have so much motorboat traffic that such masts tend to wear in the deck and step. Even fully-stayed masts take a beating this way in small craft nowadays; something gets a little loose and things begin to wear from the constant thrashing. Some hulls eventually suffer in the garboards from all this man-made commotion. I grant lowering a heavy mast each time a boat is brought to is too

121

much of a chore and has some risk if it's sloppy. I suggest lowering masts in craft with masts no more than 16 feet long. With bigger spars, the rig should be designed to stand, though even so it's wise to keep the rig light and simple enough so that with help the stick can be put in upon fitting out and taken down on lay-up for some minor repair without calling on a crane. Even on fair-sized open boats of classic model, I like to try to arrange for a gate in the partners.

Setting and lowering a lugsail is most simple. The sail has a single halyard, very little gear, yet a good spread of sail. Reefing is simple too. And it's a rig that can be stowed very rapidly in a hard chance.

The only trick I see to making a lugsail is to realize that, by the nature of the sail's setting, the luff takes a good strain, so that the sail should have a stout luff rope with a little stretch to it. A lugsail stands better and lasts longer if cut vertically.

The dipping lug, much favored in Europe among the sailing fishing fleets in the past, is probably the most efficient sail of all, as long as you stay on one tack! That it has to be lowered each time on going about makes it impractical for pleasure sailing, particularly in narrow waters. A rare instance of its usefulness might be for someone situated in a trade wind belt where he was always making long cross-wind runs, in which case it would pay off wonderfully.

The same comment might be made about the lateen rig; it's fine for monsoon sailing in a dhow but generally unhandy in a small craft along shore. The revised or canoe version of the lateen, as now seen by the hundreds on sail boards, seems most awkward in that on easing it off in a puff, nearly the whole weight of spars and sail is suspended to leeward of the craft. I found that this was so long ago, and the same

A Concordia sloop boat, one of the author's most popular designs. (Photo by Norman Fortier.)

boat with a sprit or lug rig was much more stable than with her original canoe lateen.

Another rig that used to be popular for some small craft was the sliding gunter. Except that the three spars required were all about the same length and would stow in the boat, there was nothing good about it. The sliding gunter is very unhandy to set and take in and is hard to make set well. Though this rig was much used for years in naval small boats where large crews were available, its use in small pleasure craft always seemed to me just the wrong thing. The crowded conditions in a small boat make the sliding gunter, with its long, unwieldy club, unhandy and unsafe.

The gaff rig and the marconi, or sharp-headed, rig are used of course, but where rigs must be portable, there is too much gear to make these practical. And, as mentioned before, any sharp-headed sail is always hard to make big enough unless the mast is very long, just the thing you don't want in a small boat with a rig to be struck.

Craft of a build and design suited to standing rigs, open or decked, or craft large enough to be called cruising boats have requirements different from those of the portable-rig boats, and for the most part the rigs suited to the small craft become unhandy in bigger boats, with the exception that the standing lug can often be used to advantage in fairly large craft. This is not to say that standing rigs, cruising or not, must be complicated and expensive. Just the opposite is true. Keep it simple — simple to build, repair, and use.

In discussing rigs with others in the past, using this approach, the reaction often is, "Will it be efficient?" A properly designed rig will be efficient and will be all that the hull is capable of using. Unfortunately, much money has been spent putting so-called modern rigs on classic hulls that are unable to use the advantages these rigs are supposed to offer. Nowadays, a "modern rig" means hollow spars, currently metal ones, special fittings, and many complications not needed on a handy day boat or small cruiser.

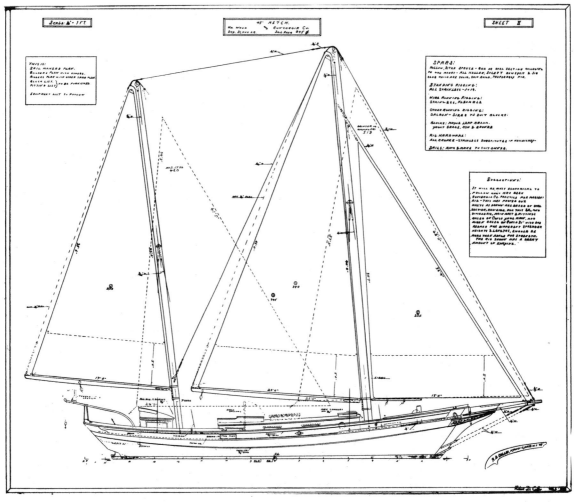

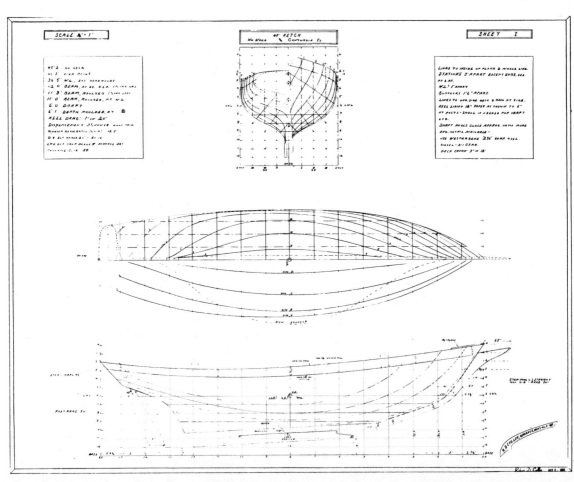

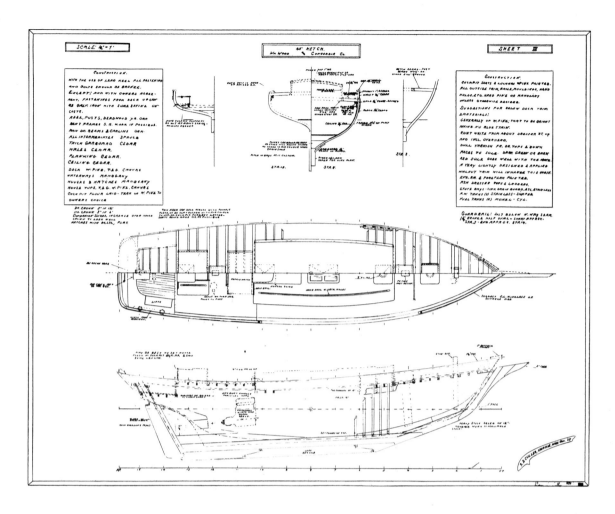

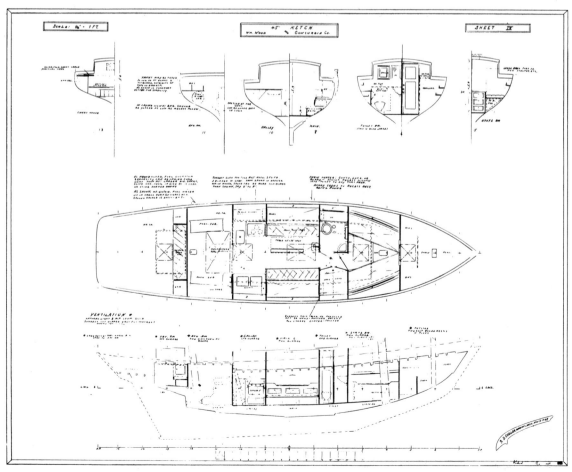

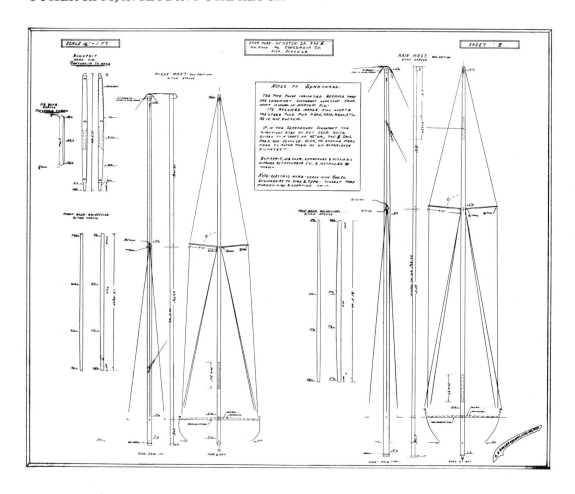

STATION		F.P.	1	2	3	4	5	6	7	⑧	9	10	11	12	13	14	15	A.P.
HTS. ABOVE & BELOW	SHEER *	6-0-0	5-7-3	5-2-2	4-9-5	4-5-2	4-1-5	3-10-1	3-7-0+	3-4-6	3-3-1+	3-2-0	3-1-6	3-2-1	3-3-4	3-5-5+	3-8-7	4-0-3
	DECK *	4-9-5 (START OF RAISE)	4-6-5+	4-1-3+	3-8-6	3-4-3	3-0-5	2-9-0	2-6-2	2-4-2	2-2-7	2-2-4+	2-2-6	2-3-5	2-5-2+	2-8-2	3-0-1+	10"END OF 3-3-7+
	BUTT III	(STARTS 0-10-4 AFT STA 3)				2-2-4	0-8-1	0-3-3+	0-10-1	1-1-1+	1-1-0	0-10-6+	0-4-5	0-1-7+	0-9-6+	1-8-2	(ENDS 1-5-0 FWD STA 14)	
	BUTT II	STARTS 0-5-5 FWD STA 2	4-8-0	1-8-4	0-1-2-	0-11-2	1-7-2	1-11-2	2-0-7	1-11-6	1-8-1	1-2-3+	0-8-4	0-2-4	0-7-7	0-8-0	ENDS 0-8-1 AFT STA 15	
	BUTT I	STARTS 0-6-0 FWD STA	3-0-3	1-10-6	0-0-6	1-3-7+	2-1-3	2-6-7	2-9-2+	2-8-2	2-6-2	2-6-2	1-11-6+	1-2-4+	0-4-1	0-7-6+	1-6-5	ENDS 0-2-0 AFT STA 15
	RABATE Δ (MIDDLE LINE)	0-0-0	0-4-1	0-8-5	1-9-4	2-9-1-	3-3-4+	— S	T	R	A	I	G	H	T	—	2-1-4	1-3-6+	0-3-3+	END HEEL OF TR.
	KEEL BOTTOM	3-7-5+	0-4-3	1-5-1	2-6-2	3-6-7	4-8-0	5-1-4	S	T	R	A	I	G	H	T — NOTE DRAG MEASURE	6-0-4	6-0-4	
HALF BREADTHS, INSIDE OF PLANK	SHEER Δ	0-0-0	1-9-1	3-2-7-	4-3-3+	5-1-0+	5-6-2	5-8-7	5-10-0	5-10-3	5-10-3	5-9-5	5-7-3+	5-4-6	5-1-4	4-9-3+	4-3-4	
	DECK		1-3-3	2-10-1	4-0-2+	4-10-7	5-4-6	5-8-6+	5-10-3	5-10-6+	5-10-7	5-10-1+	5-8-2-	5-5-7	5-2-6	4-10-3	4-4-2	
	WL 0	START EXT. RAB.																
	WL 1		1-6-0+	1-2-3+														
	WL 2		0-11-6+	2-9-3+	4-1-3	5-0-4	5-6-1											
	WL 3		0-4-6	2-2-5+	3-8-6	4-9-5	5-4-4+	5-9-1	5-10-2+	5-10-5	5-10-5	5-9-6	5-7-6+	5-5-1	5-2-1+	4-10-1	4-4-2+	
	WL 4			4-7-1+	3-3-3+	4-4-7	5-2-0	5-7-5	5-9-7+	5-10-6	5-10-7	5-10-1+	5-8-2	5-5-6+	5-2-4+	4-9-1	3-6-5	
	WL 5			0-11-4	2-5-4	3-9-0	4-8-6+	5-4-1-	5-7-5	5-9-1	5-10-4	5-9-6	5-6-6	5-3-2	4-8-2+	2-10-0		
	LWL 6			0-5-3	1-7-3	2-11-1-	4-3-5	4-9-5	5-2-6+	5-5-0	5-6-6+	5-4-7	5-0-2+	4-3-1	2-6-0			
	WL 7				0-8-7+	1-10-1	2-11-5	3-10-0	4-4-5	4-8-1	4-8-1	4-3-1	3-5-0	1-11-0	0-3-6+			
	WL 8					0-9-2	1-7-1+	2-4-5	2-10-4+	3-2-3	2-11-4	2-4-6	1-6-2	0-8-4+				
	WL 9						0-6-7+	0-10-5	1-1-4+	1-3-2+	1-2-5+	0-8-6+	0-5-1+	0-2-2				
	WL 10										0-5-2	0-5-1	0-4-5+					
	WL 11				KEEL	SIDING	12" - NOTE	TAPER	FROM	HALF BREADTH	PLAN.							
	WL 12				"	"	"											
	RABATE				AS	DEVELOPS	ON	FLOOR.										
	KEEL BOTTOM	FAIR TO 1/2" STEM FACE AT LWL.					12" SIDED.			FAIR TO RUDDER STOCK-6" HEAD-4" HEEL								
DIAGONALS - INSIDE OF PLANK	DIAG. A		0-10-7+	2-6-0	3-10-0+	4-0-4+	5-7-6+	6-2-4+	6-6-6	6-8-7	6-9-1	6-8-1	6-5-3+	6-1-1	5-6-4	4-8-7+	3-8-7+	
	DIAG. B		0-5-6+	2-0-1	3-3-2	4-2-7	5-0-2	5-7-0+	5-11-2+	6-1-/	6-0-3+	5-9-2	5-3-6	4-8-6+	3-11-2+	3-0-1+	1-11-0	
	DIAG. C		1-0-0	1-11-4	2-9-2	3-4-4+	3-10-1	4-1-2	4-2-1-	4-0-7	3-9-5	3-4-3	2-8-4+	1-9-7+	0-9-7			
	DIAG. D				0-8-6+	1-0-2	1-3-5	1-6-0	1-7-1-	1-6-6-	1-4-5	1-1-1	0-9-0					
	KEEL DRAG FR. BASE	SEE PLAN STEM & FORE FOOT RISE-			AT KNUCKLE 2"								1"					

* SHEER IS UND. SD. RAIL CAP.
+ DECK IS UND. RD. DECK -TOP OF BEAMS AT SIDE
Δ ALL TO INSIDE PLANK & MIDDLE LINE - RABATE DEVELOPS SLIGHTLY CURVED FROM IT.

OFFSETS - WAL.WOOD - 45' KETCH - CONCORDIA CO.

The 45-foot ketch has a handsome hull.

Such a rig is expensive in terms of first cost, up-keep, and repair. Unless the craft is a racer, the great efficiency is seldom of much real use. The rig is only efficient by the wind at any rate, and the hull must be made up to it. Once the sheets are started, the modern rigs become real dogs; the farther off the wind, the worse they are. None of them are easy to handle if they have sufficient area without light sails. Usually, if the modern rig has enough area to work well in light going, its center of effort is very high, the area is too narrow on the base, and more often than not there are sheeting problems that require expensive gear to overcome. Often the boat does not steer as well on all points of sailing as she should. Some folks may doubt this statement, but I base my words on having made several conversions from modern rigs back to what I thought were more sensible rigs. The boats were better handling all around, a couple decided to become self-steerers, and all steered better and carried sail better. Some were even better to windward, for they stood on their feet and went where they looked, instead of being hove down and sliding off. The lack of pointing ability of the revised rigs was largely overcome by better sail-carrying ability and easier helms.

For a utility boat, a properly cut sail is of great importance for good sailing and handling. Racers of real experience know all about this; otherwise they couldn't stay in competition. A sail of proper cut, intelligent setting, and the right sheeting, makes the boat go. The trouble with so many high-aspect-ratio rigs (this just means the mast is too damn tall) is that it is difficult to make their sails set properly, and it requires considerable gear to do it. Quite all right for a racer, but not really practical for ordinary use. Why make a chore of it?

Just why you see so many craft now with no topping lift is hard to understand. I suppose it's the racing thing again, but for easy and sensible handling, a topping lift is needed to hold up any sort of boom at all. The lowering of a sail with a boom down on the stern sweeping around or overside is one of the most lubberly sights seen today (along with the present prac-

tice of setting the jib first and taking it in last, so the whole foredeck is in a state of menace casting off or coming to). I think I can say, without too much contradiction, that seamanship has degenerated very much in the last twenty-five years. Just why is hard to say. The nice handling of a boat under sail is now looked upon as a difficult thing, and is even at times made fun of. Actually, seamanship is only common sense applied to the tools one uses, in this case a boat. Possibly that's just the trouble; common sense is no longer felt to be needed in our modern society. A fellow gets into trouble on the water and the U. S. Coast Guard will bail him out. And Uncle will look after him in his old age. But I disagree.

On small boats and fairly light displacement boats of two-masted rig, I use simple rope lifts; wire is not needed. Some folks prefer to make the end fast on the boom, lead the lift to a block aloft, then down the mast to belay. Others make the end fast at the masthead by reeving it through a hole with a stopper knot (why use a fitting when a hole will do?), then down through a hole in the top of the boom, and along the underside of the boom to a cleat in a convenient position. This is a single-part rig and is enough unless the boom is very long and large for the size of craft. No sheave is needed in the boom; a nicely rounded hole does quite well. I think it's a fine point whether the lift makes fast forward coming from aloft, or on the boom coming from the boom end; it depends on the particular rig and simply on the owner's preference. The aloft lead, coming to a fairlead and then aft makes good sense in a small boat. In a two-mast boat or small day sloop, having the running end aft would often be handier.

Lifts for large booms may need a two-part purchase, either forward (and this seems a common practice in Europe) or at the after end of the boom, when it then will pay to use a sheave in the boom. Large sloops and fishing schooners in this country mostly used the single lift, often with many parts of tackle on the boom end arranged in such a way as to prevent twisting up; that is, it was done with single blocks above and sheaves set in the boom, all as widely spaced fore-and-aft as was practical. It can be argued whether this would be the best rig on a craft with a small crew. These vessels required large crews for fishing, and such things as lazyjacks were not needed where many hands who knew their work were available.

Coasters were intended to be run short-handed. They used the double lifts, port and starboard, usually in conjunction with lazyjacks, and the purchases were hung under the trestle trees aloft, with the hauling parts leading to the deck. This was about standard, except in the West Coast lumber trade, where they had their own methods. There are few big sloops left, but there are some schooners of modest to somewhat large size by present standards. On these vessels, the double lifts, rigged in their traditional way, are still the thing for today's small crews; they are as important to the handling of the vessel as is her rudder.

A lift on the boom of any size should be frequently inspected and kept in good order at all times, for the breaking of a lift in a hard chance can be a major disaster. Picture most of a crew strung along a main boom, possibly 70 feet or more long, turning in a reef or stowing sail. The lift parts as the vessel lunges into a big one. No one there has a chance. By all means keep a good lift, even in a small boat.

I have had considerable experience with the gaff rig and some of its slight variations, particularly the short gaff using a single halyard for both throat and peak. Some folks think the one-halyard gaff cannot possibly work, but it does, and wonderfully well. All kinds and shapes of boats are not necessarily suited to it. The regular gaff as used on a catboat can be most handy and efficient, and of course on other craft too. There is a lot to be said for the catboat, and at the moment it seems to have a following again, with a catboat association, many builders competing, each with his own version of a catboat, usually a moulded creation. Catboats in the past have often been considered brutish things to handle, especially if of some size. Granted, many things inherent to a very

wide hull with a big rig stuck right in the eyes of her do cause difficulty in a breeze. The builders now turning out these boats seem to have made little effort to overcome any of this, except to follow the modern approach of reducing sail area, until the boat is dull in light going. My own feeling is that cats were over-developed for racing up to the time interest in them died out many years ago. This development made for big rigs and very wide, boxy hulls to carry them and produced craft that were not easy to use for ordinary sailing.

Whether or not a person likes a cat is beside the point; he must admit the rig is fairly simple for the area it can spread. I think for present-day use the cat can be greatly improved. I would give a catboat a fairly modest beam as cats go, more deadrise with some reverse in the sections, high, light quarters, and some overhang aft. I would give her generally sharp lines with some slight increase in hull depth, and would use a fair amount of inside ballast, or outside ballast if expense were not important. I'd want a good amount of outside deadwood, and along with the sharper lines a somewhat smaller centerboard and a rudder that was not oversize. She would have a fairly sharp hull of modest displacement. Such a catboat would sail very well with a smaller rig. The gear would be a bit lighter. A lot of the brutishness of the over-developed cat would vanish, and I feel, if the designer had any art in his pen, the boat would be far better to look at than some of the cats now being built.

Sloops never seem to go out of style, though interest in particular types waxes and wanes. The Friendships have had quite a following lately. I much admire the type. Certainly those who developed these sloops knew what they were doing, and the boats very much suited the work they were to do. By nature, the Friendship sloop requires a big rig. There have been some slight variations in the true type recently, to improve them (it's hoped) for today's pleasure sailing. My own feeling is that the Friendship, with the big rig, mast far forward, sharp entry, and heavy quarters, though right for a working craft, is not just the thing for the weekend sailor. Some designers, as I say, have attempted to improve the type for pleasure sailing, notably the well-known Maine designer, Murray G. Peterson, who turned out small, classic sloops of yacht quality. These boats are most docile and handy, and very easy to look at.

My own preference in small sloops is for what used to be referred to as a deep centerboard. Fine-lined and not too bulky, such a sloop does not need an outsize rig to move her, yet has plenty of sail to make her go in a light breeze. The fact that she will have to reef now and then is taken as a matter of course. She would have a gaff rig, naturally, for reasons previously given. Whether she has a plumb stem or clipper head is mostly a matter of how you feel about it.

A centerboard cluttering up the small cabin is of no matter whatsoever. If the rest is right and she's sweet to the eye and nice to handle, I learn to live with what is below. So many craft nowadays, regardless of size, are designed around a cabin. They look it, too. Some folks seem to care little how well a boat sails and what she looks like as long as the cabin is big, to store beer in mostly. Seems a shantyboat might do just as well.

The idea of a very large sloop is intriguing, though the practicality in today's economy makes you forget it, even though the pictures of great stone sloops and Hudson River craft are fun to look at. What often happens when a certain sloop design becomes just a little too big — that damn main boom you know — is she is made a yawl. Until recently, modern yawls were very popular and had some advantage under rating rules for racing. The original reason for the rig, however, was too much main boom on a big sloop.

I've spent many a year with yawls, both the old type and those induced by rating rules. Can't say as I really cotton to the rig, always feel I'm really in a sloop, though there's nothing at all wrong with that. To convert a big sloop to a yawl to make her easier to handle makes sense. But for me to design a yawl from scratch (unless the client just must have it and no other) makes no sense at all. The cost of the added

mizzen, or jigger, as it's sometimes called, is nearly as much as a ketch mizzen, and it gives far less return.

It seems most anybody thinks he likes a ketch, whether or not he knows the whys and wherefores of the rig. The ketch is said to be easy to handle, thus it must be a good rig! The designers of ketches have problems, notably trying to get enough sail area to drive what often is a bulky hull. Beyond a certain point, there is nowhere else to go but up in figuring a rig, particularly when using the Marconi rig. You end up with very tall masts and narrow sails that tend to set poorly. Often such a craft is hopefully intended for long passages. These tall narrow ribbons are just plain wrong for such use. Sail area in a ketch being hard to come by, she should have a rather easy-moving hull with moderate displacement. Often you see designs that are just the opposite—deep, wide, and heavy. Combine such a shape with a tall, narrow rig that won't "sleep" on what's probably a bouncy hull, and you have a poor design.

For a ketch, I like a rather narrow hull, sharp and easy of line, not of heavy displacement. She may not be overly roomy and so should have more length than a man might think he needs at first. And she should have a simple rig, which need not be massive, for the boat will move well and not put great strain on it. She needs a strong rig, but it need not be heavy in the sense of having huge blocks and big lines and stays. These are not needed with an easy hull. In other words, I like a fairly "slight" hull, compared to the often-pictured world-girdling ketch, a stout, bulky thing with a very heavy, short rig. The craft should be handsome and delicate of line, for by the nature of her design she's well suited to a pretty shape. Might as well make the most of it!

Now just how do I go about fitting a proper, light rig, with enough area, and keep it simple and handy? I'll tell you what to do, but none of it is original; I never seem to do anything original, unless combining things done many times before may turn up something a bit different. The rig to be described is suited to hulls about

*A short-gaff ketch rig driving a comfortable hull to windward in a
breeze. (Photo by Norman Fortier.)*

28 to 45 feet long. For shorter boats, the ketch is not necessary; for longer craft, other rigs are better, or so I think.

I like both masts to be solid sticks about the same length, though the foremast (some call it the main) should be of bigger diameter than the mizzen, as it carries more sail. I place them similar to the masts in a Chesapeake bugeye, and give them considerable rake by present standards, but not as much as in the Bay craft. A bowsprit is essential. The booms are about the same length. Short gaffs controlled by single halyards are light, simple, work extremely well, and get area without undue mast length. A single headsail is all that's needed, even in a 45-foot boat; it should set on a one-third-length club, not a full-length one. Right here I often get noise, for few folks seem to know about this short club. Rigged right, it tends for itself; it was standard in the oystering fleets of Chesapeake and Delaware Bays. Oyster dredges often made more tacks and handled more sail as a day's work than some yachtsmen do in five years. Their gear works if you learn it, which takes all of ten minutes, with an open mind.

Standing rigging should be wire: a jibstay, rove through a bee hole in the bowsprit end to become the inner bobstay; an outer headstay to the bowsprit, backed by the lighter outer bobstay. (This stay also carries the lazyjack iron.) For foremast shrouds, a single one on each side, on craft from 28 feet to about 36 feet, a pair each side on bigger boats. On the mizzen, a single shroud each side is adequate even on a 45-foot boat. There should be a spring stay. Three halyards, three sheets, and three light lifts, and that's about it. The rig has a minimum of wire, lines, blocks, fittings, and ironwork; it has considerable area, modest weight and windage, and, of course, simple upkeep and repair. The rig is an efficient driver, and, due to the shape of things, the sails ahead don't backwind the mizzen, a failing of some ketches. If you like light sails, the rig is laid out so that a big reaching jib works well in the fore triangle, and it will fit exactly as a mizzen staysail too. Or you can spend money and have two; it does not matter which bag you grab, either sail will fit, and they are real jazz in light going!

There is one drawback to this sort of rig for those preoccupied with cabin space and arrangements below. The masts must be placed just about so, and they govern the placement of the deck houses, and there must be two houses, unless the boat is on the small side. This, in turn, sets some limits on the accommodations. The layouts I've used vary somewhat according to length of boat, naturally. They have proven practical, offer some privacy and at times necessary segregation, you do not step on the cook, and there is storage space. The bigger the boat, the better the layout.

I find this rig tends to invite self-steering if the hull has it in her. The rake of the masts seems to have a lifting effect on the boat when running off, the sails "sleep" in light going, and jibing a sail on what's now considered a heavily raked mast is remarkably easy and simple. The sails hoist and lower very easily, and experienced sailmakers tell me it's much easier to cut a well-setting sail to a raking mast. The old timers knew all about this.

The rig has a minimum of standing rigging and turnbuckles. The bobstays can be of chain. The iron work is simple and easily made, and it should be galvanized iron, not bronze. Blocks and running gear, as mentioned before, are few and simple. There is a minimum of windage aloft. Lacings or hoops can be used to hold the luffs to the masts; I think it's just a matter of preference. The lacings work so well, offer so little windage, and are so simple and cheap that I see no need to use hoops. The sails are so small and light that a twelve-year-old boy, once he "learns the ropes," can handle them with considerable snazz in ordinary weather. The spar-making for such a rig is about as simple as you can find, and the spar material is available.

I don't say this is the only kind of ketch rig. A normal gaff ketch with, say, a sharp-headed mizzen is a seamanlike rig. If the boat is at all bulky, she will need a main topsail to get enough area for light going. If you like light sails, there is the chance for a light jib topsail as well as a mizzen staysail on this rig. Most ketches today are sharp-headed or Marconi-rigged on both masts. For reasons already given I find Marconi sails the most difficult to work with on a ketch. To begin with, the system of rigging requires more stays, fittings, and, of course, spreaders than with gaff rig. Efficient or not, you end up with a lot of windage and more weight than you might suppose. The cost of such gear has gone up considerably too. The tracks for mast and boom, masthead fittings and sheaves for wire, goosenecks, and outhauls that these rigs require, along with all the other paraphernalia that goes with them, are not cheap. Usually there are hollow spars, of wood or metal. Winches, wire halyards with wire-to-rope splices, and a thousand other things thought necessary for such a rig can make it cost as much as a whole cruising boat of simple nature. Even the amount of bronze screws used up on one of these rigs is quite an item.

My own approach to using a true Marconi rig on a ketch, if it's insisted on, is: Sail-hoist to boom-length no more than about 2 to 1; some rake to the masts; a rig generally long on the base, which calls for a bowsprit and some boom overhang aft; and considerable in the way of light sails to help along what is a rather under-canvassed hull in light weather. By now we have spent a whale of a lot of money, and have a rig that is workable and that does not look too bad, but does not have the ultra-modern style. It all works out this way: the Marconi sails are no better than the simple, short-gaff sails, and sometimes not as good when the vessel is under working sail only; the rig is not difficult to handle, but is not as handy as the short-gaff rig; and it has cost far more than the simpler rig would. In case of an accident or repairs of any kind, the Marconi rig must rely heavily on some shipyard. Yearly maintenance is much more expensive. The Marconi rig is not really suited to being left in the boat all winter if you see fit. All in all, the Marconi rig is the hard way to do it.

And that, my patient reader, is what I think of ketches.

XIII

The Schooner Rig

We all can't own big boats, yet some of us can, and anyhow, they are fun to dream about. There have been big sloops, big yawls, and bigger ketches, yet to my mind the schooner rig is the most suitable for a big boat. Everybody seems to like a schooner, in dreams at least, yet many folks think of the schooner rig as being difficult and complicated to handle. The opposite is the truth of it. Fewer men can handle more vessel with a schooner rig than with any other. It was the standard rig of coasters, pilots, and fishermen for craft of any size. Though fishermen usually had plenty of manpower and their craft were rigged accordingly, the schooner rig was very handy for them. The vessel could be shortened down for the skipper, cook, and a boy to handle when all the dories were out, and she often took some handling when it breezed up and it was time to pick up the dorymen.

The schooner rig is not suited to a craft under 40 feet long, in my opinion, though a few successful schooners smaller than that have been built. In craft 45 feet long and bigger, the rig comes into its own. I speak not of the rigs of the racing schooner-yachts of the past, a class by themselves with very small foresails in proportion to the rest of the rig, but of the coaster or pilot boat rigs, with a large foresail and a modest mainsail. Such were the working rigs of working vessels. Some say, and I very much agree, that such a schooner rig is the handsomest rig

there is, and, assuming a proper schooner hull under it, may be one of the finest sights the marine world can present, next to a fine, deep-water square-rigger.

Some schooner designs of late don't take into account that a real schooner rig must have a suitable schooner hull under it. Schooner hulls can stand considerable variation in general appearance as long as certain characteristics compatible with the rig are not overlooked. When sticking to the true, smaller schooner rig, a main-topmast two-master, or a three-master if you can find someone who can afford one, I find the schooner a very easy rig to work with design-wise. It is no trouble to get plenty of area, yet have the vessel manageable in bad going. The rig is easy to stay, and, though it may look complicated to some folks, is easy to build, and build stoutly, too.

You have a main topsail and fisherman staysail for light canvas, though in a way these are much more like working sails than the light stuff on other rigs. A topsail and fisherman are simple to use, once you are instructed, and there is no going aloft to hand the topsail in small schooners, as is often thought. The old schooner men worked all that out long ago. In large schooners, yes, you had to go aloft and like it, but then these great vessels are sort of out of range for most people and of practical interest today only in that they point out many interesting things

A real schooner has a lot of head gear.

about smaller schooners. In a small schooner, say, 40 feet long, I feel a single headsail is all that is needed and is probably more efficient than two under-sized headsails. In schooners 45 feet long and more, the old jumbo and jib with the jumbo or fore staysail set part way out on the bowsprit seems to work best. If the vessel is a flying jibboomer with two-part head gear, this jumbo goes to the end of the bowsprit proper and the jib sets on the jibboom end. If the vessel is still larger, a fore staysail set to the stemhead will work. A fore staysail or jumbo that is too narrow and too small is a hateful, useless thing.

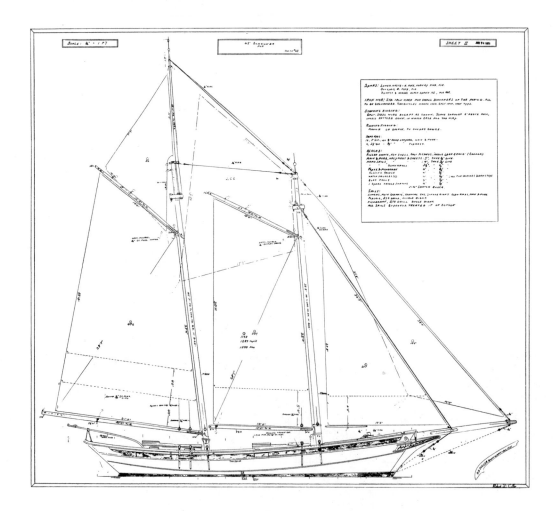

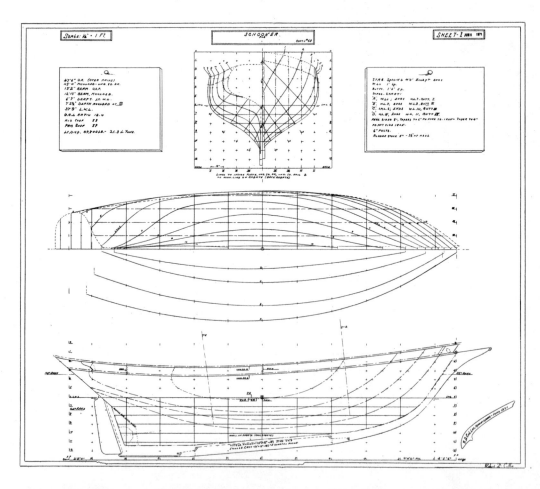

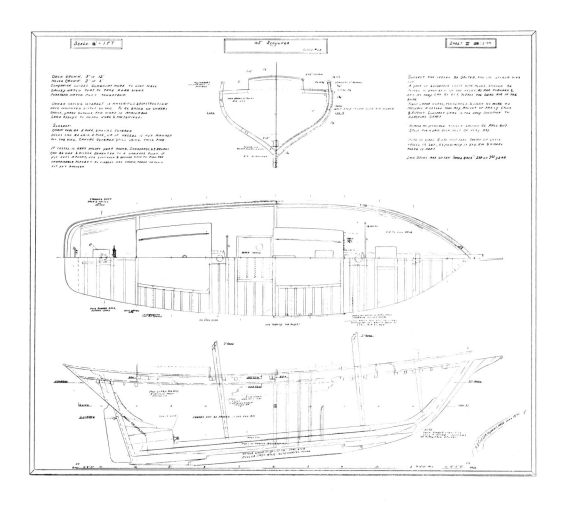

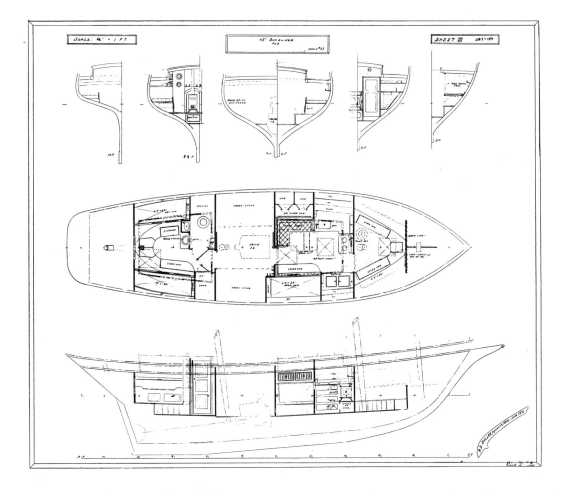

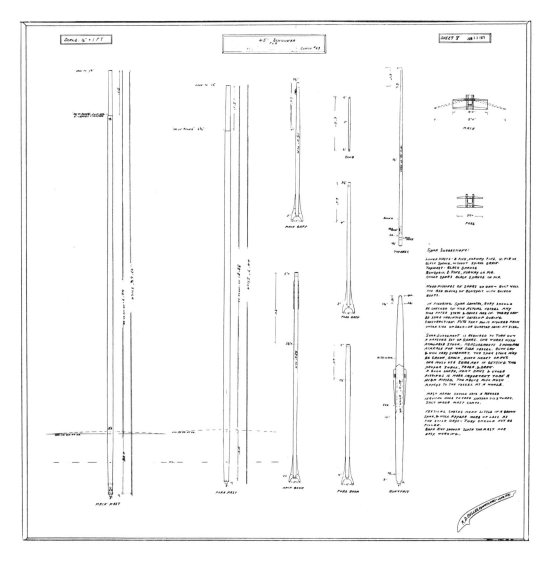

Spar Suggestions:

Lower masts - E. Pine, Norway Pine, W. Fir or black spruce, without spiral grain.
Topmast - Black spruce.
Bowsprit, E. Pine, Norway or Fir.
Other spars black spruce or Fir.

Wood fittings on spars oak or ash - bolt well thru the rab blocks or bowsprit with bronze bolts.

In figuring spar lengths, bury should be checked out the actual vessel may thus upper stem & decks may vary. There can be some variation between during construction. Note that mast is figured from under side of deck or quarter deck at side.

Some judgement is required to turn out a natural set of spars. One works with available stock. Measurements shown are suitable for the size vessel. Both can & will vary somewhat. The spar stock may be grown, sawn, bored heart or not. One must use some art in getting the proper shell, taper & grain. A good shape, many days & proper natural is more important than a high finish. The above also much applies to the vessel as a whole.

Mast heads should have a rugged vertical hole to take linseed oil & tallow, salt when mast coats.

Vertical checks mean little in a grown spar, & will appear more or less as the stick drys - they should not be filled.
Gaff jaws should slush the mast for easy working.

STATION		FP	1	2	3	4	5	(M)	7	8	9	10	11	AP	
HEIGHTS ABOVE AND BELOW LWL	RAIL UPD.SD.	5-11-2	5-7-0	5-0-4	4-6-7	4-1-6	3-9-7	3-6-6+	3-4-6	3-4-0	3-4-7	3-6-6	3-10-3+	4-2-2	
	DECK UPD.SD.	4-11-6	4-7-3+	4-0-4	3-6-6+	3-2-0	2-10-2	2-7-3	2-5-1	2-4-1	2-4-7	2-6-7	2-9-5	3-2-0	
	BUTT. I		4-1-2 A	0-10 A	1-9-3+ B	2-8-6 B	3-2-4 B	3-5-0 B	3-3-6 B	2-9-4+ B	1-9-3 B	0-6-1 B			
	BUTT. II			2-3-2 A	0-3-7 B	1-7-2 B	2-2-4 A	2-5-2 B	2-3-6 B	1-9-5 B	1-0-4 B	0-0-2 B	1-1-7 A		
	BUTT. III				1-7-6 A	0-3-7+ B	1-2-6+ B	1-6-7 B	1-5-6 B	1-1-5 B	0-5-3+ B				
	BUTT. IV					2-5-7 A	0-5-4 A	0-0-7 B	0-1-6 B	0-3-6 B					
	R.A.B.	4-11-6 A	1-5-6 A	2-2-2 B	3-5-0 B	3-11-4 B	STRAIGHT	DRAG		5-3-2+ B	STRAIGHT	5-3-2+			
	KEEL BOTT.	3-1-1 A	0-3-4 A	3-1-2 B	4-4-2 B	5-2-2-8	5-6-2 B	STRAIGHT		6-6-0 B	6-6-7 B	6-6-7 B			
HALF BREADTHS	RAIL IN SO.PLK.		2-4-7	4-4-2	5-6-5	6-1-2	6-2-3	6-2-6	6-1-3	5-11-4	5-6-4	5-0-6	4-5-1	T.R. 2-11-0	
	DECK IN SO.PLK		1-9-5+	3-11-2+	5-3-6-	6-0-7	6-3-6	6-5-1	6-3-6	6-1-2	5-8-6	5-2-7+	4-7-2	T.R. 4-11-0	
	WL 0					℄	B	TOP	SHEER						
	WL 1		2-0-0	4-3-6											
	WL 2		1-4-7	3-11-0	5-4-7	6-1-3								T.R. 3-6-0	
	WL 3		0-10-1	3-5-3	5-1-4	6-0-7	6-3-5	6-4-0	6-2-5	6-0-2	5-7-4	5-2-1	4-7-1	T.R. 2-11-7	
	WL 4		0-4-0	2-9-6	4-8-6	5-10-6	6-3-7+	6-5-4	6-4-2	6-1-6	5-9-4	5-3-2	4-6-2	T.R. 4-0-1	
	WL 5			2-1-3	4-1-1	5-5-7	6-1-6+	6-4-2	6-4-2	6-2-0	5-9-2+	5-0-7	2-7-6	T.R. 2-5-2	
	LWL 6			1-5-1	3-3-7	4-10-1	5-8-3	6-0-5	6-1-6	5-10-5	5-3-3+	3-1-2		T.R. 0-5-6	
	WL 7			0-3-4+	2-4-2	3-10-4	4-9-6	5-3-0				0-8-6			
	WL 8			0-2-7+	1-4-0	2-6-2	3-4-6	3-10-1	3-8-1	2-9-2+	1-4-4	0-4-0			
	WL 9				0-5-1	1-3-0	1-9-6	2-2-6	2-0-3	1-5-2	0-8-5				
	WL 10				0-1-7	0-6-4	0-10-4	0-10-7+	0-7-5+	0-2-5+					
	WL 11							0-3-0	0-3-2	0-3-0					
	WL 12														
	RAB.		SEE NOTES PLAN I FOR TAPERS												
	KEEL BOTT.														
DIAGONALS	DIAG. A		1-9-5	4-1-1	5-8-7	6-11-3	7-7-5	7-11-3+	8-0-2	7-9-2	7-2-6+	6-4-1	5-2-6+	5-0-2	F
	DIAG. B		0-9-6+	3-0-3	4-6-3	5-6-2	6-0-6	6-3-2	6-2-2	5-9-4	5-1-0	4-0-1		2-9-5	
	DIAG. C			1-3-7	2-5-2	3-1-6	3-6-4	3-8-6	3-7-3	3-2-4+	2-5-0	1-3-0		0-3-7	
	DIAG. D				1-0-6	1-7-1	1-11-4	2-2-0	2-1-6	1-10-5	1-4-5	1-7-5			

OFFSETS, 45' SCHOONER #63.

R.D.CULLER, HYANNIS, MASS.
JUN 24 1971
Robert D. Culler

The Russell *was built to the author's design for a 45-foot schooner at Lash Brothers Yard at Friendship, Maine. (Another photo of her appears on page 141.) The plans on the preceding pages are of the* Fiddlers' Green, *a similar vessel to the* Russell.

A schooner's mainsail is her real driver. Her foresail is her salvation in bad weather; this sail's performance when it blows must be experienced to be appreciated. Some old schooner men used to say if they had to go with rotten sails, let it be so, but never the foresail.

There can be several variations, mostly in detail, in the schooner rig, and yet stay true to type, and I suggest strongly to any coming young designer (and to some who are already established) that you stick to the schooner rig as it was. The minute you get away from the traditional proportions, the rig fails to work in practice, though it may look fine on paper.

Probably no other rig in this country has had more thorough development than the schooner. No one knows how many schooners have existed or how many variations have been developed for different trades and waters. Many vessels shifted from one trade to another as economics dictated, but, generally speaking, there were definite schooner types for definite uses. Of course in many cases, the dictates of the trades made the differences slight. Packet schooners were apt to be good sailers if built for just that trade. Very big cargo capacity was not as important as the ability to make somewhat regular passages. Pilot schooners were the nearest thing to yachts in that they carried no cargo. Their work was competitive, so they had to be fast, and they had to be very able, as their area of operation was full of hazards. Land was never very far off, they were among much shipping, and they had to be on station regardless of weather. Many yachts have been based on pilot boat models.

When we think of fishing schooners, we usually think of the Gloucester type, and it was a rather definite type in its later days. There were many other fishing schooner types, however: oystermen, menhaden fishermen, Gulf snapper schooners, Western cod and halibut fishermen, and sealers, just to name a few. And of course there were the coasters. These, in their heyday, were often designed for a particular trade, or maybe two so that the vessel had work in the off-season of one of her trades. Sev-

eral very definite and useful types of coasters were evolved, to suit certain cargoes and waters. In the last years of their sailing, most coasters took any work they could get, and many a deep-draft vessel found herself in want, for she could not get a cargo up some rivers, though she had been just fine for offshore runs. All this intensive development of schooners over many years showed what was what, both in hull design and rig. Certain variations in rig suited certain hulls and uses.

Having been so fortunate as to be exposed to the working schooner before she died, and having designed some successful schooners for today's uses, some of my notions about schooners may be pertinent. Let me note that I'm talking about small schooners, say from 40 to 85 feet in length. If anyone thinks these are large vessels, I say they are toys compared to most schooners of not so very long ago. Many folks just don't realize how much boat most working craft were, and, in most cases, how few men it took to work them. I knew an old schooner skipper who ran quite a fair-sized vessel in the Carolina-Chesapeake lumber trade. She "carried 175,000 o' boards," and he sailed her with a man and a stout boy; he being the man — quite a man. In summer, he used an idiot boy because he could get him cheaper!

Say a fellow is planning to have a schooner, a very small one. First he should consider if he can afford it, and if he can devote the time to her once she's complete. And I say right now, if you are able to build and sail a schooner, that's living! Then what about draft? She may be deep, or a fairly shoal, keel vessel, or a deep centerboarder, or a shallow one. You decide how and where you will mostly use her. Personally, I have a weakness for the deep centerboarder, if she can be of some size and other things agree.

The Russell *full-and-by with everything set and drawing. She is the result of the author's design efforts, the Lash Yard's skill, and the owner's money. Somehow she looks worth it!*

If she must be small and of modest displacement because of economic and manning problems, if draft is no great concern, if she will be used mostly along shore, I tend to favor the Chesapeake pungy schooner, though no one else seems to. These craft are descended from the Baltimore clipper schooners and are famous for several things, some of them drawbacks by present standards. They are handsome, in fact can be just daintily pretty, are known as smart sailers, and, if you stick exactly to their traditional form, are not overly expensive as small schooners go. The pungy rig, while very much a true schooner, is somewhat simpler and lighter than most as to gear and fittings. The pungy hull is also simpler than most, though she is very shapely. I've never found good looks to run up the cost in a schooner hull. The pungy has a rather uncomplicated stern, though it may look fierce to one not used to its construction. Though building this stern takes an artistic eye and some adz work, it eliminates framing and a built-up rudder port and simplifies the taffrail work. If properly designed, these craft steer very well, so are suited to a tiller.

The pungy's faults, if you consider them that, for yachting purposes are much the same as the drawbacks these schooners had as working craft. Being noted sailers, they tend to be wet. The draft must be fairly great for the vessel's size and displacement, the latter being quite moderate for a schooner. The moderate displacement leads to a lack of room below; a pungy was never a big carrier. Though she is deep-heeled, with considerable external deadwood, the pungy is high-bilged, and so not an easy craft in which to get real headroom, especially aft. For cruising coastwise where draft is not an issue, and the pungy's draft tends to be no more that that of any keel yacht of comparable size, I feel the drawbacks are of no account, compared to the good points of such a vessel.

Early pilot boats were much like the pungy's ancestors, and as the pilot types developed, I think they, like the pungies, became vessels of a type well suited to use as schooner yachts today. Several of my cruising schooner designs have been based on the late pilot boats, though of course due to present economics they have been much smaller, and hence subject to modification. I find the stern often used in pilot schooners, with the rudder port coming through a slightly immersed transom, very well suited to schooners of small size. It's strong, good looking if properly built, is buoyant and dry in rough water, and, I think, aids much in getting a nice run aft.

Saying the latter reminds me of the observations of several old-time schooner men. They all more or less agreed, though each had his preference, that a vessel could be full forward, or fine, or somewhere in between, she could be flat-floored or sharp, wall-sided or not, deep or shoal, or have any of the other combinations and variations, and still be a good ship; but not one of these experts had ever seen a vessel with a poor run that was worth a damn! I very much agree, and a designer should cultivate the ability to shape a good run, and should see to it that the builder does not "lose it" in lofting and setting up. These things can happen.

Pilot schooner yachts take kindly to the clipper bow, and also, of course, to the more-or-less plumb stem, which many originals had. It now seems the plumb stem is out of fashion. And by the odd and strange stem profiles you see now in both sail and power craft, including what seems to pass for a "modernized" clipper head, it seems many designers are groping for something they can't seem to find. Howard Chapelle and others have pointed out that the rules governing the design of a clipper head are absolute, though the size, shape, and details can vary infinitely. From the looks of some efforts now, it seems that these rules have been forgotten.

John G. Alden did so much with schooner yachts based on the later fishing schooners that these craft and his work have spoken for themselves. Suffice it to say that they were, on the whole, outstanding, but, like many good things, have gone out of fashion for the time being. Also like many good things, they could be "discovered" over again. Having been much exposed to these particular craft in the past, I still think they have a lot to offer for serious cruising.

A Maine designer, and a very good friend, the before-mentioned Murray Peterson, designed cruising schooners based on the small coasting schooners. These little schooners have been around a long time now, and have proven their sound conception. They are able, and some have done considerable voyaging. Very appealing to the eye, they stand out in any harbor scene and are just plain nice to be around. Possibly a small coaster or packet is one of the best types on which to base a cruising schooner yacht.

By the nature of the requirements of most owners, nearly all of these modified traditional schooners tend to be keel craft. The accommodation is almost always a big matter, and a centerboard in a small vessel is usually felt to offer problems to the arrangement below and is seldom accepted. A designer's lot would be much happier if at least two bunks were left out of these small schooners. It's hard to get across to a client that as these two bunks are intended to be occupied, they bring on other problems of space: fresh water tankage for two more, space for their vittles, and more ice or a bigger electric reefer and more juice to run it, two more tooth brushes, longer towel racks, more lockers for dunnage — well, you take it from there! What often happens is that the vessel's tonnage increases to hold it all, and the auxiliary power and the rig become bigger to drive the bigger hull. By now there has been talk to the point of hoarseness, much paper has been used, and many lines drawn. And then it's finally out to the yards for estimates. It will cost far more than the owner thought, though the designer knew very well it would. More often than not the whole project is abandoned. I have, for the most part, had no luck trying to think cheap for a client, though when he first approaches me, he's very apt to make a show of poverty. Then, once things are started, he's apt to run wild, and nothing will make him see the light, except being smacked full in the face with an estimate! Sometimes, if we are lucky, we start over again, with, say, a small, alongshore sloop.

Draft can be a big problem if a proposed schooner must use very thin waters. As mentioned before, a centerboard can be much in the way in a small schooner for some uses. A really big craft by today's standards makes the use of a board much simpler, but economics usually knock this idea in the head right off. Yet there is precedent in past schooners for small centerboard craft. Some of them were real old pancakes; just so it was a little wet under foot they could sail, and do it well. If a man is stuck with thin water, he soon adapts to craft suited to it, forgets full headroom, and learns the wonders of a good big wooden centerboard and the way of life that goes with it. In many ways I think it's better than the deep-draft life. Commodore Ralph Munroe, Vincent Gilpin, and others have preached the dogma of shallow draft, so I won't go into it, except to say there is no reason at all to give up schooners and cruising just because the waters are shoal. One advantage of shallow waters is that they are to some extent, still uncrowded. Besides, it's fun to have some guy row over and tell you that you're anchored in only four feet of water, "and the tide drops a foot here." Thank him kindly and look dumb. Cripes, you are only drawing two!

The feeling among many folks nowadays is that these very flat ones are unsafe, that to be any good a sailboat must have a chunk of weight on its keel. I have even met people who thought square-rigged ships and big steamers had outside ballast keels! Without going into the technical aspects of ballast, hull design as it pertains to ballast, and the reasons why outside ballast is used or not used, I will say simply that commercial craft never had it. This statement can be qualified a bit by saying a later fishing schooner or two experimented with outside ballast, a pilot schooner or two added it, and certain small working cutters in Europe used outside ballast to some extent in the later days. In this country, at least, these experiments were not repeated.

Many folks have a great fear of capsizing. I think every type of craft built has rolled over in the past and will continue to do so in the future. Some came back, some did not for various reasons, not always the fault of the design.

THE SCHOONER RIG

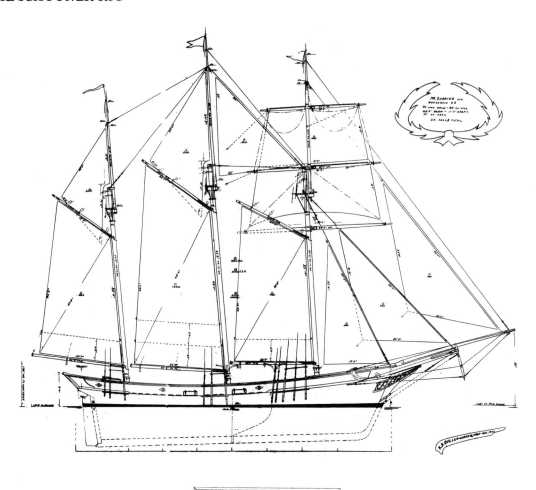

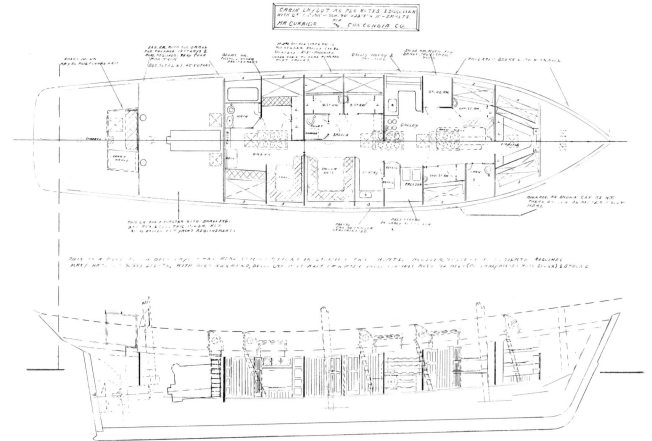

Since the beginning of boats, shoal craft have been around, and a study of them from early times to the present shows their record to be remarkably good, just as good, apparently, as that of the deeper vessels. Shoal craft have been everywhere, done everything, and it seems, made it pay. Captain Bligh made his remarkable 4,000-mile voyage from the Friendly Isles to Java in an open, shoal boat, the *Bounty*'s launch, granted that he was a master at his profession. Many others have made long cruises in shoal boats also, as in Bligh's case not always from choice. A study of these things makes you aware that the boat, whatever kind she was, did fine; the real problems were grub, water, and exposure. Furthermore, these craft often did a lot of looking after themselves because their crews became incapacitated. If a person is unreasonably afraid of capsizing and shoal boats, he might stay ashore and take his chances on the highways. Freeways frighten me, for I don't know what I'm doing on them. In trouble with some old shingle of a boat, I may not know what's what either, but if she's let alone, she has a way of coming through, and the chance of being sideswiped by some nut changing lanes is slim!

More often than not, the idea of a schooner is, for many reasons, doomed to be always a dream, yet sometimes there is a way. Usually the stumbling block is money. In the past in working craft, the same problem caused the development of a type, with several variations, that was economical to build out of easily obtained materials without necessarily using highly skilled labor. A cheap schooner of this type might be an enlarged sharpie, a pointed-bow scow schooner, a full-scow schooner, or in effect, just a large, flatiron skiff. That such craft were practical is shown by the records and pictures of them from various parts of our coast and the Great Lakes. Some of these vessels were slooped rigged; many others had the normal coasting schooner rig, with the slight variations peculiar to each locality. The idea of such craft might be hard to accept nowadays, but once understood, they make sense for shoal waters and comparative

cheapness. Some of these flat-bottomed craft were quite good looking in a businesslike way. So they can be today; it's a matter of the designer's ability and the builder's artistic skill. Nowadays, the sailing ability of a flat-bottomed schooner will be questioned, but many a skipper of a deep-draft boat has found out, quickly and decisively, that with started sheets a scow can leave him behind in short order. By the wind with much of a sea, the flatties did not do so well, yet with her shoalness and ability to cut corners, many a smart scow schooner could just lay the harbor on one tack, and was soon in and to a wharf, crew maybe ashore in the local barroom, while the deeper vessel, with maybe better windward ability, had to stick to the deep water and take hitch after hitch to make the same port, often finishing after dark with a failing wind. Yes, in waters suited to them, these sharpie and scow schooners got around with dispatch.

Many of these craft took more weather than they were really intended for, and in open water, and came through without undue trouble. I remember one of these incidents well. The schooner was about 85 feet long, cargo capacity about 150 tons. She had a totally flat bottom, though she had a pointed bow with a nice clipper head. In profile, she looked like any other coaster beginning to show her age. Her rig was that of the usual two-masted schooner with main topmast and flying jibboom. She was said to have the most prettily proportioned rig on the Chesapeake Bay. She had a hard chine with fore-and-aft planking and massive logs for chines. Her stern looked like a high-cut skiff stern. She was, on close inspection, wall-sided. Her deck layout was that of the full standard coaster of her period, with donkey engine, davits, motor yawl, and low quarterdeck. She was said to "draw 4 feet light, 6 loaded." Of course her centerboard was a massive contraption. In the schooner trade, fast-failing due to competition from trucks, she was still able to get a cargo, and "trade the rivers" when deeper schooners went hungry. Often she carried road materials, further to hasten her own end.

One winter evening she was struck by a heavy

northerly with snow, and lost her sails in attempting to make a lee and anchor. Then she had no choice but to scud. The weather was getting colder by the minute, and the visibility was poor to non-existent. During the night, she was driven out to sea between the Capes, without hitting anything, thanks to the abilities of her skipper, who was black and a licensed steamboat captain. She was now in a situation for which she was neither built nor equipped, and she was aging. She drove off quite a way, when the wind let go, leaving a miserable sea of course. Then the wind shifted to east and built up to a gale. Her skipper and very small crew managed, with some salvaged rags of canvas, to scud her back into the Bay again in torrents of rain. She was found by the Cutter and brought in to a safe berth, and given the opportunity to buy new sails that she could ill afford.

That this scow-skiff hull could cope with all this points out its abilities, for, without intending to, she was playing a tough game — Winter North Atlantic. I thought this a small epic of the sea, and sought out her skipper. Besides exposure, much work, shortage of stores and firewood, there must have been much mental strain all around, flat-bottomed vessel or no. Her skipper's words were short and to the point. "I never worried for the vessel. If the wind hadn't changed, I don't know where I woulda went to!"

I feel, for the right waters and for the man with the right outlook toward them, these scows or flatties, schooner-rigged for the hell of it and because it makes 'em look very good, have a lot to offer as a cruising boat, sometimes floating home. They are one way of getting about in interesting waters.

And that, I think, is just about enough of schooners.

The rigs I've discussed, from very small boats up to large ones, are based on much development and testing from the economic angle. I've noticed that to depart much from "just like it was" leads to complications not at first realized, for these rigs are wholes, and to disturb one part sets off a chain of problems that ends up by causing none of the rig to work right. If this sort of boating and tinkering with what some folks say are things outmoded does not appeal to you, by all means stay clear of it and stick to something that was developed last night; the originator may well know his stuff, and it could be good. I think going thoroughly modern is so much better than taking something known to be good that you don't really like, then botching it up by trying to change it around into something you do like. If you don't feel at least some kinship with the men who worked simple boats in the past, there's no point in wishful thinking about the kinds of boats and rigs they used. But if this sort of thing does appeal to you, then you've come down with a fascinating disease.

XIV

Water, Stoves, Anchors, Fuel, Centerboards, and Cabins

There are so many things about boats and ships that no one can ever begin to know all about it, let alone write all about it. There have been Monumental Works on marine subjects; I marvel at the amount of labor it must have taken to compile them. Yet even these books don't and can't cover everything. Each man's experience gives his understanding and approach different meaning. Besides, boats and ships are so specialized. Just the subject of tugboating can fill books, and has.

I simply give some experiences, ways, yarns, and methods, some of them highly local, all of them to do with boats and vessels I've been exposed to. Making the point again, none of this is new, some of it is useful, and much of it has been forgotten.

When going out in a small boat, with whatever means of propulsion, even for an hour or two, there should be some sort of water jug. You may well stay longer than you think, from choice or necessity. I sort of like odd-shaped bottles, and some of these tend to go with an attractive boat. It's best if the water bottle is protected in some way, and it can be fun to cover it with some sort of ropework. The covering can be fancy if you lean that way, or can simply be some fishnet triced around the bottle or a canvas cover sewn on. Many folks nowadays just grab some sort of plastic jug; it holds water and is not easily

stove up, but to me, at least, is not an attractive way of carrying water.

For a long day-trip or an overnight cruise, naturally the container can be bigger, and here the plastic thing may be better. A cabin boat that is small can often use some sort of portable "tank," something to be taken ashore and filled, or possibly several such tanks. Whatever is used, it needs a rack on board so it can't fetch away, and the rack should hold the container high enough to put a cup or pot under, for these things can have some sort of spigot on the bottom. In the past, some of us used new 5-gallon kerosene cans with a small spigot soldered on next to the bottom; these made quite a water supply for a small cruiser. On larger craft with built-in tanks, monel now seems to be the best. At one time tin-lined copper was the best. Some now say a fiberglass tank is the thing; others say the water from them always tastes lousy!

My own experience is that I've never had any trouble with galvanized iron water tanks, this comment based on twenty-three years using the same tanks. In the realm of tugs and big ships, plain iron tanks are used. My experience was that we cemented the tanks once in awhile. They were big enough to be crawled into, and, upon overhauling, they were drained, opened up, scaled if need be, scrubbed out and flushed, and then cemented. We used Portland cement only, mixed with water about like a thick soup and painted thoroughly on the tank sides with a "cement brush," which was about like a calcimine brush. The water from these tanks was always sweet and clean. This, of course, is only of interest to small-boat men as sea lore.

The water cask is now considered outdated, though I think for extended cruising it could still have its place. It's hard to damage, can be taken ashore in a yawl boat, and is a handy container for extra water or for doubtful water to save contaminating the main tanks, for the cask is easily cleaned out. Like many things used in the past, a new cask has a ritual surrounding its preparation. Get a cask of suitable size, if you can find one now, preferably of oak, and if it has galvanized hoops, so much the better. Cut an oblong hole where the bung is, big enough to put a dipper or small pot through. Or, if you use a spigot on the bottom, leave the bung be, and put a lanyard on it. If you use the dipping hole, put a stout canvas flap over it, tacked on one long side only. Sew a stout bolt or rod into a pocket along the other long side to keep the flap in place. In the past, when harbors were cleaner — or maybe people just didn't care — a wood toggle was put in the hole, line attached, and the cask hove overside and swamped, for it was thought "river water" helped in the seasoning. After a week or so, the cask would be taken on board and washed out, then taken ashore in the yawl to be filled, and then set aside to "go bad." After several cleanings and fillings, this going-bad ceased, and the cask was considered seasoned and fit for use. A chock was made to hold it, and a place chosen to lash it down. It was painted, and often in a decorative way. Such a cask was the water supply for the men in a small coaster or sailing oyster dredger, and it worked. What you did in very cold winter weather, at least what was done on craft I was on long ago, is interesting. The cask was on deck and should have frozen, but did not. A dry salt cod was placed over the dipping hole and a heavy scrap of old sail thrown over all. It worked; don't ask me why; I don't know.

Many large sailing fishermen had big wooden tanks below decks, usually built of cypress, and some deep-water sailing vessels had them too. They were, from all accounts, highly satisfactory. For that matter, many of us remember the old wooden tank that the windmill pumped to. Think about wooden tanks when building a cruising craft and cash is short. I use wooden tanks in my shop, one for quenching, and one as a reservoir for the steam box; they never leak. They are built with a "draw," so freezing does not hurt them.

Nowadays many sizes of metal tanks can be bought "stock," and should be considered in making a design or planning a layout below deck. Nothing is now cheap, including these tanks, which usually have had a pressure test, but there is much saving over custom-made tanks of odd shape. Something that is often overlooked is that a tank way down low, maybe in the bilge in a deep boat, with a long fill pipe will have a heck of a "head" if filled right up, and may rupture unless very stout.

Among other things, water is used for cooking, which brings up galleys, be they a sort of box with small stove and other gear to use in an open boat, or something more elaborate for a cabin craft. Without a stove, there is no galley; with one, it's official even though it may be an unhandy nook, or just a shelf.

Nowadays there are all kinds of portable stoves running on several different fuels. Some are risky in a close space. Each man to his choice; I still prefer the Primus using kerosene. It has the drawback of requiring a priming fuel, usually alcohol. Some curse these stoves, for they never learned to preheat them properly.

No one has yet made a cabin comfortable in wet, chilly weather with an open-flame stove. All you get is foul air and condensation, and often a headache or worse. Even a very small cabin boat, if there is possibly space for it, should have some sort of solid-fuel stove, no matter how tiny. These stoves can be bought, but a small stove, or a large one for that matter, can be made of sheet metal, a few rivets, and some stove bolts by anyone handy. It will burn sticks of wood, using sand for a grate. If you do this, remember there is a necessary relationship between the draft vent and the stack; examine a few small stoves to learn about this. A miserable Northeast day and one of these stoves is the difference between living and wishing you were home. Some folks say they won't have a solid-fuel stove because it's messy; to some extent it is, but it's "clean dirt." For myself, I would sooner live in squalid comfort than be miserable in bad weather. Besides, you can heat a kettle on a wood or coal stove, make toast, simmer a pot, and do many other things, including dry socks. Such a stove is very nice, too, when tinkering in the cabin on weekends in winter, and for spring fitting out. After a cold morning under a bottom, scraping, it's nice to have a warm place out of the wind to work on the lunch box comfortably. All this is, I think, a very good part of boating. As soon as you do these things all cold and wet, boating is not so good.

Sizable cruising craft naturally have more elaborate galley set-ups, though getting too elaborate does not seem to bring worthwhile returns. A craft that is able to do some real cruising and have the galley in operation in most kinds of weather is the dream of many. Here again, for certain climates, a solid-fuel stove, or at least one on the range principle with plenty of iron, an oven, and a stack, is needed. In many cases today, such a stove will be oil-fired. In practice, the type of fuel is not the main thing; it is the slow, steady radiation of heat that is important. The first thing any range needs is a good stack draft; without a good draft, there is nothing but trouble. Many folks may shy away from a good cooking range, though intending to do considerable cruising in latitudes where it's really a must, because of experience with a stove that had a poor draft.

In working up a design for a cruising boat, I often find that the client has quite set ideas on a cabin arrangement, sometimes without realizing just what goes on in use. A sailing vessel has air circulation from aft forward at anchor, and most of the time at sea. This is most noticeable in classic models, maybe because they tend to have plenty of sheer and deck layouts that favor

this reverse circulation. Most folks want the galley right by the main companionway, basing the choice on "light, air, and ventilation, besides being handy to the deck." My experience has been that this is the worst possible place for the galley in a craft of offshore capability and some size, say 36 feet and bigger. In port, the cook is in a line of traffic; everyone is stepping on or around him. Some air gets in, and all the hot stuff goes forward. What air tries to get out the companionway because it's hot is bucking the vessel's natural draft. Some pleasant ape wants to sit in the companionway and shoot the guff; he blocks both light and air. His remarks like, "Cookie, what's cooking?" get tiresome. If you give him potatoes to peel, he does it right there.

At sea, having the galley aft is worse yet; there are comings and goings, often in wet oilskins, and there are dollops of spray as the hatch is slid back. Worst of all, under sail, there is poor stack draft with the galley aft. On one tack at least, and more often on both, there is a downdraft from the sails, and besides, there is not room enough for a proper smokehead. The old-timers knew all about this, and their stove pipes were near the forward end of a cabin trunk, be it after cabin or forward house, and the smokehead was usually in the form of a long tee, from one side of the house to the other, with turned-down elbows on the ends. Iron straps or rods supported these ends and also prevented lines from fouling them. The point was that since the stovepipe was limited in height by the foresail or mainsail, both when set and when stowed, the pipe was made as long as possible athwartships to gain draft. A very long pipe, even horizontal, increases draft, and the turned-down elbows prevented down-drafts from the sail directly above. At the same time, the pipe being as close as practical to the mast, the part of the boom above the pipe did not get very far outboard, even before the wind. This tended to keep those drafts that did come from the sails fairly constant regardless of point of sailing.

There was often a hatch directly over the cook's head. This hatch worked in favor with a vessel's natural ventilation, from aft forward,

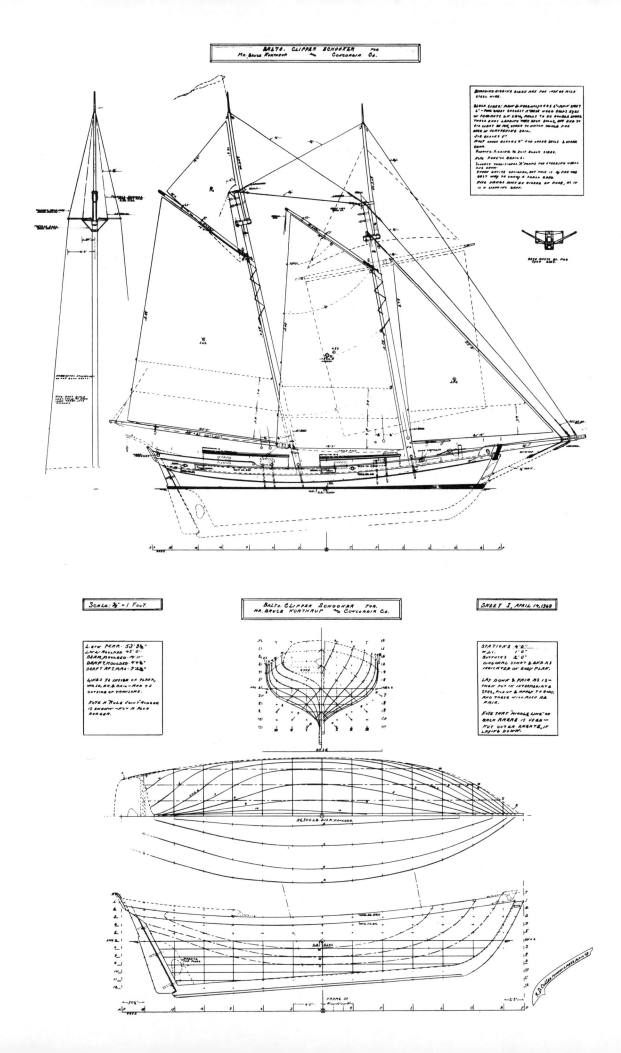

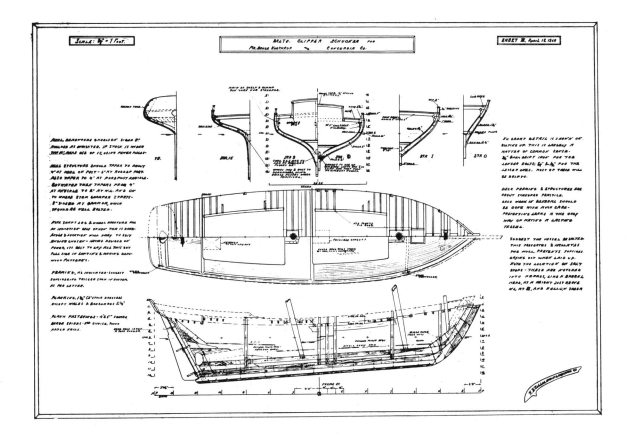

and the hot air in the galley further helped ventilating. The system is not bucking nature. I have had it pointed out that a galley forward is bad on account of much motion at sea. In practice I've not found it so, at least in designs based on classic models. Having the galley forward was standard on all sizes of sailing vessels in the past, and you see nowadays many motor fishing vessels whose galleys really are little different from those of the days of *Captains Courageous*, except for the oil range and a reefer.

I think I speak from experience on these matters; it's been said I was considerable of a cook; at least there was never much left, and someone else was usually willing to wash up. I go into such things as galley arrangement just to make it clear that in planning, designing, or having designed a vessel with serious cruising in mind, this kind of thinking can have a great bearing on the vessel being successful later on. No designer or builder can have full experience in all things pertaining to vessels, but they can and

should be very much guided by what worked in the past.

Another important factor for the success of any vessel meant for serious cruising is her ground tackle. Many kinds of anchors have been invented, quite a few relatively recently, yet only one or two of the recent ones have stood the test, and these, like all anchors, are not perfect. Each kind of anchor has its best or worst conditions of holding power. We don't seem to have come very far ahead with anchor development in 500 years. Most everyone agrees that every vessel should have a really big anchor and cable of some kind for use when the chips are down, yet the big hook is often very unhandy to put overboard quickly. There was a rule, now mostly neglected on account of "the work," that in seasons of bad weather or in unfamiliar waters, the big hook was always put down first as a matter of course; some used it regardless of seasons and conditions. These men seldom if ever drove ashore; they had no mad scramble during the night to get a too-well-stowed big anchor overboard. Instead, if they felt they needed a second anchor, it could be gotten out calmly and in an orderly manner, as the vessel was not in immediate danger of dragging.

If a wise skipper, thinking this way and having a vessel built or an older one overhauled for some adventure, dumps the ground tackle question in a designer's or builder's lap, it's no big problem. All that is needed is a method of letting a big anchor go, sufficient power by man or motor to heave in and cat it, and a way to stow the cable. It's all been done uncounted times before, yet to fail to prepare for these simple operations in a new craft and then find (if you have been lucky and have not driven ashore) that these things must be done, can be a most expensive proposition. It's better to do it right the first time.

Another sometimes underestimated part of a cruising boat is the fuel system for her engine, if she has one. Fuel problems can mean not only discomfort and inconvenince, but also, of course, sudden disaster. A good many years' working around fuel tanks has taught me many things. Way back, when even big engines were gasoline, or possibly distillate, the first-class fuel tank was considered to be copper, unless large tank size made this metal impractical. I remember no more engine trouble in those days than there seemed to be later on, though the cause of trouble changed. Gas does not smell now like the old stuff used to, and the old stuff probably was not much good, though the engines used then did well on it. Something in the gas changed, and copper tanks started forming gum. So now it's monel, and, in some cases, plain steel for diesel oil. For the most part fuel tank installations are now made to Coast Guard recommendations; for certain uses they must be. In some classic boats it's best to have the tank on deck; even though it's covered on top, there can be full ventilation around it. I feel a shut-off valve at the tank, always a good idea, is the thing here. Always use it. Shut down the engine; shut off gasoline.

I've found that shutting off the gas and running the carburetor dry is bad business. Sometimes when the gas is turned on again, the carburetor float will stick and flooding results. Flooding is no good at all with the present system of remote starting; you get ready to fire up and never know she's flooded!

The engine should be very accessible (few are now) and when you start it, you should be right at its side — no remote starting. What happens is, you get right next to it, and smell before doing anything else. The difference between open air and engine gas smell is easily noticed. Look and check things over for a few seconds. What's that juice washing around in the pan? water? gas? If it's oil, check the stick. If all seems okay, fire up. The throttle and clutch lower ends should be handy or extensions put on them. There should be a cut-off valve at the engine too, right next to the pot. Folks running their engines this way have little chance of blowing up. I'm well aware that this thinking will not go over with some folks in these days of Step-On-It-And-Go. Some people bring the auto outlook aboard their boats, but remember that the car has most of its guts hanging out in fast-moving air; that's what keeps it from burning up.

In my distant past, most engines were stemwinders; a few had starters; all had to be cuddled up to if starting was intended. It was all very backward, I suppose, but we did not know any better. We started and stopped these hunks of iron totally by feel on the darkest of nights, and even made hasty repairs in the dark. In some "trades," lights of any kind were very much frowned on. Some remember when the only beer was known as "3.2." Starting in the dark of a wet and drippy night, we learned some things quickly. There is often a stream of red sparks from the starting gear ring. If the starter cover is not on just so, there is much blue light at the armature. A connection you didn't know was a bit loose sparks a bit. A big-bore "six" with dual ignition has a lot of wires and plugs; the whole business often glowed and crackled till she got a bit warm. Try it some miserable night, in the dark of course.

I still like to cuddle up to start a gas engine,

even if it's the most modern type.

Though it's done, I don't care for the syphon pipe tank in a diesel, as, over a long period, or even in a short time if you are unlucky, water and crud collect until they come very close to the bottom of the intake. After a winter lay-up you fit out and try the engine at the dock; it's fine, and you start for the home port. It's early spring and it's windy, with the tide horsing up against the wind. There's lots of thrashing, and soon she gets a blob of the gunk. You clean filters, get going, and soon it happens again, and again. Wallowing in the trough with this smelly stuff is no fun. I know because I've gone around Point Jude this way. It's better, I think, to feed off the bottom of the tank, and catch the mess a little at a time, by plenty of attention to the filters; if it can't build up, it can't cause as much trouble. There is much to be said for the old Navy type of filters, those that are dual in the same line, with separate cut-offs. You clean one while you run on the other. Cooling water filters work well this way too. The system isn't cheap, but it may save piling her up.

Centerboards seem to have nothing to do with fuel systems, yet, like them, they have some relation to making the boat go, at least somewhere near where she looks. Nowadays, and in cabin boats in particular, centerboards and wells seem to be designed mostly to suit the cabin, and not primarily to help the sailing of the boat, or not for strength, simplicity, and ease of maintaining. Therefore, centerboard boats tend to get a bad name in some boating circles. Even in open boats we find some poorly designed centerboards nowadays. In so many craft, open or not, dropping out the board, either ashore or afloat is most unhandy and difficult. There is no need for this. The centerboards in small, open craft can usually be arranged to be removed from either the top or bottom of the trunk; it's often unhandy to lay the craft on her side to remove the board from the bottom. In cabin craft, taking the board out through the top of the well can often be impractical, and few railways now have easily removable sills or a hole under them for dropping a large board. Or, if you beach

out, you can't get the board out through the bottom.

The "old way," which now seems forgotten, was simple. We are talking of very large, heavy boards, such as were used in schooners, bugeyes, and big sailing bateaux, 2 to 4 inches thick, and 16 feet long or longer, but of course the same system works with smaller boards. There was a stout eyebolt on the top of the board at each end. The well cap was made to remove easily over these eyebolts, and halyards were dropped down through hatches and hooked on to the eyebolts, along with a stout lazy line to each. The vessel was put in water of sufficient depth to clear the board, a strain was taken on the tackles, the pin, which was a simple affair, was punched out, and a couple of wood plugs driven into the pin hole, one on each side. The board was then lowered clear of the keel, the lazy lines following. The lazy lines then were fished out from under the vessel, using the yawl and a long boat hook. Just the bights of the lazy line were taken aboard the vessel, not the ends, which were of sufficient length to stay fast in the hold. The bights were racked off, or other falls secured to them, and a strain taken. The original falls were slacked off, and naturally the board came under the lines or falls alongside. The board was then hoisted up to the rail against fenders and the vessel taken to railway or ground. At the railway she was hauled with the board alongside. Then the board was slacked down to the sills if the tackles were long enough, or to blocking. The outboard side was scrubbed, then the board was pried past center if need be, and gradually lowered outboard, flat, so the inboard side could be tended. Repairs, if any, followed, and the board was, of course, painted. Also, the well was swabbed out. After launching, the procedure is reversed to bring the board back up into the well. You might think this would take some tricky fiddling, but if the water is quiet, she comes right back where she belongs, hauled up by falls on the lazy lines, with no fuss.

Some craft had the centerboard pin slightly above the waterline when in light condition, so it could be driven out without the usual temporary flood below. To me this is most sensible, and I've designed a number of craft this way. Just why a centerboard pin has to be complicated, expensive, and inaccessible I fail to see. Some present designs show complicated machining, bushings, stuffing boxes of a sort, threads, and what all, often for a 14-foot boat! Small working craft often used a tapered hardwood pin and just a plain hole in the board. Bigger boards had crudely bushed holes, made with just a stout piece of flat iron rolled in a circle without a weld, just a butt, and driven into a tight hole in the board. Sometimes the pin was threaded with a nut, more often not in the large sizes. A big pin would often consist of a stout bolt with a large head and a forelock on the other end. A forelock is simply a punched hole, usually oblong, a big, stiff washer, and an iron wedge, that was driven through the hole to set up against the washer. The bolt head and forelock washer set against stout hardwood blocks, often square, with thick leather washers under them, and they were quite tight! So much for simplicity, which many centerboarders do not have nowadays. These under-the-floor, hidden boards, while suited to gold platers and racers (where they give much trouble at times), have no place in practical, economical cruising boats.

Centerboard pennants often cause trouble, just because it's not understood what goes on and can happen at times. A centerboard is made to kick up when something is struck, or if purposely used as a brake or temporary hold-off on coming alongside in shoal water. A rope pennant does fine in a small craft and is easy and cheap to replace. If the board is let down below the well, it's very apt to jam the pennant on striking something. I think chain is very bad this way. And even if the board is not lowered too much, chain piles up and once jammed is most difficult. Wire, being stiff, does all right, but needs watching; sometimes it rots out fast. Big coasting schooners used a stout iron rod or "monkey tail" hoisted by a tackle from aloft. This never jammed, which in those big craft would have been a big problem. Rods of various patterns have been much used in small craft, especially in beach boats that tend to get gravel in the wells. I like rods, with one exception; in a fast-sailing boat you like to fuss with board adjustment. If the board is part way up, the rod won't lie down and house properly, and lines get caught under it.

Any centerboard well, large or small, that is totally capped should have a hole in the cap, with a plug, of sufficient size to allow pushing, or even pounding, down the board with a stick if something goes wrong. A stout dowel will do for a small boat; a large craft might sometimes require a stout oak 2x and a sledge. Jamming, from many causes, can happen. If the board is get-at-able, there is seldom much problem.

Many folks think a metal "board" is the answer; I find it not at all so. Some class racers use metal centerboards, so it's the law there, and, like other racing things, you put up with it. Metal boards kink easily or crimp on the edge, and, of course, jam. If they are built stoutly enough not to have these faults, they become so heavy that they require strong mechanical means of handling, usually a winch. This is not an economical approach. For some reason, a boat that has been using a wooden board successfully will not sail as well with a thin metal one, even though the well is narrowed to suit. I really don't know just why this is, except that in practice thick control surfaces, and this includes rudders, seem to help, though just the opposite would seem the case. My experience has been that the very extreme streamlining of both boards and rudders, at least in the ordinary run of boats, does no good and sometimes causes harm, most notably in steering and handling. Blunt, or even nearly square, edges seem to require less area for a given board or rudder. I find I much prefer a very long, shoal board to a short, deep one. I suppose the long, entering edge has a way of steadying the boat and making her hold on. On the other hand, the very narrow, deep rudder, which is not always practical on a shoal boat, seems to do the most work easily for its size and has less leverage on the steering gear.

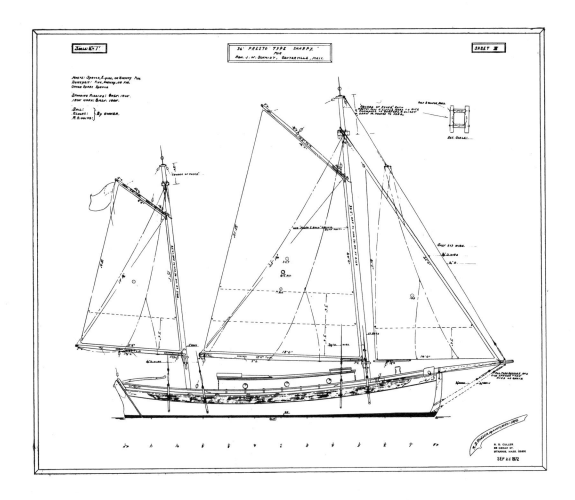

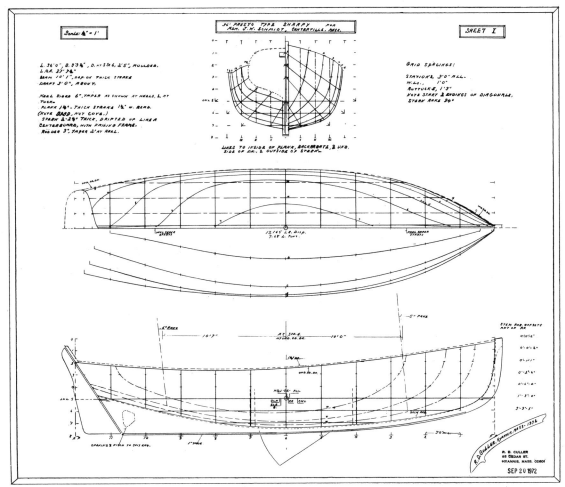

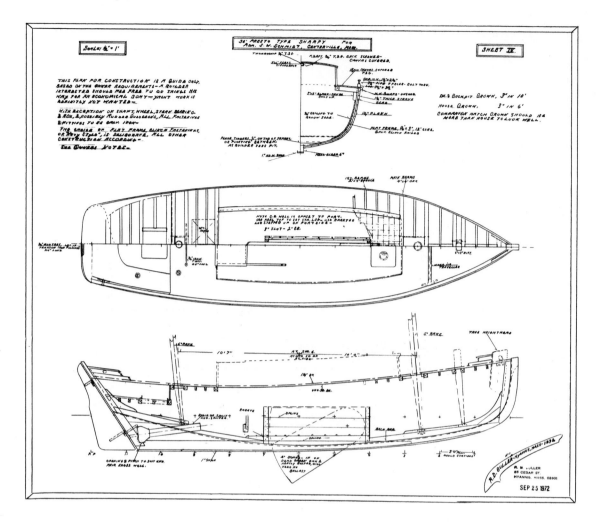

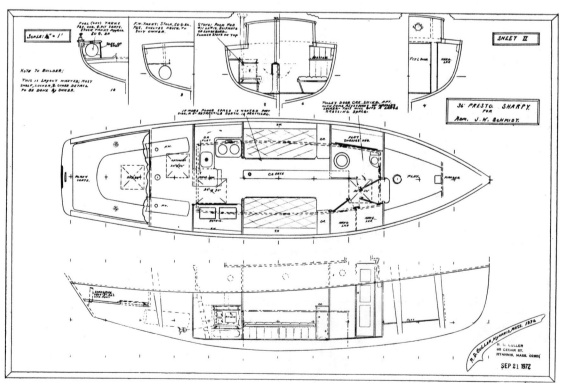

STATION	FP	1	2	3	4	5	6	7	8	9	10	11	AP	
UND. S.D. DECK	4-7-6	4-2-3	3-9-0-	3-4-0	2-11-6	2-8-3	2-5-7	2-4-2	2-3-6+	2-4-2	2-6-2	2-8-7+	3-0-4	
BUTT. I		1-0-2	0-7-7	1-4-7	1-10-0	2-1-0	2-2-1-	2-0-7	1-8-7-	1-2-5	0-5-3	0-5-0	0-10-7	AT TR.
BUTT. II			0-8-2	0-7-4	1-3-6	1-8-3	1-10-3	1-9-1	1-5-3	0-10-2	0-1-1	0-8-7	1-2-7	AT TR.
BUTT. III				1-3-2	0-4-0	0-10-6	1-1-6	1-1-4	0-9-5	0-2-2	0-8-6+			
RABATE		0-9-5	1-5-4	1-10-2	2-1-6	2-3-7+	2-4-7-	2-3-2	1-11-3	1-5-1+	0-9-1	0-0-0	0-3-2	AT TR.
KEEL BOTTOM	0-3-6	1-4-2	1-11-4	2-4-3	2-7-4+	2-9-2	2-10-4+	2-10-7	STRAIGHT 7		2-11-3	TO HEEL		
UND. S.D. DECK	0-1-7	1-10-4	3-2-2	4-0-6+	4-6-1	4-9-2	4-9-6	4-9-0+	4-5-7	4-5-6+	4-1-4	3-7-6	3-2-4	
W.L. 1	0-1-7	1-10-0												
W.L. 2		1-7-4+	3-2-3	4-1-0	4-6-0									
W.L. 3		1-7-4	3-0-0	3-11-2	4-5-7	4-9-1	4-9-5	4-9-0	4-5-6	4-5-6	4-1-2	3-7-0+	3-0-6	AT TR.
W.L. 4		1-2-7	2-8-0	3-8-2	4-3-1	4-7-0	4-8-0	4-7-7	4-6-3	4-3-2	3-10-3	2-11-3	1-7-0	AT TR
L.W.L. 5		0-8-3+	1-11-6	3-2-0+	3-10-6	4-3-1	4-4-5	4-4-4	4-3-1	3-10-6	2-8-0	0-1-7		
W.L. 6			0-10-2	2-0-2	3-0-7	3-7-7+	3-10-7+	3-10-7+	3-6-0	1-11-3				
W.L. 7				0-7-6	1-6-4	1-11-4	1-6-0	0-1-7						
W.L. 8		USE AS BASE IF DESIRED												
RABATE	AS COMES - 3" HALF SIDING - 1 1/4" PLANK													
KEEL BOTTOM	0-3-0	0-1-0	0-2-2	0-3-0							0-3-0	0-1-2	0-1-0	AT HEEL.
DIAG. A	0-3-4	2-2-3+	3-7-6	4-6-6+	5-1-7+	5-5-7	5-7-7+	5-7-2	5-5-2	5-1-6+	4-9-1	4-2-2+	3-8-2	ENDING
DIAG. B	0-3-7	2-0-2	3-4-2	4-4-0	4-11-4	5-3-6	5-6-0	5-5-7	5-3-4	4-10-4+	4-2-5	3-4-7	2-11-2	"
DIAG. C	0-4-0	1-8-4	2-10-0	3-8-1	4-3-4	4-7-7+	4-10-0	4-8-7	4-4-5	3-9-7	3-0-1	2-1-0	1-8-0	"
DIAG. D	0-4-2	0-8-1	1-3-2	1-9-7+	2-2-5	2-5-3	2-6-5	2-5-1	2-1-0	1-6-1	0-10-3	0-4-0		"

TO INSIDE OF PLANK · FEET, INCHES, & EIGHTHS, + OR -
OFFSETS HAVE NOT BEEN CHECKED, SO THERE ARE BOUND TO BE ERRORS -

Centerboards of my experience in big working craft were not ballasted. Being built of green oak and being heavily bolted they had sufficient weight. In small craft and even in sizable pleasure boats that winter ashore, ballast in the centerboard is required. In small boats, almost any wood is usable and strong enough for the board; lead makes up for its happening to be light. I have made small boards out of almost anything that's on hand. It's best to use narrow planks and plenty of bolts. Wide boards tend to warp in spite of much bolting, whether or not the board is taken out for the winter. Some people put a hardwood shoe on a small softwood board, though I prefer a metal band. Wood end pieces, supposedly to stiffen the board, have, in my experience, been a waste of time. Also, they tend to get loose; the swelling and shrinking of the horizontal planks, coupled with end-grain fastenings, make them not altogether practical.

Plenty of drift bolts, "fastened wild," that is raked this way and that, hold everything securely in a centerboard. You often see drifts in any kind of structure nowadays put in carefully parallel with each other. The trick is to put them in raked all differently fore-and-aft, the only care being to keep them in line in the plane of the board, so you don't "bore out." Many folks think boring for drifts in thin wood is difficult (by thin, I mean 3/4-inch to 1-inch) yet if approached properly, it's not hard. A straight-edge short enough so it does not foul the drill is clamped to the side of the work; it can also be set to the wild rake, though that is not critical. The electric drill for this job should be of modest speed. The trick, if any, is to have the drill properly sharpened; one side doing all the work throws things off. Take care in starting, for the first inch is the critical one. Feed easily, and clear often. For big bolts, say ½ inch and up, the barefoot auger is used, as it runs the truest. Everyone bores out occasionally. So what? Plug off and try again.

I've used about everything to bolt up centerboards in a pinch, everything except square rod, for I have not yet learned how to bore a long, square hole. I don't care for copper or bronze, as it has little holding power, though this can be improved by putting the bolt in a vice and making sharp burrs along it, similar to those on a coarse wood rasp, using a very sharp cold chisel. Unless these bolts are of hard metal (and then they don't burr so well), they don't stand driving into sufficiently tight holes. Galvanized bolt iron, from ¼ inch up, is probably best. Plain black iron rod seems to last a long time in a centerboard for some reason. On small boards made with narrow stock, I often use 6oD galvanized spikes with the heads cut off. These seem excellent and "draw" wonderfully, as they are usually very rough. Softwood should have a somewhat tighter hole than hard stuff, not much tighter, but some. What I say here pretty much applies to building rudders, except that they should be hardwood if possible, and narrow stock is even more important, as rudders get exposure to sun and kick around in an open boat.

Some folks think a centerboard should be of plywood. If you make a plywood board, lay it out to the stiff way of the stock; this applies to rudders, also. Plywood is not pleasant to work; edges tend to splinter, and there is much time taken to "seal the edges." Any metal binding is hard to fasten into the end grain. So the notion comes to fiberglass it. Time and stock are now more than doing it the old way, so why bother?

Since I've said centerboards ought to be designed solely to make the boat sail at her best and never mind what the well does to the cabin arrangements, maybe some thoughts on cabins would be proper. Of course a cabin can be anything from a small cuddy or "hunting cabin," often removable and just a place to get out of

the wind and chuck gear out of the wet, to a big layout suited to considerable cruising. Somehow, the light cabin house which can be bolted on in spring and fall, or used in winter, and then removed in the hot months, is seldom seen nowadays. Yet it makes a lot of sense and is easy to build. For land sakes make it low and good looking! Remember, just a while back you did not have any cabin, so don't attempt a palace, just a shelter. Such a cabin much extends the use of many small boats. The Rhode Island Box is of similar nature, just a shelter to squat in when operating an outboard in cold weather with a half lid that folds back so that you can stand up at times. I suppose this kind of shelter has not created more interest because most boating stops on Labor Day, and the usual molded stock boat is not suited to easily fitting them. Most people miss a lot by conforming.

A real cruising cabin is another thing. It requires some sort of drying-out stove (my previous remarks indicate this is not complicated unless you want to make it so) and it has to be tight. Everything else can be poor, but if the trunk and deck are tight, you make out pretty well. Good light is usually essential, except you don't want too much daylight in bunks. I make no fixed statements as to cabin arrangements; some work, some don't. A good position for the stove and the why of it has been mentioned. A cabin to spend a lot of time in is like a home ashore; have it as you see fit.

I've noticed so many times that some of these domains are most cheerful regardless of the time, weather, and other conditions, and remain so even if you are confined below for long periods. Others, with excellent joinerwork, expensive fittings, and all the things you would think would make a nice cabin, somehow fall short, and Cabin Fever develops quickly. On trying to analyze the differences between cabins, some things become apparent. In the interest of a "clean look" and a certain style, maybe, in one "cabin-fever cabin," nearly everything was awkwardly placed. The toilet room was especially unhandy. Somehow things were planned for a contortionist throughout. Simple things, like taking a shave in port with all quiet, or a supper for a lone man, almost become productions instead of simple chores. Underway the set-up was plain hateful; a lee bunk on only one tack, plenty of light, but when sun, skylight, and the usable bunk happened to line up, a watch below in daytime was worthless. And so it went. Nothing was quite right, but all was beautifully built.

I've been in other cabins, some in pleasure craft, some in working vessels, where everything felt just right and, what's more, worked right. Most real offshore craft tended to be not overly bright below. The bunks were quite sheltered or recessed. A spot of bright sunlight sweeping around below as the vessel plunges is not at all restful to those turned in. Such things are worth thinking about if you're planning real cruising.

Few folks realize nowadays just how nice and well appointed for their time some of the working vessels' cabins were. The larger the craft, the more elaborate the cabin, as a rule, though some of the small ones were pretty nice. They all seemed homelike and workable, their "design" being based on years of experience.

For cruising, much thought should be put into arrangements below decks. A counter that is all wrong as to height, width, and depth, though covered with Formica and shiny metal bindings and all, is no good. A plain pine board that is just right is what counts; you can fancy it up later. Though there may be a cabin plan drawing for general guidance, as the interior is built, the pieces should be mocked up and tried for height, clearance, and usefulness; fewer mistakes will be made. The mock-up can be simple; just a few sticks and small nails, a shoal box, some boards to shim it up, and a couple more pieces of board. Kneel, stand, reach, and try; it all tends to work out.

My usual method of placing a toilet bowl is this: Once the telephone booth is built, I place the pot about where it seems to want to be, block it for height, and then set the boatowner on it. We fuss, shift, and change the shims. Finally it seems all right, and the location and height are carefully noted. When the bowl is finally installed, the fellow is usually happy with it; after all he decided its location himself. Many other items in the cabin can be located just this way, by trial. No cabin plan, even though carefully drawn, can be wholly accurate, due to the fact that such accuracy depends on the craft and her scantlings being built exactly as drawn, which is not quite the usual case. Most builders come pretty close. A designer with much cruising experience tries to show the things that matter in making his drawings. Some parts are difficult to show. Drawings of some minor detail could get so elaborate as to cost more than just standing by to see that the job is done right, along with some quickie sketches on a board for a workman. Building a good cabin takes some art, like building many other parts of a boat. Staying simple makes it all work better.

Having owned one vessel for over twenty years, having traveled considerably in her, and having made a home and a living of sorts with her, I was much sought out by others planning a cruising boat. Certainly, they thought, I must have worked out many wrinkles, and there were sure to be a lot of "gadgets," which there were not. The craft for her size was a model of simplicity. This was often disappointing to people, and much searching would be done for something that might be considered a wonder gadget. If something caught their eye, it was not really a gadget, but an expedient just to suit the vessel, and probably useless in another. It is so easy for the inexperienced, though well read, to miss the point.

There naturally should be some plan of the basic cabin arrangement, showing locations of the main "furniture." Once that much is installed, the cabin is usable. Some cruising in an unfinished but usable cabin often makes the further details come forth of themselves, and this procedure can save some mistakes. The kind of surface finish you finally end up with comes of its own too; you find where the chafe, finger marks, and sharp corners are.

However it's done, whether plain or fancy, I've found one very valuable method of putting any cabin together. Assuming floor, bulkheads, main lockers, and such are in, I try as much as possible to make everything else as units, which go in with screws, or sometimes bolts, if the unit is heavy. Later on, if changes are made or a big refinishing job has to be done, these units simplify the job very much. Pieces easily can be gotten out of the way of the paint brush, and the units can be taken home for overhaul. If you have ever tried to remove a complicated glass rack that was built in place (takes more time to build that way) with toe nailing, blind fastenings, and all, you appreciate the unit system. Often taking out a unit is the only way to clean up properly a spilt mixture of molasses, catsup, and, say, black pepper in some compartmented rack. You unscrew it and take it out to plenty of water.

There is one thing I learned in racer-cruisers in an effort to keep a sweet cabin. After a heavy summer of campaigning, these boats get much salt below. There is hasty stowing of wet sails, you often stop up a big, wet spinnaker below decks so as to be ready for the next run down wind, wet oilskins come below, spray gets below, the craft is over-pressed and knocks down, rolling bilge water up into the lockers, and so on. In spite of constant attention, she's well salted below by lay-up time. The yard boss knew my methods; he hauled me out near the hose, or arranged an extension. The bilge plug was pulled and the yard watchman was informed that the craft was to stay totally open as to hatches for a few days regardless of weather. All soft goods and linen were taken ashore, washed, and stored. Other gear that couldn't be wetted was taken out; these items were not many, for most things can stand fresh water. A

good rousing fall Nor'wester was waited for. It soon came, so full wet-weather gear was donned, including boots, and the hose was dragged aboard with full pressure, the more the better. All current being off and the batteries removed, the hosing started — overhead, down back of ceilings, and from ends to middle, all floor boards up, washed on both sides, and all lockers and drawers. Silverware, cutlery, all stuff which was around loose was dumped on the bunk flats and got blasted. Engine and wiring were especially hosed down, and finally the stream was sent down into the bilge, being sure to wash every last crumb out through the drain. In all, this took about two or three hours' work, as it was very thorough. All the salt was gone.

Then let the dry wind work two or three days, tidy up, and put the cover on. The wiring never corroded, the engine was free of rust, and the highly-finished woodwork glowed; the craft never sweated in winter, and the cabin never needed to be "dried out" for any painting or varnishing or other work. The idea is to blast everything, inside and out, with fresh water, in good drying conditions. The amount of junk that came out of the bilge drain each season was astounding, a great wad of blanket lint among other things. I was of course considered a revolutionary by others who stuck to the rag and the bucket of soon-befouled water and could not possibly reach the places that really count.

So there, patient reader, are a few miscellaneous ways and means of doing things around a cruising boat. As I keep saying, none of these notions is original with me, but, as I also keep saying, I know from my own experience that every one of them will work.

XV
Paints, Oils, and Goo

Since the beginning of boats, there have been paints and such things used to help keep them tight, preserve them, and decorate them. Nowadays, we see almost unlimited products of this nature, nicely packaged in cans, spray tins, squeeze tubes, and other devices. In the not-too-distant past, there were a lot of these products too, not so prettily packaged. Few of these old standbys are still around, or, if they are, they appear in a different guise. I wonder if many were really much good. I also wonder about the new products and try one once in awhile.

The ancient goos applied to boats were what Nature provided. Asphalt was just fine. Animal hair, tallow, gums from trees, and, no doubt, these things combined, were in use. Industrial development brought other materials, most of them still available and still good, though many are about forgotten in the rush to try something new. Most of these old standbys are cheap, and they are easy to use.

Kerosene is the boatbuilder's friend. Plank soaked in it overnight bends remarkably well. Even if you're going to put a plank in a steam box, it helps first to soak the plank in kerosene. The stuff will go right through thin plank in a short time. It probably is somewhat of a fungicide and seems to be the base of many wood preservatives. It tends to drive the moisture out of green wood. A large, green timber, if heavily soaked in kerosene and then placed in the steam box, though no bending is intended, seems to dry out remarkably well, and with little checking. I'm sure the sterilizing effect on the sap is a benefit.

Kerosene seems to come in three grades nowadays: lamp oil, which is water-clear and doesn't smell like kerosene; stove oil; and something that is quite yellow. They all seem to work on wood. Lamp oil costs the most, but I see no advantage to it, except for lamps and primus stoves.

I can't imagine a builder getting along without kerosene. I use it, with a very little lube oil added, for whet stones. It's standard for freeing saw blades, hand or power, from gum. It's often used mixed with linseed oil to "drive the oil in the wood." It does. Mixed with melted tallow, it's most handy for keeping machinery tables in shape, and makes for an easy and steady feed. It's also fine for the temporary lay-up of a saw table or similar gear. The metal gets dusty, but there is no rust. This tallow mix, applied very sparingly to clamp screw threads works just fine. It's also excellent for hand saws in use or laid up, and for any other tool to keep it bright. When working long leaf or any other fat pine, kerosene, with or without the tallow, is a necessity. Without it, tools gum up and become ineffective, and power tools wander and burn. A sanding disk, drum, or belt that gums up can be cleaned easily with plain kero and a wire brush, and this can be done several times. The kerosene seems to have no effect at all on the binders used in today's sandpaper.

Tallow is also most useful and was once much used. Nowadays not many folks know how to come by it or even know just what it is. It's simply grease from the trimmings of meat. Some few butchers still do some trying out. Most everyone eats some meat; the fat trimmings from it, saved and tried out, will make your own tallow. Heat the fat scraps slowly in an iron skillet; don't get it smoking much, if any. Pour off the grease into a container. It will be somewhat dark. Later on, simmer this grease in a big pot with plenty of water for quite awhile; the dark stuff will settle out. Don't boil, simmer. Like all good things, it takes time. Then let it get cold, and the solid tallow can be lifted out. There are, I suppose, three main kinds of tallow that are common. Mutton, which is said to have the best properties of all for some uses; beef, which may be the most common; and that from pig. There are no doubt many others, somewhat rare, and I've had no experience with them. There must be bat tallow, which might be useful in witchcraft!

Tallow is great stuff for adding to kerosene. It has launched no end of ships as a grease for the ways. In the far South in the great heat of summer, it's often impossible to keep tallow on the ways, as it simply melts off. Other slippery stuff is then used, sometimes green bananas. No, I'm not kidding one bit! For oar leathers, the steps and partners of rotating masts, and for other crude shipboard lubrication, tallow can't be beat. It's great on gaff jaws, hoops, mast lace lines and such. It's also good as a grease for serving marline. When working with tallow while rigging, you never seem to get chapped hands or those splits common to much outside work. Most boat gear screams for lubrication; tallow does it.

Mixed with white lead, tallow has been the standard stuff in vessels for years for protecting metal, especially when laid up. For instance, large turnbuckles are packed in this mixture, parcelled with canvas, and painted. This mix

is also fine for filling rents in big timber during construction; it has the property of "bottoming out" in the crack instead of just bridging and is most easy to work with. In the past, white-lead-and-tallow has been used as a bottom paint on iron vessels, as it seems to be somewhat anti-fouling, probably because it wears off as growth forms. Worm, of course, is no problem in a metal hull. Many steam engines and other bright machinery were smeared with this stuff on laying up; it gave fine protection, yet was not difficult to remove when fitting out.

Tallow and slaked lime make a good, cheap, seam filler for some old boat that is past her prime; you know she will need a lot of tinkering with the seams, and the stuff goes in easy and is simple to get out for recaulking. Boiling hot tallow will, more often than not, cure an unreachable leak, such as a split keel, or defective king post, centerboard well, or deadwood. This particular use of tallow takes some experience and knowledge of construction. A few holes are bored in likely places and the hot tallow run in. It seeks out rents, cracks, and worm holes. I've seen the tallow run right through at the start of a pour, which is fine, as you have found the trouble. Slack off, let it congeal, then pour slowly, slacking off again as necessary. When she shuts off, fill right up; you have it licked, unless there is another bad place somewhere along. This same system works fine in a split shaft log. Sometimes the conditions are such that you will want to use a high-pressure grease gun, using grease fittings screwed tightly into holes you think will catch the leak, and for the gun the best mixture is, again, white lead and tallow. The great pressure will tend to heat the tallow. Keep pumping until the stuff shows somewhere. If the pump fetches up, take it slow. Often the goo will begin to show in the most unlikely places, around nail heads, out of end grain of wood, and in seams you thought looked tight.

Though I've used tallow for years, I still marvel at its properties. For some reason that I don't know, it acts as a dryer for an old-time canvas treatment that is famous for its slow drying. A chemist friend can't tell me either, though he knows it works. It does not get rancid if properly tried out, even though stored for years. I have a "gub" of tallow from a launching over forty years ago. It's a curiosity and sort of ossified now, but it does not smell.

A can of tallow kicking around the shop does not spill like oil, and is just the thing to dip an auger in, or the end of a long drift before starting. When moving a heavy weight, a couple of greased timbers under it makes things go real easy. I know of some yards who move all their

craft on grease, though for a sandy, windy place like Cape Cod, it's impractical; ten minutes and the grease is full of grit. Tallow and white lead, or graphite and some light oil make a thread-cutting oil that is not bad at all, if you don't have the real stuff. I use this often in some metal turning, and it's fine for the lathe centers. This same mess, mixed rather stiff, is handy for assembling machinery, especially on threads; it comes apart easily a long time later, as there is no rust. There are so many uses for tallow I just have to keep it around.

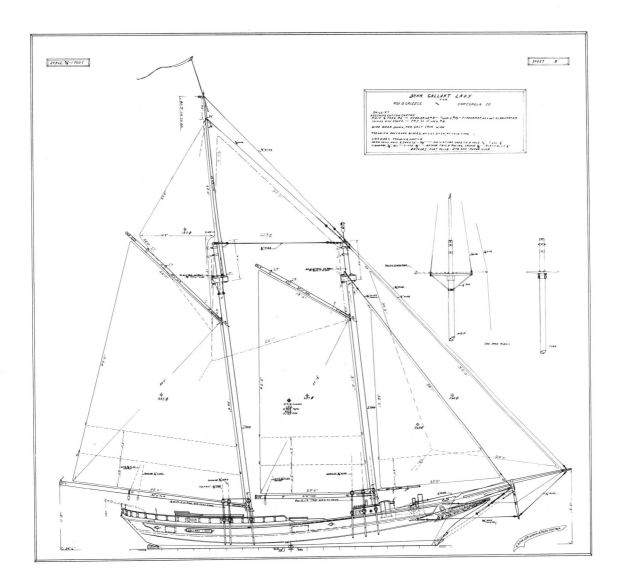

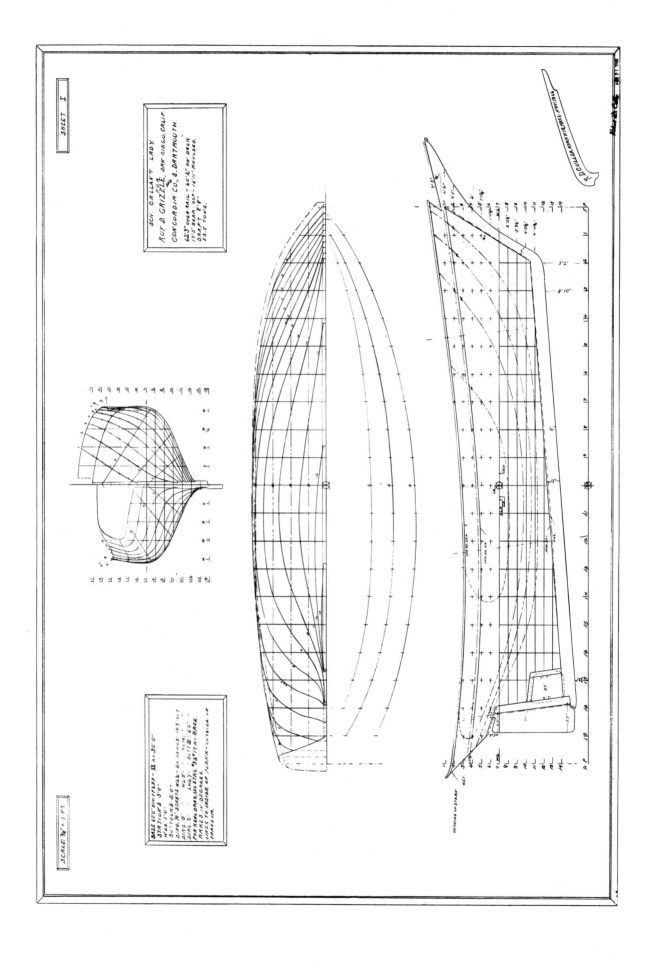

SCALE 3/8" = 1 FT.

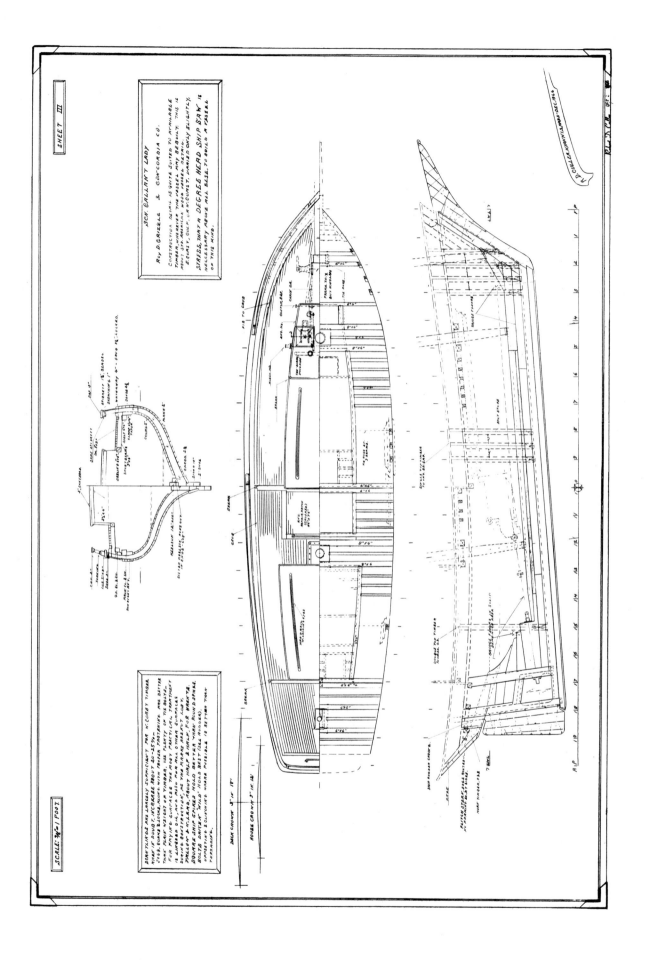

SHEET III

SCH. GALLANT LADY

Roy D.GRIZZLE & CONCORDIA CO.

CONSTRUCTION DETAIL IS QUITE SUITED TO AVAILABLE
TIMBER. WHEREVER THE VESSEL MAY BE BUILT. THIS IS
ABOUT STD. AMERICAN WOOD VESSEL DETAIL.
E.COAST, GULF, OR N.COAST, VARIED ONLY SLIGHTLY.

STRESS, THAT A DEGREE HEAD SHIP SAW IS
NECESSARY ABOVE ALL ELSE. TO BUILD A VESSEL
OF THIS KIND.

SCALE: ⅜"= 1 FOOT

DECK CROWN 3" IN 18'

HOUSE CROWN 3" IN 18'

D CULLER, HYANN. MASS. DEC.1964

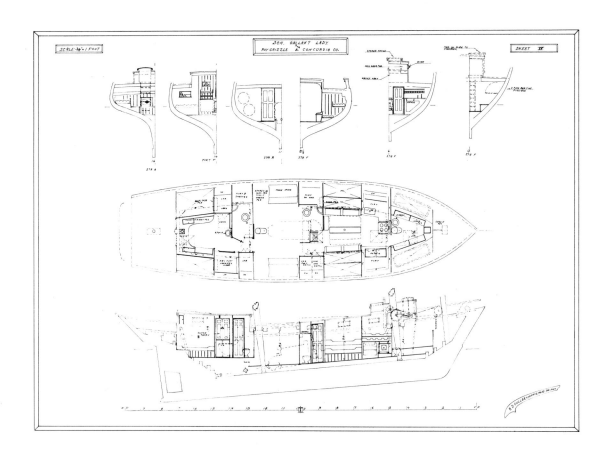

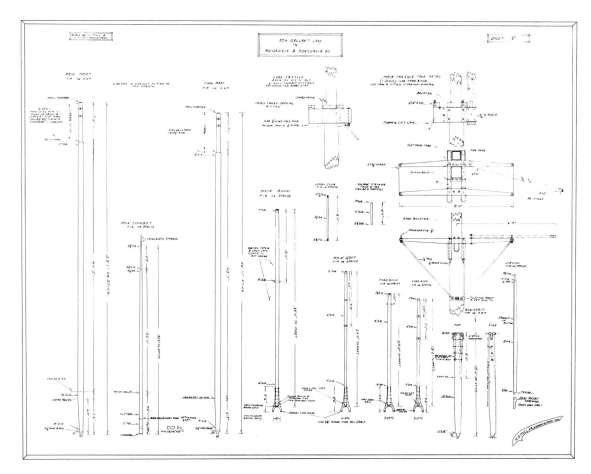

OFFSETS - SCH. GALLANT LADY.

	STATIONS	FP	1	2	3	4	5	6	7	8	9	10	11	12	13	14	15	16	17	18	19	AP
HEIGHTS ABOVE BASE	SHEER. UND. SD. CAP	17' 8"-6°	17' 3-1	16' 10-4	16 5-3	16' 0-6	15' 7-7	15' 3-2	14' 11-4	14' 7-4	14' 4-4	14' 1-7	13' 11-7	13' 10-3	13' 9-4	13' 9-4+	13' 10-3	14' 0-0	14' 2-3	14' 5-5	14' 9-7	15' 2-1
	DECK. UND. SD.	16' 0"-8	15' 6-3	15' 1-3+	14' 8-3+	14' 3-1	13' 10-4	13' 6-2	13' 2-3+	12' 10-4	12' 7-2+	12' 4-7-	12' 2-6	12' 1-3	12' 0-7	12' 1-0	12' 1-4	12' 3-1-	12' 5-4	12' 8-6	13' 0-4	
	BUTT. I		14' 2"-6°	11' 1-7	8' 11-4	7' 7-6	6' 10-2	6' 4-3	6' 1-1-	5' 10-7	5' 9-6	5' 8-7	5' 8-6	5' 8-5	5' 9-4	6' 1-0	6' 9-3	7' 9-4	8' 3-0	10' 7-5	11' 9-5	
	BUTT. II			13' 1-3	11' 7-0	9' 8-7	8' 6-0	7' 8-4	7' 1-6+	6' 9-3+	6' 6-2	6' 4-6	6' 4-6+	6' 6-1	6' 8-6	7' 1-4	7' 9-7	8' 8-2	10' 9-2	11' 11-7	12' 3-0	
	BUTT III				14' 11-7	12' 6-4	10' 8-0	9' 3-5	8' 5-1	7' 10-3	7' 5-7	7' 3-5	7' 3-3+	7' 4-6	7' 7-7	8' 0-3	8' 7-1	8' 4-7	10' 4-6	11' 7-4	12' 10-6	
	BUTT. IV							14' 6-3	12' 0-4	10' 2-3	9' 4 2	8' 11-7	8' 10-4	8' 10-6+	9' 2-2	10' 1-4						
	RABBET	USE "MIDDLE LINE", OR BACK RABBET - STRAIGHT FR. 2½" FWD. OF STA. #2 TO 1'3¾" FWD. STA #18																				
	KEEL BOTTOM	KEEL STRAIGHT, 16" BELOW "M.L."-OUTER RABBET BECOMES A FAIR CURVE. (SEE DRAG HTS, 5° PITCH.																				
HALF BREADTHS	SHEER	0' 11"-0°	3' 9-0	5' 6-1	6' 6-4	7' 3-4	7' 9-6	8' 1-0	8' 3-0	8' 3-5	8' 4-2	8' 4-3	8' 4-3	8' 4-2	8 3-0	7' 11-6	7' 6-1	7' 1-4	6' 8-1	6' 1-7	5' 5-7	4' 9-1
	DECK	0' 3-4	2' 11-3	4' 8-3+	5' 0-0	6' 10-7	7' 5-4	7' 10-3	8' 1-2	8' 2-4	8' 3-6+	8' 4-7	8' 4-6	8' 3-3	8' 1-7	8' 1-0	7' 9-4	7' 5-0	7' 1-3	6' 7-5	6' 0-7	
	WL 1																					
	WL 2		2' 3-3	4' 5-6																		
	WL 3		1' 8-6	3' 11-0	5' 6-0	6' 7-4	7' 4-3															
	WL 4		1' 8-5	3' 2-1	4' 10-6	6' 2-3	7' 0-7	7' 8-1	7' 11-6								7' 7-5	7' 4-7	7' 1-1-	6' 7-6	4' 8-4	
	WL 5		0' 6-6+	2' 6-7	4' 3-4	5' 8-3	6' 9-3	7' 5-6+	7' 11-4	8' 2-3	8' 4-1-	8' 4-1	8' 5-0	8' 5-4	8' 3-3	8' 1-2	7' 9-6+	7' 5-11	7' 2-6	6' 6-6	3' 1-0	
	WL 6			1' 10-4	3' 6-4	4' 11-7	6' 2-3	7' 1-7-	7' 9-0	8' 1-4+	8' 4-7-	8' 5-0	8' 5-1	8' 4-4+	8' 3-1+	8' 1-0	7' 10-0	7' 5-7	6' 9-6	4' 4-4		
	LWL 7			1' 3-5	2' 8-6	4' 2-3	5' 5-4	6' 6-6+	7' 4-4-	7' 10-6+	8' 2-3	8' 4-2	8' 4-7	8' 4-4	8' 3-1+	8' 0-1	7' 7-6	6' 11-1-	5' 0-4			
	WL 8			0' 9-0	1' 11-4	3' 3-3	4' 6-5-	5' 8-3+	6' 7-2+	7' 3-5-	7' 8-5	7' 11-5	8' 1-1	8' 1-1	7' 10-6+	7' 5-7	6' 8-6	4' 11-5	1' 5-6-			
	WL 9			0' 6-3	1' 3-7-	2' 3-7-	3' 4-6	4' 5-6	5' 5-3	6' 2-3	6' 8-2+	7' 0-3	7' 1-3+	7' 0-4	6' 8-6	5' 11-5	4' 5-7+	2' 3-7	0' 8-6			
	WL 10			0' 3-5	0' 9-4	1' 4-5	2' 1-2	2' 10-0	3' 8-2	4' 3-7	4' 10-6	5' 3-3+	5' 4-1	5' 1-6+	4' 7-4+	3' 7-5	2' 4-6	1' 2-6	0' 4-7+			
	WL 11						0' 7-5	1' 1-5	1' 7-4-	2' 1-3+	2' 6-5+	2' 11-1	3' 1-2	2' 11-4	2' 6-4+	1' 11-1	1' 3-5	0 8-5				
	WL 12										0' 6-2	0' 11-3+	1' 2-2+	1' 3-2	1' 3-1	1' 1-3	0' 10-4	0' 6-4				
	WL 13														0' 4-0	0' 5-6+	0' 4-2					
	WL 14									-AT KEEL-												
ALONG DIAGONALS	DIAG. A		1' 11-1	3' 9-2+	5' 1-5+	6' 3-4+	7' 3-2	8' 1-3	8' 9-0	9' 3-4	9' 7-5	9' 10-1	8' 11-4	9' 11-5	9' 9-7	9' 6-5	9' 1-5	8' 6-4	7' 9-3+	6' 8-4	5' 5-5	
	DIAG. B		0' 6-5	2' 1-6	3' 4-5	4' 5-0	5' 3-1+	5' 11-3	6' 5-6	6' 10-4	7' 2-0	7' 4-2	7' 5-4	7' 5-4	7' 4-1	7' 1-1	6' 7-7+	6' 0-0	5' 1-1	3' 9-3+	2' 1-2	
	DIAG. C			1' 3-5	2' 3-3+	3' 1-7	3' 7-7+	4' 1-2	4' 5-5	4' 8-6+	4 10-7	5' 0-1	5' 0-4+	5' 0-4	4' 11-4	4' 9-3	4' 4-5	3' 9-2	2' 11-0	1' 9-4	0' 6-0	

NOTE: REPEAT AGAIN, LINES TO INSIDE PLANK, UND. SD. DK. & RAIL, & TO MIDDLE LINE — OUTER RABBET & BEARD DEVELOP → WILL

KEEL SIDED 10", START TAPER TO 8" AT STAS. 4 & 16

(BEARD; MIDDLE LINE; RABBET)

MEASUREMENTS II FEET, INCHES & EIGHTS THUS, 7'-4"-3° - ADD OR SUBTRACT FOR + OR -, 1/16"-

ALL TAKEN FROM BASE & ℄ - SEE PLAN NOTES FOR GRID SPACING & ENDINGS -

DECK CROWN 3" IN 17' - (SEE CONSTRUCTION)

Robert D. Culler NOV 22 1966

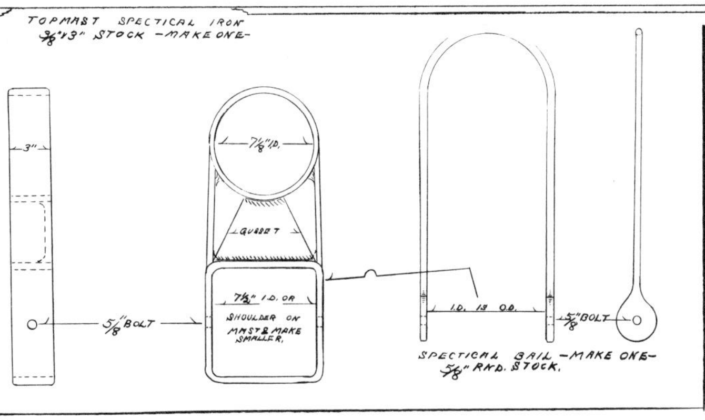

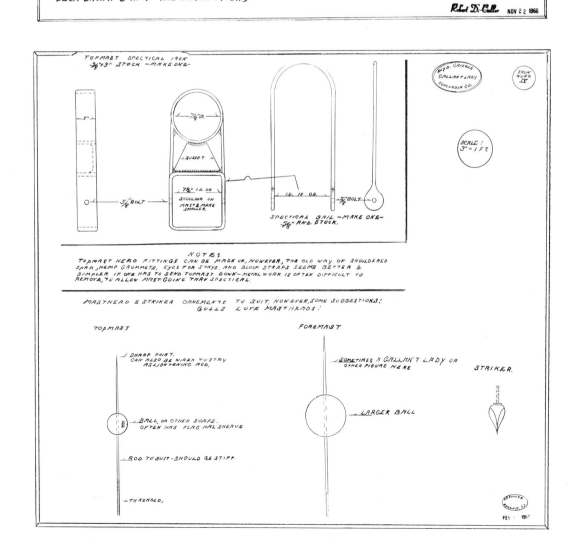

TOPMAST SPECTICAL IRON
3/8" x 3" STOCK - MAKE ONE -
3"
7 1/8" I.D.
GUSSET
7 1/2" I.D. OR
SHOULDER ON
MAST & MAKE
SMALLER.
5/8" BOLT
I.D. IS O.D.
5/8" BOLT
SPECTICAL BAIL - MAKE ONE -
5/8" RND. STOCK.

ROY D. GRIZZLE
GALLANT LADY
CONCORDIA CO.

IRON WORK IV

SCALE: 3" = 1 FT.

NOTE:

TOPMAST HEAD FITTINGS CAN BE MADE UP, HOWEVER, THE OLD WAY OF SHOULDERED SPAR, HEMP GROMMETS, EYES FOR STAYS, AND BLOCK STRAPS SEEMS BETTER & SIMPLER IF ONE HAS TO SEND TOPMAST DOWN - METAL WORK IS OFTEN DIFFICULT TO REMOVE, TO ALLOW MAST GOING THRU SPECTICAL.

MASTHEAD & STRIKER ORNEMENTS TO SUIT, HOWEVER, SOME SUGGESTIONS;
GULLS LOVE MASTHEADS!

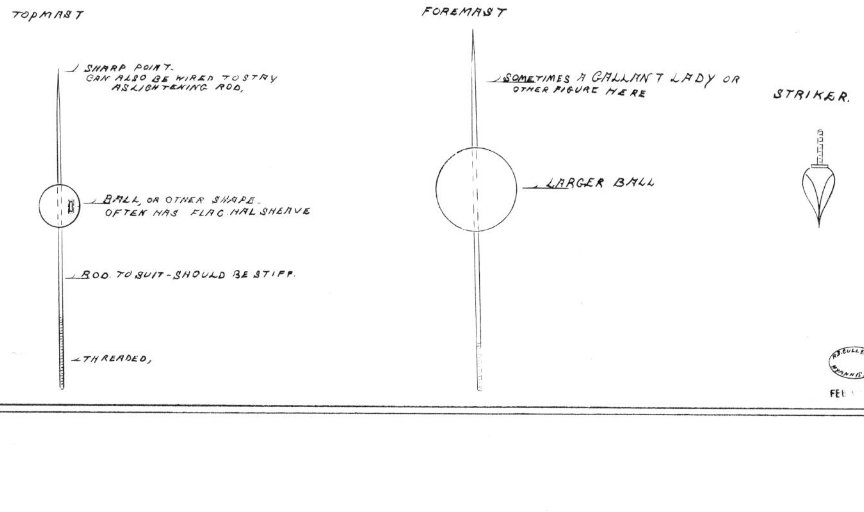

TOPMAST
FOREMAST
SHARP POINT.
CAN ALSO BE WIRED TO STAY AS LIGHTENING ROD,
SOMETIMES A GALLANT LADY OR OTHER FIGURE HERE
STRIKER.
BALL, OR OTHER SHAPE.
OFTEN HAS FLAG HAL SHEAVE
LARGER BALL
ROD TO SUIT - SHOULD BE STIFF.
THREADED,

R.D. CULLER
HYANNIS, '67

FEB 1967

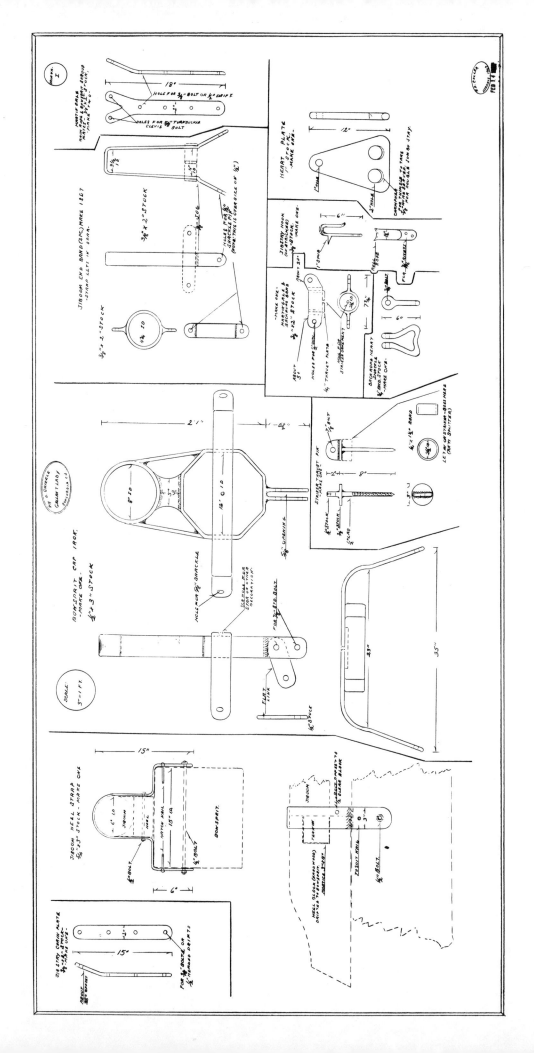

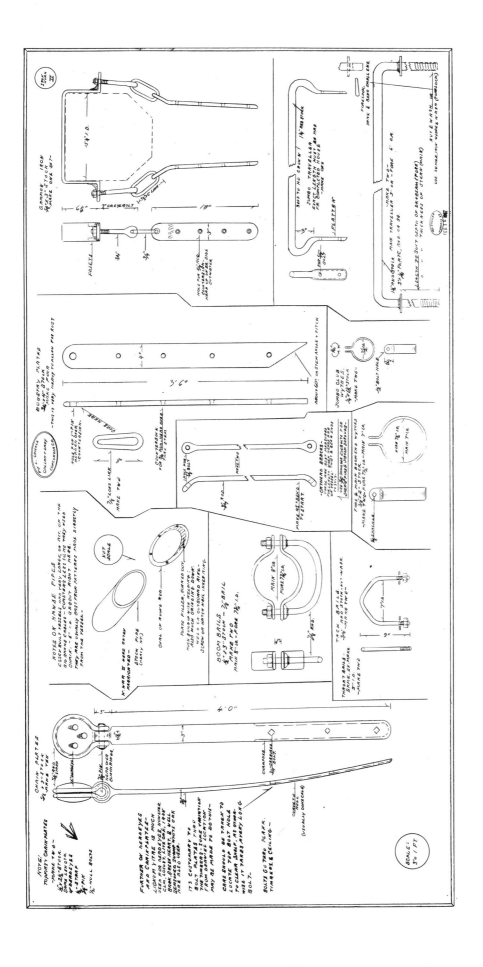

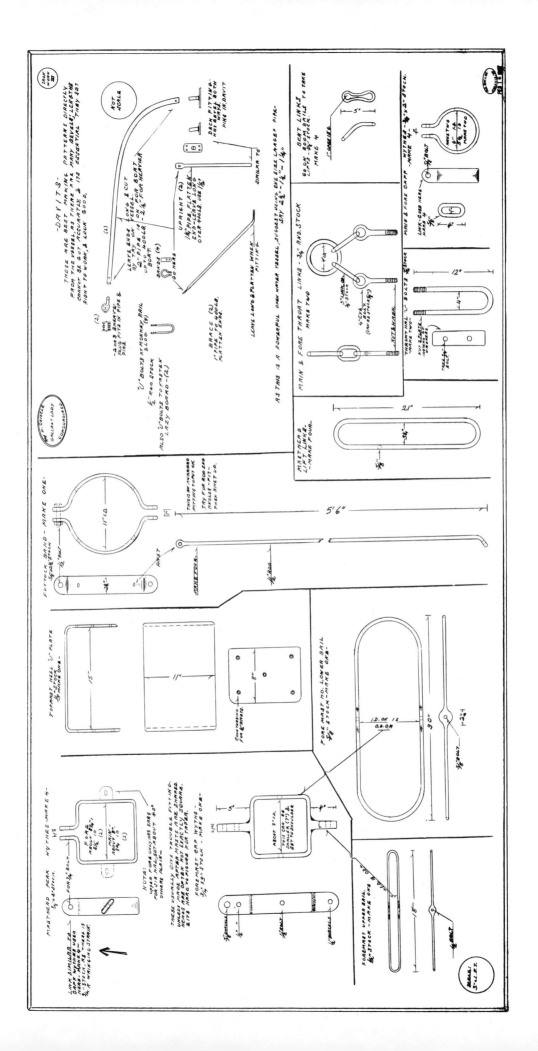

Pine tar is another necessity, now little appreciated. Its main use was the protection of rigging, and nothing since developed does as well. It has many other uses, one being around pig pens, which is sort of out of my line. If you put pine tar on the threads of an anchor or mooring shackle pin, it can always be backed out easily even years later, and turnbuckle threads treated with pine tar never seize. Some uses of pine tar seem very odd; one old skipper of a handsome little schooner years ago was always complimented on the whiteness of his paint, and he was quite open about how he did it: one tablespoon of pine tar to a gallon white paint! No one cared to try it, but maybe that's just what he did.

Pine tar is still available; usually it must be thinned. Turpentine or alcohol work fine; kerosene or gasoline do not, unless very hot, which is taking a big chance.

Knowing few folks will be interested in tarring rigging nowadays, I won't go into it much, yet if rigging is to last, it should be tarred. On new craft you can tar several times the first year to build it up; after that, tar once a year each early fall in northern climates, and don't spare it. I've known a vessel thirty-six years old with all original wire and hemp lanyards, all still in fine shape from being tarred. I've seen the serving lifted for inspection on a lower splice fifty-two years old; the rigger said it was a shame to disturb it. This was another monument to thorough tarring. Just how to make up a gang of rigging that will last, in the old-time way, is explained in detail in works on rigging, all of them considered out of date. The rare person wanting to do this sort of rigging will find out all about it on his own and learn many interesting things, and his rigging job may well outlive him!

Some open boats require trimming ballast, not so much for stability, though that comes too, but to get them down in the water or balance against the weight of the crew. Lead costs plenty, is at times unhandy, and can be too concentrated a weight for many craft. For a boat that may haul up often, lead can sometimes be

a finger-pinching business to handle. The old sand bag still has a lot going for it. If you want to get rid of the weight, open the bag and let her go. Some localities have only gravel or shingle, but it's just as good as sand. Some folks say a ballast bag filled with gravel or shingle lasts longer than a sandbag, probably because it ventilates better. Being in a sandy locality, I use sand, and the bags are pine-tarred. This tar seems to make them go five or more years with ease. The bags can be dipped or brushed; then let them dry well and they are not sticky. For tarring canvas, pine tar should be mixed quite thin. Any object tarred, ballast bag, rigging, or anything that should be dry to use, should be placed outdoors. Drying in a building, especially in winter, just does not work. Often pine tar is put on too thick; several thin coats do much better. Like tallow, pine tar seems indispensable. I can't see just how a builder or boatman can do without it, or if he does, he's missing a lot.

Black asphalt paper-shingle stickum is readily available and cheap, and is most waterproof. It's very handy for underwater seams and nail holes, and it comes about as near to working in a wet seam as anything made; in fact it will work, though naturally a dry seam is better. Copper paint takes kindly to black asphalt stickum, though most other paints do not; the stickum will bleed through to some extent with ordinary paint, so stay below the copper line with it. Asphalt stickum tends to "settle," even in an overhead seam and in fastening holes, which is fine in a new boat. Any low places can be flushed up later when the craft has found herself. I assume this settling has something to do with the tenacious way the stuff stays in place. With care, and several shallow applications, a very bad gouge in a plank can be furred out with this goo and it lasts. It's very easy to apply, even if the weather is sort of chilly, and it has the property of skinning over fairly quickly.

I've tried other similar asphalt compounds, but that made for sticking shingles seems to give the best results. It tends to flow when bedding down underwater fittings, so you get the fastenings tight right off and a good "bleed" all around is readily apparent. This is most useful stuff. In the past, a well-known maker of bedding compounds had a black one that stuck in wet seams and that was much liked by all who used it. It came in cans with his trademark. A pint cost about what a gallon of the shingle stuff does. I think it was the very same thing!

Linseed oil and turpentine are so old and so familiar to most folks that there is no point in dwelling on them. Many things I've mentioned here and in other writings require their use. You will always be using linseed oil and turpentine in various combinations. This is getting close to paints, on which much has been written in the past and is written yearly in many boating publications.

Paint manufacture has changed somewhat through the years, and many paints once much used are no longer around, at least in any quantity. Much is made of paints just for marine use, and in many ways these are fine. Most marine paints tend to a very hard finish, and for good reason. For the most part, they stay white or hold their colors very well. Many are difficult to refinish when that time comes and tend to "build up" through the years. Being hard, many marine paints are difficult to sand, at least to the point of keeping the surface from building up too much. The very high gloss of some of these paints tends to show defects in hull smoothness and, at times, even in fairness. I have no quarrel with these paints, or varnishes either for that matter, if they are used in the right places for the right effect. However, due to their nature, many of these marine paints have a short shelf life once the can is opened and a little used, for they all seem to dry quickly and there is often much skimming over in the cans. Lifting off these skins for short touch-up jobs must remove some of the important stuff in the make-up of the paint each time.

What I now say will no doubt be considered treason, but so be it. For many wooden craft, especially if more or less of classic model and with a fair hull, a high shine, or even a very smooth finish, adds little or nothing and often detracts from appearance. I'm aware, of course, that modern marine paints come in other versions than high gloss. But there is the consideration of do-it-yourself refinishing and the cost of materials. For many more years than I care to count, for exterior use on classic wooden craft, I've used nothing but good-grade, outside, oil-base house paints. The results have been first class; the boats look as they should, are easy to refinish, and the materials are economical. House paint seems to have a longer shelf life than marine paint, and so can be bought in larger cans with more economy. I think house paint is a must on a canvas deck, as, if properly done, there is little build-up.

Every time I bring up this approach, using house paints on a boat, I get a lot of noise from boat owners, paint salesmen, shipyard people, and others. Many boat owners are certainly experienced; I think I am too, by now. Paint salesmen and shipyard guys sell paint, and, to give them their due, they mostly have to do their work in unsuitable conditions and please some owner with shine — maybe his craft is the type for it — so quick-dry stuff that covers is just what they need, especially in spring.

I look at it this way: A fine 8-metre yacht should be dressed in the style to which her type is accustomed or she will look shabby. She is largely a big, unbroken surface of delicate line; any slight defect shows up badly. A classic craft, with much beading, bulwarks, seams that show, and other trademarks of her type, looks dowdy if highly glossed, yet if finished in the somewhat subdued effect of house paint, she looks the part. A 200-year-old colonial house finished in high-gloss marine paint will not look right; it cannot reasonably be made smooth enough. The fancy paint will not "chalk," and when the time for refinishing comes, there is real work to be done. My pitch for house paint is: First cost is less; refinishing is simpler; shelf life is usually longer; it looks fine on the right craft, though on the wrong one it does not.

Some of us still think oil-base paint, usually white, gray, or red lead, sometimes all three in some combination, well thinned with turps, is better as a primer on new work than the "undercoaters" often used, which dry quickly, are often hard, and "drive into the wood" not at all. Many old notions die hard, right or wrong; new ideas come along and require many years of use for acceptance. Some of these never make it, probably because they weren't practical to begin with. Turpentine has great ability to drive into wood, taking some pigment with it. Why, I just don't know, unless turps, being made from wood, just wants to go back where it came from!

By the way, pine tar comes from wood too.

Compounds, paints, oils, and similar things can be gone into at length until it sounds like the "Book of Ten Thousand Formulas." What little I've mentioned here has stood the test of time, and works. Whether a person wants to use any of this or not is his own choice; the point is, these things are still around for those who do want to use them.

I think now I have stirred enough paint.

XVI
Sailors, Old and Young

To get afloat, for whatever reason, you have to have a boat or vessel of some kind. This means someone, or a gang of people, has to build it, and this starts in a boatyard or shipyard. These places have, through the centuries, developed their own humor, which has often made light days of very heavy work. My experience has been that yards that don't have any humor don't amount to much. Things drag and there is a big turnover of help. Such a yard is generally not a happy place from the workman's standpoint. Just how a yard's sense of humor develops, I don't know, but when you see it building up, things are going fine. Most of the humor is simple, a lot of it is crude, and some is unprintable though very descriptive. Many workmen get nicknames due to their build, way of doing things, or some other oddity, and this includes the boss. Vessels building or in for repairs, their owners, and often their designers all get the same treatment. I think the crowd was unhappy when a him, it, or her showed up that was so utterly normal they could not pin on a suitable name!

I remember "Old Knife Bottom;" everyone dreaded her hauling up, as they feared "dropping her," and once she was hauled, even with all precautions taken, you felt uneasy working anywhere near her. In her long life, she never did fall, though other vessels of flatter model did, in various yards. Having witnessed one

"drop," I can say it shakes all hands and the vessel, and it can be fatal to man and ship. If the craft is repairable, she carries the stigma of it the rest of her life. Future buyers view her with suspicion and beat down the price. There are, of course, recriminations all around, a considerable expense to someone, and a lot of work. Most yards manage to live down such incidents, however.

Though there was damage to the vessel I saw fall, there were no injuries. The incident produced some crude shipyard humor. The accident started with a strange tumbling sound from the shores and blocking simply being spit out from under her. There was a great rattling crash as things fetched away below, she bounced and trembled for a spell, and then lay still. It was near sunset. There was a moment of dead silence all over the yard. We knew "Old Up" had been painting under her, no one else. No one wanted to make the first move. Then there Upshure was, about 75 feet away, a big, very elderly black man, slowly turning to look back, paint pot and brush in hand, highwater pants on, not much of a shirt, and toes sticking out of his shoes. A lot of skin showed, and it was the strangest color. One look, and he walked woodenly out the gate into the sunset and never came back, nor the paint pot nor brush either. This broke the tension, and the relief made it seem funny. All hands jumped in and stayed late to straighten out the mess, or at least make a start on it. Nowadays they would demand overtime, and not appreciate the sight of the old black, still in one piece, departing into the sun's glare.

Some vessels get lurid descriptions of their whole hulls, or parts of them. One round old thing became "Missus Bruisewater;" one had "a run like a bucket;" and another's stern was described impolitely. Another craft was so shapely she took the name of one of the country's leading beauties of the time. One regular caller for bottom work was described as still unfinished; someone in the distant past had forgotten to put on the four ball-claw feet!

One dull craft went through the water "like a brick through wet sand," and when it came to going by the wind, another was so close at it that the galley smoke came straight aft and choked the man at the wheel. My, she could go to windward!

One old sailing windbag, named after a political windbag of the distant past, came in to get her seams mended after a long lay-up, for she was going to work again. She was hauled and doctored so much that she was actually quite tight on launching. Then new lanyards were rove and her rigging was set up, the rigger finished about quitting time. Next morning, she was on the bottom, with only the top of her house and her perky jibboom showing. The setting up of the rigging had pushed the masts down enough to open the ancient garboards. Strangely, she was not at all difficult to raise, due to know-how with ancient vessels. Her rigging was slacked up, a very low tide taken advantage of, there was much pumping, and up she came. Setting in the mud had sealed her off. She eventually sailed, with very slack standing rigging, and made a trip or two, though her days were numbered, as the sawdust and manure ran out at an inconvenient time.

Every old-time yard had access to a shipsmith, and the one I speak of was right next door, on a shell pile hard by the Creek. The shop and its owner were right out of a story book. The building, now long gone to make way for progress, would today be a museum piece; it even had a tree spreading over it and all sorts of scrap and nautical gear sort of propping it up. Its owner, Captain Oliver, was a perfect specimen of an old-time blacksmith. His build was fantastic; he was big all over, and the shoulders, chest, and arms were massive in the extreme. They were surmounted by a head with no apparent neck at all. His feet were bad from long years of standing, and he walked with a sort of mincing shuffle. A bachelor, and very softhearted to all living creatures, his oyster tong shaft annex, filled with hard pine shavings, was a home for all the lost, the cast-out, and the ailing cats, kittens, ducks, pups, and others needing help. Every day he went up the street with a great bag of vittles for his charges, and more often than not stuff for the ailing. It was surmised much of his hard-earned money went to some unfortunates in the village, especially children.

This huge, much-liked, and powerful man was, of course, highly skilled. His feats of welding were wonderful to watch; such a shop always had loafers and onlookers. He was also very artistic, and the decorative iron work he turned out was famous, all done with the hammer and forge. I don't think he had ever heard of a welding torch, and if he had, would have cared less. He knew his trade and knew that he did.

Captain Ol liked loafers and visitors and didn't mind their learning how he made things, except for his six-strand, decorative iron rope. This he made in secret. Three, four, and five-strand you could watch being formed, but the six was something special. For heavy work, he employed a powerful black man part time. The heavy thud of the striker sledge and the ring of Oliver's signal hammer directing the blows let the village know something big was going on. He readily admitted that forging an anchor for a 65-foot vessel was hard work for two men, yet he did it. He would not weld with "a new fire," waiting until "after dinner" for it; at which time, and on till quite late, he could put iron together about like working putty, without ap-

175

The author, putting his rig away after a sail.

parent effort or stress, and all of it was perfect; laps, butts, splits, jumps, and all the other welds. It mattered not if it was a mast band or a broken truck spring. The flux for all this welding was plain sand, from a small spot on a certain beach; nothing else would do.

Captain Ol was famous for being able to weld six pieces of iron to a seventh, all on one heat, and finish it off too. This he did rapidly, over and over again, when making oystermen's grappling anchors, all of different weights and five or six-prong, according to the fancy of the owner. Though made entirely of scrap, they always weighed as specified when finished! These sessions always drew the crowd. Smiths wear a large leather apron to protect against the flying dross, scale, molten sand, and whatnot that flies in all directions, sometimes twenty feet or more, when making a weld. There is also a loud pop or small explosion as the weld "takes." This six-weld business was a most interesting process, based on a thorough knowledge of the trade, great manual dexterity, strength, and a long reach.

One "observer," not too bright in the head, got pretty close, and, as the first blow of the weld started, received a slug of white-hot in an important part of his britches! This happened long before the days of rockets, but there was a Whoosh, and a blast-off, and a big splash in the Creek. This Brought Down the House with howls and roars of delight. I think this was the

only weld Oliver ever botched; he threw down his tools and jigged about the shop, playfully belting anyone within reach. The fellow who went in to cool off never quite lived it down, and, in the retelling many times over, his leap grew to a full 75 feet!

Captain Tom was a "character," and lived up to the part, especially in summer for the benefit of the Rusticators. He had started his career as a Bound Out Boy, that is, he was apprenticed for a given number of years to do as he was told by a tycoon who owned plenty of ships and land. This consisted of considerable experience in the owner's vessels in the West Indies Trade, a big thing in those days.

Tom also spawned numerous children. When asked how many, he said, "Eighteen head, if they're all a' livin'." When asked just how many were living, his answer always was, "Well Sir, I don't rightly know." His abode was tumble-down and his boat not much better. Tom was an oysterman in his later years. He seemed never to wash and was covered with dried mud from the "grounds." When chided about this, he said "erster mud was good for rhumatiz." Maybe it is, for he was a spry old chap. Summers, Tom often built skiffs as part of the efforts of a small boatyard where he was sort of a man of all work. By present-day standards in skiffs, his were pretty good, and he loved to have strangers stop and watch, so he could put on his act. This consisted of much serious "measuring" with thumb, fingers, and hatchet handle, and the transferring of all these dimensions from skiff to board and back again, to the accompaniment of mystic symbols in chalk. This chalk came from a pile on shore up the Creek, said to be ballast left by some foreign craft, no doubt from the Cliffs of Dover. Finally, Tom would get a rise out of some Rusticator, such as, "Don't you ever use a rule?" Tom was set for the kill. "Nope, never had no learnin', can't read a rule, but if I'd learnin', and could read a rule, I'd be the best boatbuilder in the Whole Big World!"

Captain Billie was of a different cut. A widower, with family grown and gone, he made his home aboard a tiny, salty craft of his own build. Short, barrel-chested, with blue eyes surrounded by crinkles, he looked the epitome of the old-time seaman in sail. He was self-taught and extremely well-read. Square rig, coasters in their heyday, oystermen, yachts, he had sailed in most of the best, and had skippered several. He was navigator, seaman, shipwright, rigger, painter, and model-maker of some skill. He was "independent as a hog on ice," as he said, taking a job here or there as the spirit moved and if he liked the set-up, for he had high standards, some of them odd, but nevertheless high.

Captain Billie was helping fit out an extensively rebuilt schooner yacht, having moved aboard temporarily from his own craft to be handy and do the cooking for himself and the straight-laced Marblehead skipper, Captain Jimmie. Among other things, Bill was quite a cook and enjoyed it. This moving aboard consisted of bringing his own skiff, "so as to be independent," and his mattress, better known as a "donkey's breakfast." When chided about this last, for the yacht had the finest of new bedding, Billie said, "I allus done it," with a tone of finality. The two old boys got on just fine for a couple of weeks, and the schooner glowed from their efforts. What with Billie's skill with the stove, life was just good. Then one fine Sunday in early June, Captain Jimmie decided it was time he explored the tiny village. Billie was not interested, as he knew it inside out, and

besides, he wanted to work on a model of a pungy that he had under construction. Captain Jimmie was gone a long time, and it got to be way after dark. I think Bill began to worry, and so did the yard owner, as he was keeping a lookout and was my eyewitness to the following goings on.

When finally skipper James showed up, he had considerable cargo; apparently he had found a friend with a jug. Being conservative and careful by nature, he was proceeding with caution, and steering fine. Without undue adventures, he made the yard path, and, though yawing ever so slightly, made the narrow, rickety dock too, and arrived at the piling where his highly varnished yawlboat was tethered. Here he sat down with extreme care, unmoored the yawl, and carefully and slowly worked her directly under his feet. It was flat calm, bright moonlight, and very low tide, with little water under the yawl's keel and all the softest and blackest mud under that. He had a foot or so drop to get into her, so was arranging the maneuver with much care. The moment came to slide in and he started, then stopped. Something had hooked the seat of his pants! There he hung, unable to slide down, and too far down to pull back. The yawl drifted to one side, and the efforts of Captain James, up or down, were to no avail. He was hung between wind and water, you might say. Suddenly there was a ripping sound as the nail, or whatever it was, tore out of his pants. Captain James pitched forward on all fours into inches of water, and feet of mud! Then there was much thrashing around recovering the yawl, getting aboard with pounds of mud, and finally making it to his vessel, which was promptly polluted with the mess, as he had to disrobe in the cockpit and clean up as best he could.

Apparently, there were bitter words aboard that night. Early next morning, here comes Billie in his skiff with donkey breakfast, seabag, tool box, and an unfinished model on top of all. He made the very picture of an old-time seaman changing berths. His only greeting was some remark about Marblehead Sots, on which he went aboard his own packet, did a large washing, and sulked the day out. Yes, Captain Billie had high standards.

Many of these old seamen had seen things at sea that they could not explain and seldom cared to talk about. When they did discuss such matters it was with considerable awe, speculation, and sometimes doubt, according to their nature, but always with wonder. They all more or less did agree that such sightings, real or imaginary, had been going on since man first went sailing. There has been much written about this sort of thing, most of it just to make good sea tales, though some serious investigation has been done too, with, as far as I know, no results at all. That these sightings exist, real or not, I have no doubt, for I have been privileged to see some myself.

I was lying in New York lower bay waiting for "a chance along" down the coast, bound South. I was in a nice vessel, well found, had plenty of grub and a good stake after a summer's work, no worries and was not at all tired, for the three or four days' waiting for a wind shift was no chore at all. It was just modest, routine ship's work, regular feeding, and plenty of rest.

Finally the wind came "down" as expected, with considerable of a squall, and, after the first edge was off, we set easy sail, hove up, and were off. We were two-handed, so it was watch and watch. The wind settled down to stay and eased enough to set the topsail, and we looked forward to a fine night and a fast passage, which it was. After a good supper, roast beef with the trimmings, and a watch below, I took the deck at midnight. It was fine and clear, though no moon, and a bit of Northern Lights, as it was early fall. The vessel was a noted easy steerer, so there was little to do except pace back and forth and nudge the wheel once in awhile. About a half hour after the start of the watch, I saw a vessel, sailing vessel that is, on our port quarter, about a mile away or less. She was by the wind on the starboard tack, standing in for the beach. She was a full-rigged brig! This was in the early 1940's, and I knew of no full-rigged

brig still sailing anywhere in the world, except possibly one or two in the Maldives trading to India, the last of their kind. What was she? Some new training craft I had not heard of? A night glass being always handy, I took a long look at her. She was about 90 to 100 feet long. Her sails were set to the top-gallants; I could not make out whether she was rigged for royals. A running light shone dimly. She stirred right along, heaving gently to the old southeasterly swell common along that stretch of coast. I judged she would pass a quarter to a half mile astern and thought fit to call the watch below, for there was much interest in this sort of thing on board.

Giving the wheel a slight poke, I slid back the hatch and went partly below to sing out where I could be heard. Just before doing so, I looked in the brig's direction and she was gone. Coming back on deck immediately, I searched long and carefully, with the glass and without, and never found her again. I pondered this the rest of the watch, and many times after, and still do. The brig seemed real, all in order, proper course for the wind, right amount of sail, and I automatically assumed she was bound for New York and had been headed by the wind that favored us. Then she vanished while closing somewhat with our course. She showed clearly in the night glass.

Now, I still don't know what I saw, except that when in sight it was real. Was it a privilege of some sort, a setback in Time; or was it just imagination? Square rig in any form was far from my mind at the moment of sighting. During the war years, I came across a book telling much of Jersey coast history, including accounts of the wrecks there. It noted the loss of a brig in the early fall many years back at about the same latitude, with much loss of life. Was I seeing a re-run of her final hours? I don't know!

Many times during The Years of Strife we had occasion to make places or ports unscheduled and unplanned, usually without charts. This was often a nervous business, though we managed to pull it off successfully each time. On two occasions, it was not difficult at all, however, though the places were just dog holes or mucky creeks. Somehow, without ever having been in that part of the world before, let alone in those so-called "ports," entering them seemed perfectly natural. I knew every inch of the places, like my back yard. Both times, my mates on the bridge said, "Been here before, aincha?" All I could say was, "Nope." I was just as surprised as they were.

There are, in the great seas of the world, places known as The Triangles, two that I know of, and possibly more. Many ships have crossed these regions, yet many enter and are never heard from again. Just what goes on in these vast areas does not seem to be understood. Perhaps they have weather conditions that we are not aware of. Some folks think there are other reasons, though they have no idea just what. We still have a lot to learn about the Sea.

(*Text continued on page 192*)

The author (foreground), taking it all in on board one of his schooners.

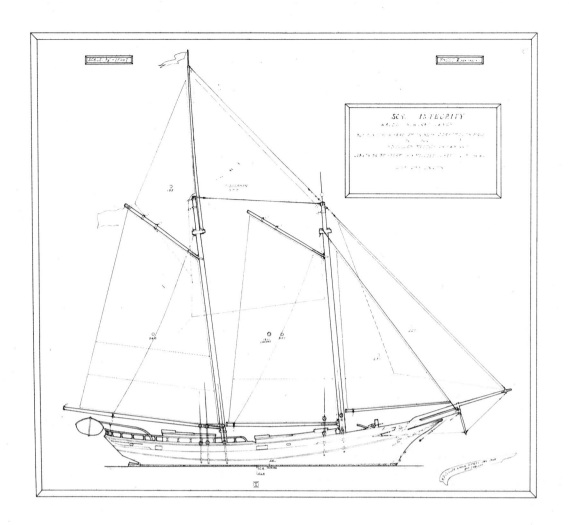

SCH. INTEGRITY
WALDO HOWLAND, OWNER

SCALE 3/4" = 1 FOOT.

SHEET III

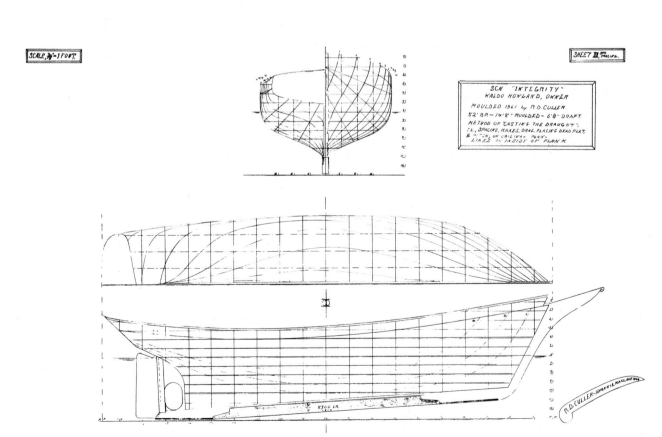

SCH. "INTEGRITY"
WALDO HOWLAND, OWNER

MOULDED 1961 by R.D. CULLER
52' B.P. — 14'8" MOULDED — 6'8" DRAFT.
METHOD OF CASTING THE DRAUGHT,
I.E., SPACING, RAKES, DRAG, PLACING DEAD FLAT,
& PITCH, ON ORIGINAL PLAN.
LINES TO INSIDE OF PLANK

R.D. CULLER—IPSWICH, MASS. JAN 1961.

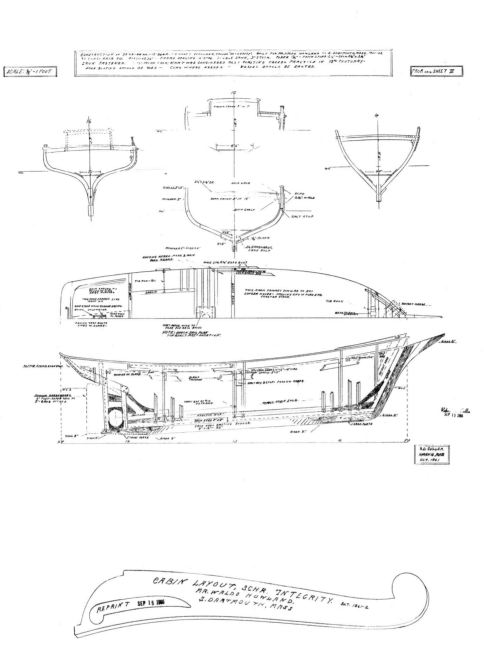

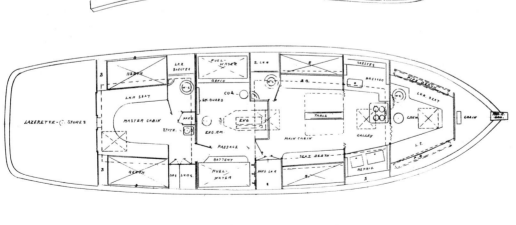

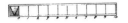

Building the schooner Integrity. *The author's hat helps him hark back to the old days and ways.*

The Integrity, *going together inside and out.*

The author (back row center in the light cap) and his gang built the Integrity *to live up to her name, which she did. The man on the left is the boss caulker, age 83.*

Her traditional details, such as the exceedingly handsome quarter rail, give the Integrity an appearance of classic beauty.

SAILORS, OLD AND YOUNG

Once rigged up, the Integrity *really begins to show her potential.*

The Integrity *on her trial sail — Waldo Howland lets his feet swing to the roll of his vessel.*

Looking back on past experiences at sea, coastwise, and in building, I have fond memories of ships, boats, and those who sailed them, yet as years advance, the idea no longer appeals of long night watches, often the wearing motion of a craft in a hubbly sea, "fog eating," making the land under difficulties, using poor anchorages from necessity with the rumble of chain on a rough bottom, and many other similar things that a sailor must take in stride. They were all right a while back, but not now. There were, of course, the very good times, and these stand out. I think I was lucky. When much exposed to crews, I had very little crew trouble. Most of the fellows were dedicated to some facet of their trade. Many were dedicated to booze when ashore, though it interfered little with their work on board. Apparently I was not born to be blown up in the Forties, though much of my time was spent in floating bombs.

I have experienced no real fires, and no man overboard permanently. The only man who fell off a vessel I was in did so in harbor, and was back aboard again in short order. I had no collisions, or even close calls, though at times there was much hooting and evasive tactics in thick weather. Many times we should have been messed up in many ways and for some reason avoided trouble. Possibly most of those I sailed with felt about like I do; when in doubt stop her, or, if under sail, lay to. Time has a way of straightening out many situations.

When I was young, I was exposed to sailing skiffs and catboats. Now, I find these just as much fun as any vessel; it's my second childhood, no doubt, and made sweeter by a background of varied experience. For many reasons, I still find much pleasure in swabbing out a nice small craft, cleaning her bottom, fussing with her simple gear, and understanding her de-

The schooner Integrity, *gaining an offing.*

sign, gear, and build. I find I get a lot out of her when we go sailing or rowing. Most good small boats have a lot more in them than most people take the time to get out.

Many folks nowadays say small craft don't offer a real challenge. To take some nice, classic, small craft, with properly cut and sheeted spritsail, around some toy sandspit in what appear to be adverse conditions — there is a favorable eddy if you know where to find it and she works wonderfully in moderate going with only the tip of the board — takes as much experience as driving some hard-pressed schooner around some tide-ridden cape, and you don't get so wet!

I think sailing and handling and thoroughly knowing a craft large enough and of a build to be called a "vessel" is the finest of things. Most of us can't own vessels, so we settle for boats, which we can and should learn thoroughly, too. In these days of many small pleasure craft, I'm struck by the short time most owners keep them;

people are always buying and selling, and never really learning about the boat they have at the moment. Many folks have never learned to reef and don't know how and when to handle a boat under short sail. These same people also seem to have little real knowledge of the gear they try to work with. Those who go out in protected waters in heavy weather by mistake or to show off soon show their lack of understanding of their craft. Some heavy-weather sailing is good, and often necessary, as it can "air on" at times without much warning. I certainly feel reefing should be learned at once and that judgment that goes with reefing should be developed.

I think much is lacking in the ways of starting young people to use boats today. They are shoved off to a bum start and seldom are set right later on. First should be taught respect and understanding of the value, monetary and otherwise, of a good boat. I think a classic type gets this across, with the help of an elder seaman, better than any. The fact that the young "apprentice" will, much later on, be using way-out racing machines or double-hulled bananas, is, for the moment, beside the point. With a proper start, he will know what to do with 'em when he gets that far.

A classic boat is not easy to arrive at, even though papa is quite wealthy. Her designer has spent much time on her; the building is quite a chore, though not at all unpleasant. She has considerable "background" even before she is launched, is usually handsome, and is therefore valuable. Cleaning, routine in-commission maintenance, and proper mooring are the first things to master. This is all part of appreciating and getting to know your boat. The craft should be rigged for and be of a model suited to some rowing and sculling. These two should be mastered before any thought is given to sailing. Learn smart and somewhat stylish pulling, skill with the sculling oar, proper shoving off and landing, and the use of the centerboard and how it can aid rowing and sculling. The important knots follow as a matter of course. The painter or the oarlock lanyards need renewing; here is a fine chance for applied marlinespike seamanship.

Oars stowed askew, oarlocks left in, bumps and scratches, these are signs of the "farmer." Besides, when the young man learns to fit out, these bruises can make quite a chore of it! When a thorough boat handler under oars has developed, and it does not take long with an interested and knowledgeable teacher, it's time to think of sail, and it will be found that the young apprentice has more knowledge of it than you might think. He has been observing other craft, knows the "fetch" of his boat at oar speed, how she drifts, and something of her turning ability; he has the feel of her. He knows about what a centerboard does, and no doubt has had passengers and coxs'n to try her rudder.

The classic craft should, if possible, have a "two-sail" rig. She is not gotten under way until all the gear is quite familiar. There is practicing at setting and taking in, and there is practice at reefing. Then she is gotten under way

under short working rig with the fores'l in the second step, and Old Bill, the teacher, giving a few, now-well-understood pointers. She misses stays a time or two, then it all comes natural, and soon the handling, mooring, landing, and getting under way in many different conditions are an open book. Boy and boat have been out in quite a breeze, under short sail. By now he knows when to reef, and why. There has been an Expedition, with some grub and a small shipmate, and it required the proper use of an anchor, which was long ago acquired while rowing.

The day comes to use the "sporting rig," both sails. It's a fine bit of weather and Uncle Bill gives his blessing and stays ashore, for the boys now know what they are doing. The small mate is now useful, can pull a pretty good oar himself, and is heard to expound on how to do a rolling hitch properly! He already has little use for "farmer" ways.

Comes fall, and the proper laying up is at hand. A clean boat, properly stored, will last. There are many lessons to learn; the sails and gear need laying up too. Then spring, and the fitting out. Things must be right, for this year we are in full charge. That gawky place on the bow needs a lot of work; have to be more careful coming to a dock!

A season or two, and this young skipper, more often than not, gets a summer job on some yacht. He's a useful hand, knowing how to take care of gear and keep a boat clean, and is aware of what it's all about in a larger craft. Besides, his former mate is beginning to take command of the small classics that taught him so much.

These boys, with such training, are quite fit to handle a motor launch or big outboard, though chances are they don't care much about such craft except to use and understand them in their proper place. By contrast, the often-seen sight of a boy turned loose in a plastic outboard, his first boating experience, is both sad and somewhat frightening. He never learns what it's all about, and is, unbeknown to himself or his parents, a menace. His boat is never anything to him but something off the shelf, easily replaced.

I think a proper training craft, and she can well do for a family boat for many years later, should not be too forgiving of the young sailor's mistakes. You learn that way. It used to be said in my youth that a lad who could sail some old scow with a packing box leeboard and a home-made sail, and do it well, could, when he got the chance, sail anything. Times have changed no doubt, but the Sea has not. Seamanship is still around too, though sometimes much neglected. Sadly, there are no more good packing boxes from which to make leeboards!

If what I have spoken of in this book is useful to hopeful builders, boatmen and sailors of the present and future, I will consider this small effort quite worthwhile. There is, of course, far more to it than the few things I touch on. I hope what I've discussed, some of it at length, some of it lightly, moves the spirit in the direction of nice boats, their building and handling. That, my readers, is what matters.

Index

Index of Boat Plans